FIVE-FINGER
DISCOUNT

FIVE-FINGER DISCOUNT

A Crooked Family History

HELENE STAPINSKI

RANDOM HOUSE

New York

All rights reserved under International and Pan-American Copyright Conventions.
Published in the United States by Random House, Inc., New York, and
simultaneously in Canada by Random House of Canada Limited, Toronto.

Grateful acknowledgment is made to the following for permission
to reprint previously published material:
EMI Music Publishing: Excerpt from "Marianne (All Day, All Night, Marianne) by
Terry Gilkyson, Richard Dehr, and Frank Miller. Copyright © 1955, 1956 and
copyright renewed 1983, 1984 by EMI Blackwood Music, Inc. All rights reserved.
International copyright secured. Used by permission.
Warner Bros. Publications: Excerpt from "When Day Is Done" by B. G. DeSylva and
Dr. Robert Katcher. Copyright © 1924 by Wiener Boheme Verlag. Copyright © 1926
by Warner Bros. Inc. Copyright renewed, assigned to Warner Bros. Inc. and
Stephen Ballentine Music. All rights reserved. Used by permission of
Warner Bros. Publications US Inc., Miami, FL 33014.
Henderson Music Co. and Fred Ahlert Music Group on behalf of Old Clover Leaf Music:
Excerpt from "Bye Bye Blackbird" by Mort Dixon and Ray Henderson.
Reprinted by permission of Henderson Music Co. and Fred Ahlert
Music Group on behalf of Old Clover Leaf Music.

RANDOM HOUSE and colophon are registered trademarks of Random House, Inc.

Some of the names of the author's friends and relatives have been changed
to protect their privacy.

Library of Congress Cataloging-in-Publication Data
Stapinski, Helene.
Five-finger discount : a crooked family history / Helene Stapinski.—1st ed.
      p.   cm.
ISBN 0-679-46306-2 (acid-free paper)
1. Criminals—New Jersey—Jersey City—Biography.   2. Stapinski family.   I. Title.
HV6785 .S73 2000
364.1'092—dc21
[B]   00-059104

Random House website address: www.atrandom.com

Printed in the United States of America on acid-free paper

2 4 6 8 9 7 5 3

First Edition

Book design by Caroline Cunningham

For Sissy and Babe

CONTENTS

FIVE-FINGER
DISCOUNT

1

MAJESTIC MEMORY

The night my grandfather tried to kill us, I was five years old, the age I stopped believing in Santa Claus, started kindergarten, and made real rather than imaginary friends.

Because Grandpa was one of two grandfathers in their family, my cousins called him Grandpa Jerry. For me, he was simply Grandpa. I had only one. The other—my father's father, the Polish grandpa we called Dziadzia (pronounced *Jaja*)—was hit over the head during a burglary in his front hallway seven years before I was born and died after slipping into a coma.

Everyone in Jersey City knew Grandpa—Italian Grandpa—as Beansie, because when he was young, he stole a crate of beans from the back of a truck. Details about his life started to bubble into my consciousness during the summer of 1970, the year my memory kicked in full force. There were stories about Grandpa "going away" to Trenton for murder. Being arrested for armed robbery. Beating my mother, her sister, and her three brothers.

Grandpa was a well-known neighborhood bully and crook, though the only stolen objects I knew of firsthand were the ones he swiped while working as a security guard at the Jersey City Public Library and Museum in the late 1960s. The fact that Grandpa was able to get a city job as a security guard—through an uncle, who knew a local judge, who was connected to the mayor—says a lot about Jersey City's patronage system and general reputation. Everybody stole. It was no big deal.

My brother inherited most of the objects Grandpa took from the library and museum—the shiny, shellacked coins with Indian feathered heads; a photograph of Abraham Lincoln; small, black Indian arrowheads; a set of encyclopedias. I always wondered if Grandpa stole them book by book or had one of his friends with a car pull up to the library and help him load them in.

The only stolen object of Grandpa's that I possess is a dictionary, a Webster's Seventh New Collegiate edition, which he inscribed to my sister the year I was born: "From Grandpa. Hi Ya Paula. Year—1965." The call numbers on the spine and the blue stamp on a back page, which reads FREE PUBLIC LIBRARY JERSEY CITY, N.J., have been crossed out in blue indelible marker, his attempt to legitimize the gift. Grandpa obviously had his own interpretation of the phrase *free public library.*

Before I started school, my grandma Pauline baby-sat for me while my mother worked as a clerk at the Jersey City Division of Motor Vehicles office, three blocks away. When Grandma died in February of 1970, my mother had no one to baby-sit, so she quit her job. Though I'm sure I missed my grandma—a saintly woman with a halo of white hair and small, pretty hands—my world changed for the better. I was suddenly the center of my mother's attention. With Grandma gone, Grandpa was at the center of no one's.

Because my grandmother had stayed married to Grandpa for four decades, she died fairly young. She was only sixty. She died on Ash Wednesday, the first day of Lent. By then Grandma hated Grandpa so much that on her deathbed, with the smudge of ashes on her forehead, she made my mother promise that Grandpa wouldn't be buried on top of her when he died. She couldn't stand the thought of his remains mingling with hers.

During her lifetime, Grandma quietly threatened to poison Grandpa, but she never did. She never even got up enough courage to leave him. I couldn't understand why she stayed with him for so long. Or why she was even with him to begin with.

Maybe it was because Grandpa was so handsome. Like my mother, he had delicate features, thin lips, and olive skin. His hairless body was covered in tattoos, like a bloom of fresh blue-and-purple bruises, which he'd gotten when he was in the army, which he joined, illegally, at age fourteen. On his leg was tattooed a hula girl, which, in his lighter, happier moments Grandpa would make dance for me by rippling his calf muscle. A blue chain was tattooed around one wrist. A snake slithered up his arm, past a cross and a red-and-blue heart. On his other arm was my grandmother's name—Pauline—underneath the profile of Evelyn Nesbit, the famous girl in the red velvet swing, a popular tattoo subject in 1906. It was a sign that Grandpa adored Grandma. Though he was known to beat his children, he never laid a hand on his wife. He loved her and even had a pet name for her—Boobie.

But Grandpa's rage was so potent that it could be contagious. My aunt Mary Ann had moved to Florida just to get away from Grandpa after almost hitting him over the head with a statue of the Blessed Virgin Mary. Uncle Robby, my mother's youngest brother, was once chased by Grandpa with a broken bottle in front of his own children. Uncle Robby, pushed to the brink of insanity during one of their fights, went at him with a five iron, then smashed Grandpa's picture window.

The violent streak hadn't been passed down to my mother so much. She cursed a lot, though. Whenever she let loose a particularly nasty string of obscenities, my quiet father would yell from two rooms away, "Shut your trap." When she was going through menopause, she ripped a phone out of the wall. But that was the only time I ever saw her do something violent.

Right after Grandma died, Grandpa turned his rage on himself, since he had no one at home to terrorize anymore. He tried to kill himself three times. He jumped out the first-floor window of his apartment but did little damage. If Grandpa had lived in a high-rise, our troubles that year would have just ended there.

But Grandpa was persistent. He tried again, swallowing twenty tranquilizers. When the pills failed to do the job, he stabbed himself with a penknife. Later that spring, he was taken to Meadowview, "the crazy house," the only one of its kind in Hudson County.

Meadowview was in Secaucus, a few towns over from Jersey City. Because land was abundant there, it was not cramped like nearby Hoboken and Union City. Secaucus, destined for office parks and multiplexes in the 1980s, was still trying to live down its reputation as a pig farm in the 1970s. When I was a kid, there were jokes about Secaucus and how it smelled like manure. A joker would stretch out one arm and hand, like in a Nazi salute, and hold his nose with the other hand.

"Who am I?" he would ask. "Superman flying over Secaucus."

I didn't get it. I didn't know about the pig farms. I was convinced that people made fun of Secaucus because of the smell rising from Meadowview.

With no baby-sitter, my mother had to take me with her wherever she went—to funerals and wakes, shopping, and to visit Grandpa at Meadowview. It reeked of urine and dirty bedsheets. Legions of mentally retarded men and women and crazy people—much crazier than Grandpa—wandered the fluorescent-lit yellow hallways.

One man had the habit of twisting his wrist all the way around, then placing his hand over his skull, pressing his thumb and middle finger to his temples. The compulsive action—repeated thousands of times—left indentations in his head. I wondered if it gave him a headache and, if it did, why he kept doing it. Another floormate of Grandpa's would lift the lid off a garbage can and replace it, again and again and again. Yet another wore a turban and was known to stand up on a chair and pee onto the dinner table. Grandpa may have been crazy, but he certainly didn't belong there. Nobody belonged there. Except maybe the guy with the turban.

On my first visit to Meadowview, I learned that I actually had two relatives in residence. My father's brother Tommy had been there since 1963, but until Grandpa was institutionalized, I had never visited him. Tommy, the shame of the Stapinski clan, was now brain-damaged from years of epilepsy. Various family members had taken turns caring for him after his parents, my Polish grandparents, died. Most of the time, they had liked having him around. Uncle Tommy cleaned house better than a woman, turning the mattresses over and cleaning the bugs out of the springs. Some afternoons he even made a few bucks cleaning and waxing the cars down at the Manischewitz factory, where his brother Joe worked.

Unfortunately, Tommy was also known for his fits of rage, which always came on the heels of an epileptic seizure. He had almost killed his brother Henry, the family bookie, bending him backward over a tub and nearly breaking his back.

Once, at our house, Uncle Tommy had a seizure and, due to some especially slippery carpet, slid under my parents' bed and got stuck there. Several uncles ran to his rescue and dragged him out before he swallowed his tongue. Another time after a seizure, Uncle Tommy ran up onto the roof of his house. The cops were called, and they chased him from roof to roof until he was caught. Then there was the time he fell down the stairs and knocked his teeth out. The Stapinskis had no choice but to send Tommy "away" to Meadowview.

Whenever I saw him, timid and smiling a shy, squinty-eyed smile that looked too much like my father's, I felt like crying. I couldn't decide which was worse, visiting Uncle Tommy or not visiting him. Being at Meadowview with him was awful. But the incredible guilt and sadness of thinking of my uncle there alone was even more painful. The most heartbreaking vision of all was one that I could only imagine, one that my older sister, Paula, had witnessed as a child: Uncle Tommy standing in a doorway with a shoe-shine kit outside the downtown train station, pleading, "Shine?" over and over again at disinterested passersby. On my visits to Meadowview, I wondered if Uncle Tommy missed his job, or if he even remembered he'd had one.

For Grandpa, I felt much less sadness. What upset me most, made me cringe, was the sight of his bloody fingernails, which were chewed practically to the cuticles. Just the thought of them sent a sharp pain through my abdomen and down to my groin. I was a nail-biter myself, but there were limits.

The sight of Grandpa must have bothered my mother, too. After convincing my father it was all right, she finally signed Grandpa out of Meadowview and invited him to come and live with us in our three-bedroom apartment that summer of 1970. Meanwhile, Grandpa would search for a place of his own. Something on the ground floor.

From the second-floor kitchen window in our apartment, my mother would watch me play. She kept a close eye on me because we lived above a tavern—the Majestic—which sometimes attracted a "bad element." During the day, the Majestic was filled with harmless old drunks and corrupt City Hall politicians, who came to the tavern for lunch—soggy pot roast sandwiches with rich brown gravy or delicious pepper and egg or cheeseburgers, which seemed as big as Frisbees in my small hands.

Patrolling the corner was the Majestic's mascot and most loyal customer, a hunchback named Vince, who wore a fedora and a long raincoat. He was the bar's first customer each day, a true alcoholic, who downed his first drink in broad daylight. To help defray the cost of his beer—which he slowly sipped like tea, savoring every drop—Vince swept the cracked sidewalk outside the Majestic every few hours, then swept the gutter, pushing the cigarette butts and other litter down past the sewer grate.

My brother, Stanley, who was seven years older than I was, usually played ball with his friends across the street at City Hall Park, a concrete plaza with a few patches of dead grass. When his friends weren't around, he would join me in a game of stickball against the graffitied wall of our three-story brick building. The rest of the time I played alone, watched over by my mother and Vince.

In winter, I built snowmen with the dirty snow out front. Instead of a broom, I sometimes stuck a discarded, empty whiskey bottle in the snowman's side. My mother yelled at me for it. We weren't allowed to play with bottles, and whenever we even went near one, my mother would retell the story of the little neighborhood girl who was found standing up, dead, a broken bottle lodged in her jugular vein. Did I want the same thing to happen to me?

Some afternoons I wasn't allowed out to play at all, especially during the riots and parades that were staged outside City Hall, an imposing building with a two-story-high arched entrance and four Corinthian columns, which took up a whole city block. Guarding the entrance was a green-bronze statue, a seated woman with a helmet on her head and her right arm in the air, who I thought was a tired, miniature version of the Statue of Liberty. My mother told me that late at night, when I wasn't watching, the lady got up and danced. Maybe that was why she was sitting down during the day. Her feet obviously hurt.

We lived on the corner of Mercer and Grove Streets. My parents' bedroom window looked out onto Grove, a heavily trafficked street, and directly at City Hall and the tired lady. Our front door was on Mercer, a one-way treeless street of battered three-story brick buildings and dilapidated brownstones. The intersection was a busy one, because of City Hall, and was easy to find through the telescopic viewing machines from the top of the World Trade Center in Manhattan, where my mother took me on field trips when I was a little older. From the top of New York's tallest skyscraper, my house and Jersey City looked a lot like that statue outside City Hall—small and tired.

Living across the street from City Hall guaranteed hours of entertainment, better than watching *Kojak* and *Cannon,* because from my parents' bedroom window I could see the political action unfold.

One afternoon I made a poster, featuring the name of a political-reform mayoral candidate. I used red and blue Magic Markers, and hung the poster from my parents' bedroom window on the day Mayor Smith took his oath of office. I was on the news that night—or at least my skinny arms were, sticking out from the sides of the poster as I waved the oak tag in the wind.

One autumn, City Hall nearly burned to the ground. Along with the Tired Statue of Liberty, we sat and watched the fire department battle the flames. I bit my nails as the pump and ladders doused the building with three-story-high sprays of water. Mayor Smith, wearing a fireman's hat, ran in and out of the building, dragging soggy files into the street, his face covered in soot.

It took all day for the firefighters to extinguish the flames and a few weeks for them to rule out arson. There were reports of disgruntled workers driving off in a red car minutes after the blaze began. Those stories were either unfounded or hushed up. All we knew was that part of the green copper roof was destroyed, its metal frame poking out like a skeleton. The bronze lady was intact, though. A little wet, but undamaged.

One year my mother made us all duck for cover when bullets started to fly at the Puerto Rican Day Parade, which always ended at

City Hall. Tensions were high during the parade every summer, and no wonder, with a mix of new immigrants from the island and the third-generation Irish and Italian cops. The Puerto Ricans would wave their single-star flags, and the white Jersey City residents, forgetting they were only a couple generations removed from immigration, would yell things like "If you like it so much, why don't you go the hell back?" I remember watching one riot from my parents' bedroom window and hearing the distinct crack of a billy club hitting a hard skull. Another summer, a local anarchist threw a Molotov cocktail at the building. That time, the fire didn't catch.

Jersey City was a tough place to grow up, except I didn't know any better. I had nothing to compare it to. All I knew was that I was well fed and comfortable in our apartment. The air was filled with industrial smells that meant home. On rainy days, the sky was thick with the pungent smell of coffee manufactured by Maxwell House in Hoboken, the next town up the Hudson. On most other days, the air was dusted with scents from the Colgate-Palmolive factory just a few blocks away. Depending on the stage of manufacturing, the air either stank with the fat from which the soap was made or it hung heavy with the perfume with which it was scented. On the worst and windiest days, the city borrowed its smell from the south, from Newark's bone-rendering plant. But on its best days, Jersey City smelled of chocolate from the Van Leer cocoa factory, a five-year-old's dream come true.

The sounds of my neighborhood were as memorable as the smells. Each summer night, the Puerto Rican men on our block would drag their giant conga drums over to City Hall Park and bang throughout the night, until we fell asleep to the Latin rhythms or until my angry father called the police. "The natives are restless," he'd grumble, trying to drown out the sounds with the ball game played simultaneously on the radio and the television.

Sirens were familiar, too, and whenever one Dopplered past, we were taught to bless ourselves and say a prayer for the person on the other end of the emergency. Mixing with the sirens were the calls of the drug dealers on our street. I didn't know that it was uncommon to have guys on your corner yelling *"Tobaccos sueltos"*—"loose joints." Junkies sometimes slept on our doorstep, and I learned at an early age not to play with the hypodermic needles they left behind. One night the family was awoken by a woman having withdrawal symptoms on our doorstep. My mother called an ambulance, not the cops. That's when I learned the difference between a junkie and a dealer: The dealers were evil; the junkies were just sad.

For revenge, or maybe just for fun, I would drop my Slinky out the kitchen window, lowering it enough to graze the dealers' heads, and then yank the metal coil back up. They would reach up to see what was there, but by the time they craned their necks up toward my window, I'd be crouched down low, both me and my Slinky out of sight. Reminding the dealers that they were trafficking in front of a five-year-old's home, I would blow bubbles from that same window, letting them drift down onto the street below. The dealers would laugh and wave up at me. I waved back, or sometimes gave them the finger.

When she got frustrated enough, my mother would stick her head out the window and curse at them. "Get that shit out of my garbage cans," she once shouted to a dealer hiding his dime bags in our trash.

"Okay, lady," the dealer yelled back. "But you don't have to curse."

My teenage sister, Paula, a petite brunette voted prettiest in her high school class, suffered the most in our neighborhood. Her dating pool was extremely limited. Whenever she left the house, the dealers would make smooching sounds and catcalls. It made me so mad that I swore I'd pour pots of boiling water on their heads someday.

There were worse neighborhoods in Jersey City, my father always rationalized, and worse taverns than the Majestic. A bar just down the street from us was known for its bloody fights. I remember strolling with my mother and seeing a shirtless man covered in blood bursting out the door, screaming. He had been attacked by another man with a carving fork. What could he have done so wrong to make someone want to stab him with a carving fork? I thought of the devil, armed with a big pitchfork, and wondered if he lived in Jersey City.

An optimist like my father, I was convinced that downtown Jersey City wasn't so bad. The piers in our neighborhood may have been burnt and rotted, but at least we had a view of downtown New York from the Majestic's roof.

When my father returned from work each day at around 5 P.M., the tavern was his first stop. Some afternoons I was out front playing, climbing the pole on our corner or killing ants with shards of glass, pretending to be a mad surgeon. Daddy would kiss me hello, then disappear into the mysterious darkness that was the Majestic. An hour later, if I was still out playing, my mother would yell down to "get Daddy." Getting Daddy was one of my jobs.

In the hot summer months, getting Daddy was a pleasure, since the Majestic was ice-cold from the huge air conditioner hanging over its bar. It was even colder than our own well-air-conditioned apartment. At the Majestic, I would push open the corrugated-metal door, chilled from the inside out, and enter a cool cave of smoke and stale beer. My father usually sat on the far side of the bar, drinking a shot and a beer, so I would have to make my way around its entire U shape, passing my father's friends and various bookies along the way. They would peel dollar bills from thick wads in their pockets and hand them to me— "for ice cream," they'd say. On a good day at the Majestic, I'd make an easy ten bucks, cramming the bills into my giant Tootsie Roll bank, which we'd gotten from a family friend who worked at the nearby Tootsie Roll plant.

Daddy kept his money folded in order of denomination: singles on top, followed by fives, tens, twenties, and the occasional fifty or hundred, which slept warmly and silently in the center. The bills were bound by a thick rubber band, never a wallet. Back in 1956, Daddy's wallet had been stolen at Schneider's bar. He'd refused to carry one ever since. He kept his roll in the left-hand pocket of his sky-blue work shirt. Above the uniform pocket and his cash was his nickname, Babe, sewn in script. The nickname came from his being the youngest boy of eleven children.

I knew a secret about him that most of the men in the Majestic didn't know: Even in summer, Daddy wore long johns underneath his blue pants, because he worked in a walk-in freezer, the Union Terminal Cold Storage, the big red warehouse right beside the mouth of the Holland Tunnel. Because my father was used to the cold, we had air-conditioning in our house, a big unit blowing waves of cold air from my parents' bedroom over my father's hairy beer belly.

When my father saw me at the Majestic, he would smile, barely wide enough to reveal his missing top teeth. (Dental hygiene was never big on the Stapinski side.) When he smiled, his slanted eyes nearly closed shut and his large nose bent lower toward his top lip. His gray hair, which in later years turned white, was slicked back by a handful of Vitalis hair tonic. His laugh was high-pitched but muffled, in the wheeze family, the result of his not wanting to open his mouth too wide to reveal his gums. He also didn't talk much. But when he did, what he said was usually either wise or witty, since he'd had so much time to think through what he wanted to say. This was the opposite of my mother and me. Like Grandpa, we got way too excited over the smallest thing and let you know about it right away.

My father spoke Polish, but hardly ever around me. I pictured him having elaborate conversations in Polish with his siblings, out of earshot. The reality was that Daddy hardly ever spoke at all, in Polish or in English. His nickname for me was Helcha, a Polish version of Helen. He never cursed, unlike my mother, and his harshest insult was "you banana." When he yelled, which was very rarely, he roared, and you ran as far away as possible. His favorite animal was the elephant, which explained a lot. Slow and patient, powerful but peaceful, never forgetful. Every year he took us to the circus at Madison Square Garden, and before the Greatest Show on Earth, he would usher us under-ground to the menagerie to feed peanuts to the silent, friendly pachyderms, his soul mates.

He was the smartest of all his siblings, and a natural-born leader. His biggest responsibility, besides his job at the Cold Storage, was serving as president of a downtown organization called the Dudley Social and Athletic Club, so named because it was located on Dudley Street, which took its name from Jersey City's first mayor, Dudley S. Gregory.

The members of the Dudley Club, which consisted of my father's brothers and all of his best friends, ran illegal raffles, a Christmas bash, an occasional polka party, an annual dinner dance called the Dudley Dinner, a softball league, and summer bus rides to a place called Bubbling Springs, a man-made lake in western New Jersey that held mixed memories for me. Since I was the youngest, I caught only the tail end of the joyous Bubbling Springs era. But my mother regaled me with stories of the good old days, when she would bring a giant tray of macaroni and Daddy would grill lobster tails, which had fallen hot off the truck at his job at the Cold Storage. Not surprisingly, the lifeguards always spent their breaks at our picnic table.

By the time I was old enough for the Bubbling Springs bus rides, the joy had begun to run out. My most vivid memories included many of the reasons the trips were discontinued: Some kid gave a duck a cigarette and burned his bill. A poacher shot all the deer on the property. They had been tamed and fenced in for visitors to pet (along with the duck). Finally, the Dudleys were involved in a four-car pileup on the way to the lake. When they got there, the car trunk carrying all the beer was so dented that they couldn't get it open. Just when the Dudleys thought things couldn't get any worse that day, a deaf boy drowned at the lake. The trips to Bubbling Springs ended soon after that. The only thing my mother feared more than me falling on a bottle was me drowning.

Despite his Dudley accomplishments, Daddy was an underachiever, following the path of least resistance. He could have been a professional bowler, a surgeon, an accountant, or the boss at the Cold Storage, my mother said. But he never wanted the headaches that came with responsibility. The Dudley Club was about all he could handle. At one time, though, he did have the ambition to run numbers, like Uncle Henry. A guy named Chick wanted to hire him to drop off some betting slips. My mother told him in no uncertain terms—likely peppered with a string of obscenities—that no father of her children would run numbers, that she would leave him if he became a bookie. She knew the embarrassment of having a father who was constantly being arrested.

If you were from Jersey City, you were either a quick-witted crook or you sat back and blended into the ugly scenery. Otherwise, you moved out. My father was too good to be a criminal (with my mother providing an extra shot of morality) and too apathetic to move. That was why we lived where we did: the path of least resistance.

Daddy carried that concept over into his wardrobe. When he wasn't wearing his uniform, he wore white shirts with a single pocket, black or brown dress slacks, and highly polished, shiny dress shoes. Colors did not adorn his body. Colors were for women, hippies, and effeminate men. My mother did all his shopping for him.

Each night in the Majestic, Daddy would lift me onto the knee of his blue work pants so I could get a glimpse of the rows of colorful bottles behind the bar. Each one wore a tiny, brightly colored cap that looked like a little birthday hat. They made it easier to pour the drinks, Daddy told me, his breath smelling of Scotch, his work clothes heavy with smoke.

"Hi, Nicky," I'd yell to the bartender, a short, balding man with a very round head and glasses. He resembled a clay figure from an animated Christmas special on TV. If there was time before dinner, Nicky would fill me a glass of soda, with a maraschino cherry, or even let me behind the bar to clean glasses on the rounded rotating brushes inside the deep stainless-steel sink.

Each night around this time, the pay phone in the Majestic would start ringing. Wives without the convenience of living upstairs were in search of their husbands. Daddy would take my hand and with his other hand grab the bag of frozen food he'd swiped from work at the Cold Storage that day. Together, we'd walk up the two dusty flights of stairs to our apartment.

On weekend nights, Daddy would usually come home on his own, drunk, and excited to watch *The Lawrence Welk Show*. Daddy was a happy drunk. On Welk's cue—*an'-a-one-an'-a-two*—he'd sweep me up into his arms and waltz me around the living room. We'd dance until the bubbles were released from Welk's bubble machine and the chorus sang "Good night, sleep tight, and may your dreams come true."

By July 1970, my father wasn't the only relative hanging out at the Majestic. Grandpa, now living with us, hung out there too. My grandfather, an unhappy drunk, sat at one end of the bar, closest to the cold metal door, and my father sat at the other end, in his usual spot. Daddy, who seemed to get along with everyone, never got along with Grandpa. No one did.

By then, beaten down by Meadowview, Grandpa seemed humble and quiet. I rarely saw him, since he was out most of the time. His presence was more like a bad smell that lingered around the house— hard to trace, but always there. A telltale sign that he was in the house or close by were the Lucky Strike butts he left floating in the toilet, gray and pointed, with black tips. I had never seen a bullet, but I imagined that's what they'd look like.

The only time I remember Grandpa getting out of control was the night he pounded his fist on our dinner table, which my mother had inherited from Grandma when she died. Maybe because of the table, Grandpa felt right at home, comfortable enough to terrorize us. He pounded so hard that the Pepsi bottle jumped in the air.

While Grandpa lived with us, my brother, Stanley, was forced to sleep on the couch. Grandpa was given his bedroom, a back room that was always dark. I hated that room even before Grandpa arrived, and rarely went back there. Its one window looked out onto a small tar roof, where pink Spaldeen balls lost from countless games of stickball sat abandoned, covered in grease from the Majestic's grill fan. Because of the fan, my brother could never open his bedroom window. And the view of the fan and roof was so ugly, the blinds were always drawn. Every few months we would peek through the slats and glance longingly at those unused handballs out there. I hoped that someday, with a little soap and water, they would be mine to toss into the graffitied strike zone on our front wall—a giant S floating in a white square.

I wondered whether Grandpa would have done what he did that summer had he been given my sister's bedroom, a bright, sunny spot with daisy stickers on the walls and a view onto Grove Street. It probably wouldn't have made much of a difference. Grandpa was just mean, my mother said. I figured he was born that way.

He was given a key to our apartment and was told to keep the front door locked because of the junkies and dealers. But Grandpa—who had been on the wagon at Meadowview—started to drink. One night he threw up all over our bathroom. Even worse was that night after night he left the front door unlocked, the hypodermic needles—and their owners—drifting into our hallway. On rainy nights, the dealers set up shop in our vestibule.

My father decided he'd had enough. He asked Grandpa to give up his key and to ring the doorbell whenever he needed to come upstairs. Once he was buzzed in, the door would automatically lock behind him, keeping the junkies and dealers out. It was a simple and understandable request. Grandpa gave up the key, but he never forgave my father for asking for it.

One afternoon in August, one of Grandpa's sisters called my mother. I remember my mother nodding, not smiling or laughing like she usually did during phone conversations. This call didn't last long, not even long enough for my mother to sit down at the kitchen table. My aunt hadn't called to chat; she'd called to say that Grandpa had a gun and that he was threatening to kill my father.

Grandpa had often threatened to kill different members of the family, so my mother shrugged it off as just another rant. But the next night at the Majestic, with my father at the other side of the bar, Grandpa started flashing his gun. My father, having downed several beers by then, didn't see what was going on. But I can just see Grandpa, looking like a disheveled George Raft in his gangster-wanna-be fedora, his silver .22 glinting in the light from the Yankees game on the tavern TV, bragging about putting a bullet in my father's belly.

Our neighbor Ducky casually walked up to my father and asked, "What's with Beansie? He's got a piece on him."

I was upstairs, playing in the kitchen with my cousin Gerri, who was staying the night. Gerri was named after her father, my uncle Jerry, and Grandpa. Aside from the name, she had little in common with Grandpa. Gerri had no mean streak like some of us had inherited. Like Grandma, she had blue eyes and fair skin and a bright, easy smile, later straightened by braces. She was five years older than I was, but she never shooed me away like some of the other big kids in our family. My sister was eleven years older than I was, and was usually too busy dating, cheerleading, and sneaking Marlboros to spend time with a five-year-old. Gerri, my favorite cousin, didn't mind playing with me.

That night, Gerri and I were playing with our Barbies in the kitchen sink, pretending they were at the municipal pool in North Bergen, the town north of Jersey City where my cousins lived. Tap water was flowing over Ken's hairless chest when the front door opened.

It was my father, who had come upstairs to tell my mother about what Ducky had said. He knew nothing about my aunt's call. And he hadn't seen the gun and still didn't know what it was for.

My mother went to the kitchen phone and dialed the police, telling them there was a man with a gun threatening to shoot someone in the tavern. She was embarrassed to tell them it was her father and that he was coming to kill her husband. All she needed to say was the magic word—*Beansie*. The Jersey City police knew him well. Within minutes, the cops were on their way, lights flashing, siren screaming, this time growing closer and closer until the ear-piercing sound settled outside our front door. It never even occurred to me to bless myself at the sound. It was all too close.

Gerri and I took a break from our Barbie dolls to peek through the dusty venetian blinds in the kitchen. I wasn't sure what was happening, but it was very exciting. I wondered if Grandpa might shoot up at us from the street, but the police frisked him and confiscated his .22 after dragging him from his bar stool.

We watched from the window of our yellow-wallpapered kitchen as the police put Grandpa in handcuffs and shoved him into the cop car, their blue arms pushing him into the caged backseat. The next day, there was a brief story on page 3 in the local newspaper, *The Jersey Journal*. The headline read MAN SEIZED ON WAY "TO KILL 5 CHILDREN." The man was Grandpa. That last phrase was in quotation marks because Grandpa had told the police who he planned to shoot: Ma, Daddy, Paula, Stanley, and me. He'd forgotten that Gerri was sleeping over. "The police said Vena talked openly of his desire to kill his family," the story read. "He said he was despondent, he had been drinking during the morning and he had a desire to shoot someone."

Since I hadn't even started school yet, I couldn't read the newspaper account. It wasn't until years later that I found the clipping in the library. That's when the drama—or the reality of it, anyway—finally hit me, written in simple black-and-white. The memory had been clear, but it was just one of a string of family crimes and tragedies, which I thought most people experienced on a regular basis.

Over the years, in family stories told casually in passing, the anecdote had been repeated again and again until it had lost all meaning, like a word said over and over until it sounds like gibberish. I had heard a hundred times how the arresting detective, Michael Borseso, told my mother that Grandpa had the gun all ready to fire that night, that he would have kept shooting until all the bullets were gone. I imagined myself in a dramatic death scene, falling to the kitchen floor. But that wasn't how the story had ended.

I knew it all by heart, like the chorus of a familiar song: He had been just a few yards from the front door, steps from being buzzed up, a quick walk past the dust bunnies and broken tiles of the hallway that my father and I passed on our way home from the Majestic on those hot summer nights.

That night, after Detective Borseso took Grandpa away, Daddy was so upset that he drank practically a whole bottle of Dewar's. My mother wasn't as upset as he was, only because she was already numb from a lifetime of Grandpa.

He was charged with threatening life and possession of a dangerous weapon. Two days later, he was out on $500 bail, probably put up by one of his drinking buddies or one of his eleven siblings. My mother soon heard he'd gotten another gun, so for weeks she lived in fear.

She tried calling a local judge, Edward Zampella, the same guy who had gotten Grandpa the job at the library, to find out if there was anything we could do to keep him away from us. But Zampella brushed my mother off and told her not to worry. "That bastard," my mother said after she hung up. If she had offered him a cash bribe, maybe Zampella would have produced some results. He was that kind of judge. Hudson County was full of them.

So Ma worried until Grandpa was finally sentenced to twelve months in the Hudson County jail. His stay there didn't last long. To get high, Grandpa drank cough medicine, and wound up throwing up blood. He was sent to the Jersey City Medical Center, where he was tied to his bed because of his violent tendencies. When they'd had enough of him, the staff sent him to Trenton State Psychiatric, where he had a heart attack.

At some point, he went to live at my cousin Gerri's house. I remember seeing him one more time while he was living there. I was seven years old. Grandpa scared me, but in the way a muzzled attack dog scares you. I kept my distance, just in case Grandpa bit one last time. He offered me a dollar bill to try and get me to come closer. I told him to leave it on the floor, that I'd pick it up later. Once he was gone, I grabbed the dollar and crammed it into my Tootsie Roll bank.

Grandpa died the next year at Kennedy Hospital in Edison, on Christmas Day 1973. My mother went to the funeral without us.

Safely buried at Holy Name Cemetery on New Year's Eve, in a plot separate from my grandmother's, Grandpa could never bother any of us again. Not physically, anyway. But he damaged us all in different ways—emotionally, psychologically, genetically. For one of us, Grandpa opened up a door to a dark place, one much darker and colder than the Majestic or Stanley's bedroom.

In time, one of us would carry on a long family tradition, one that didn't start with Grandpa and wasn't confined to just our family. As I grew, I realized that crime was—and still is—a rich Hudson County tradition, floating from one generation to another, like a defective gene in a dirty pool.

2

LUCKY NUMBER

The day I was born, my whole family hit the number.

Back then, Ma, Daddy, Stanley, and Paula hadn't yet moved to the apartment over the Majestic but lived a few blocks closer to the Hudson River. That first apartment was on Sussex Street, right across from our parish church, Our Lady of Czestochowa (OLC), the parish for all the Stapinskis.

Uncle Henry Stapinski, my father's oldest brother and the family bookie, lived just a few doors down from us, in a bachelor apartment, where he kept his "office." Henry's desk and the apartment were a complete mess. The television and radio always played simultaneously, broadcasting two different games. A pillow was kept on his hard, wooden chair for support, to protect his back, which Uncle Tommy had almost broken.

His desk was piled high with copies of *Sports Eye* newspapers, the local papers, lists of numbers, receipts, and large piles of cash in mostly small denominations. There were two phones on Henry's desk—not for efficiency, but because he was lazy. One was broken. He just never bothered to fix it.

Uncle Henry didn't spend much time in his bachelor apartment. When anyone in the neighborhood wanted to play the number, all they had to do was find Henry, loitering on some neighborhood corner, and tell him their number, which consisted of three digits. It was easy, easier than playing the Pick-6 or Pick-21. There was no waiting on line at a convenience store or filling out an SAT-like card and handing it to a man behind a deli counter.

Some people in Jersey City played the same number every day for decades, hoping the odds would finally catch up with them and reward them for their loyalty. They were the people spooked by stories of a gambler changing his number midlife and the next day that number finally hitting. Others based their bets on birthdays, anniversaries, dreams they'd had the night before, psychic predictions, addresses on doors, license-plate numbers of cars that ran into them or their family members. If it had three digits, it was up for grabs and was considered potentially lucky.

No matter how a gambler arrived at it, the number was written in Uncle Henry's small flip-up notebook. Each page was perforated down the middle, with the number and the amount wagered written on each side—one side for Henry, one side ripped out as a receipt. For obvious legal reasons, the gambler's name was left out of it. Uncle Henry would shake your hand at the end of the transaction and slip you your receipt in exchange for your money.

Playing the number was a community activity, and in my case a family affair. Nobody ever cheated you out of your winnings, and you never cheated anybody out of your losings. People paid up or else they got hurt. Uncle Henry never broke any kneecaps himself, as far as I know. Someone else took care of that.

Unlike the lottery, the daily number had a kind of dignity. It wasn't chosen from a cheesy air-generated Ping-Pong ball machine by an aspiring model/actress on a local TV station, but by cutting off the last three numbers of the total mutuel handle at the track that day. Gamblers found the number by looking in the horse-racing pages in the local paper. In Jersey City, crowds would run to the Palace drugstore each night to buy the *Daily News* as soon as it came off the truck. The number would spread through the neighborhood by flashing fingers, from corner to corner, like baseball catchers communicating secret signs. For those at home, the number would come by phone at around 7 P.M.

Ours was one of the first phones to ring, since the bookie was, after all, Uncle Henry. His call was a thrill each night, and as soon as I was old enough to walk, I would sprint to the kitchen, reach up, and grab the receiver before the first ring was even through.

Whenever he called, Uncle Henry never said hello, just in case he was being bugged. Just, "Henny. 325." Or, "Henny. 478." Always in a mumble, no matter what the number was. Before hanging up, I bellowed the number through the house for everyone to hear. It was my nightly ritual and moment in the spotlight. When my mother's boss from the DMV called to get the number, I was the one to tell him. I had no idea it was illegal. I just knew it was really important. Being the bearer of information gave me a thrill.

Back in the days before I was born, bookmaking was so popular that the bookie would come into the trash-strewn courtyard of the tenements and whistle to get the gamblers' attention. As rats hid in the bushes, housewives would lean out the back windows to toss out their coins or crumpled dollar bills. Their numbers would drift like the smell of fresh-baked bread from the warm kitchen windows, landing in the bookie's pad. The bookie would make out the slips and leave anonymous receipts in the dented hallway mailboxes. Those were the days of penny spreads, when you could bet a penny on a number boxed and straight, and win a dollar back.

In my mother's day, the local bookie was Mr. Zeller, who owned a custom dress shop and a candy store. Mr. Zeller was a gentleman and stood at the counter in the candy store, dressed in a three-piece suit, pretending to sell only old candy, Royal Crown Cola, and loose cigarettes, called loosies. All day long, customers would come in to play the number, saying, "Zellie, give me a nickel on . . ."

One day, Grandpa sent my mother around to the store to find out what the number was. She found the dapper Mr. Zeller standing with two big guys, dressed in suits just like his. "Mr. Zeller, my father wants to know what the number is," my mother politely said. Mr. Zeller almost dropped dead. The two men were FBI agents.

Unless the feds were breathing down their necks, the local police hardly ever came down on bookies. Dudley Gregory, the city's first mayor, helped institutionalize gambling in Jersey City. He was known as the Lottery Man back in the early 1800s, because of the local 50/50 raffles he held. (Just another reason for my father's Dudley Club to be named after him.) The questionable money he raised was used to build churches, schools, prisons, and roads, and no doubt to line his pockets. But it was because of Mayor Frank Hague that gambling was so ingrained in the daily life of Jersey City's residents. Hague, who ruled for the first half of the twentieth century, was one of the most corrupt politicians in the country, and certainly the most notorious in the city's history. His main income came from controlling the county's illegal gambling rings and an elaborate telephone and telegraph system for off-track betting. It was known as the Horse Bourse, and it was the Wall Street of the gambling world, the center of the horse-betting universe. Hague was its master.

A tenement would be gutted and filled with telephones and adding machines, creating a central betting system that could handle lay-off bets from around the country. In other words, if a bookie in another city didn't have the capital to cover a bet, he would call Jersey City for backing. Each neighborhood was also allowed a certain number of illegal dice and card games, in return for giving Hague a percentage of the take. A bagman from the police department was assigned to each neighborhood to collect his take from the game organizer or bookie.

With the number, the dream was to hit it big and get the hell out of Jersey City. But the odds were against you—even if you won. The odds of hitting the three digits were, mathematically, 1,000 to 1. But bookies only paid 500 to 1. So they rarely lost, unless the whole city hit the same number on the same day, as it did in 1958, the day after a commuter train fell off the bridge that linked Bayonne to Elizabethport. The five-car, two-engine Jersey Central train, a Bay Head–to–Jersey City special, was carrying a hundred passengers, among them George "Snuffy" Stirnweiss, a former New York Yankee. There would have been more people aboard had it not been a holiday—the first day of Rosh Hashanah.

The driver didn't notice that the vertical lift of the bridge, opened earlier to allow a sand boat to pass, was still open. So the train took a dive. The two diesel locomotives and first two passenger cars sank down into thirty-five feet of water, killing four crewmen and forty-four commuters, Snuffy included. One car was left dangling from the edge of the trestle for over two hours: car number 932.

When pictures of the disaster were published in the next day's newspaper, 932 was prominently displayed on the side of the car. Everyone in Hudson County played 932 that night. When the last three digits of the mutuel handle turned out to be 932, the bookies couldn't get over it. They had to pay 500 to 1 to practically every gambler in Hudson County, which included almost every man and woman who lived there. Bookie losses from the train number were $5 million countywide. Since the disaster photo appeared not only in *The Jersey Journal* but also in the New York *Daily News,* bookies in the entire metropolitan area lost upward of $50 million.

The train-wreck hit was a freak occurrence, of course. Most days, the bookies made a nice profit. Because of the crummy odds, the number couldn't make a bettor too rich. Unless a large sum of money was bet, the payout was small. People rarely had large sums of money to play with in Jersey City. If they hit, that little extra money helped, but it didn't drastically alter their lives.

There actually was such a thing as being too rich. The problem with the huge jackpots of the legal lottery was that once people hit, they weren't sure where to go or what to do with all that money. The beauty of the number was the hope, the dream. Once it became a reality, it could never live up to that fantasy of sipping tropical drinks on a boat in the Bahamas.

For instance, Ruthie, the school crossing guard at OLC, hit the lottery and became a millionaire overnight. Her life's job, crossing kids in dangerous traffic on Henderson Street as they walked to school, became an impossibility. People would laugh at her if she continued wearing that silly hat, shiny blue crossing guard coat, and white belt across her chest. So she quit. Relatives Ruthie hadn't heard from in years began to call, asking for "a loan." There were those who wanted money for an investment in a sure thing and relatives who simply wanted the cash up-front, no strings attached. How to divide it? Where to move? Would she make new friends, rich friends who would be ac-cepting of her Jersey City accent and manners?

It was all too much for Ruthie. She died of a heart attack several weeks after hitting it big. It was not a story people wanted to hear, since it detracted from their lofty dreams and hopes of a better life. They were better off playing the number, even if it was against the law.

Uncle Henry, whose bookie career spanned three decades, went to jail only three times. It wasn't that he eluded the cops. Uncle Henry was an easy target: He was huge, weighing in at an easy 250. Watching him eat was a sporting event in my family, an amazing physical feat in-volving raw power and stamina. He could inhale a dozen pierogi in less than sixty seconds. And then there was what my kind Polish relatives liked to call his "lazy eye." Uncle Henry was cross-eyed.

Though the police knew that the illegal number was an integral part of the region's economy and social fabric—and were paid well to think that way—they had to do a sweep now and then to make things look good. Every few years, they arrested a bunch of bookies in Jersey City—about thirty-five in all—and sentenced them to perform com-munity service at St. Lucy's homeless shelter, near the Holland Tun-nel. On Sundays, my brother went with Daddy to visit Uncle Henry at St. Lucy's, which, for that short time, became a virtual dormitory for the local bookies. Each one had his own tiny room, but they ate meals in a common meeting room and shared a television set. After two months, they'd be back on the street running numbers.

The first time Uncle Henry was arrested wasn't for numbers but for destroying traffic tickets for friends while working in the Jersey City violations bureau. The name Stapinski appeared in the police blotter story in the local paper—the first time a Stapinski had been on the wrong side of the law. There was talk that the family name was tar-nished forever. But then Henry started running numbers, and no one seemed to mind, not enough to stop placing bets with him.

Uncle Henry was, as my family would say, "a good egg." A grade-A extra-large egg, but a good egg. As homely as he was, I felt a certain af-fection for him. Whenever I saw him, he never failed to peel off a fiver for me. I always felt sorry for him, since he was the one who Uncle Tommy had tried to kill following one of his epileptic fits. Ironically,

Uncle Henry was the only one who still went to visit Uncle Tommy regularly. You had to love him just for that. Your retarded brother tried to break your back, and you go and visit him every week.

But Uncle Henry's soft spot for Tommy wasn't the only reason I felt a special connection to him. Uncle Henry took the bets the day I was born, scribbling my family's hopes into his little notebook, one number at a time.

When my mother was six months pregnant, she had her tea leaves read by my cousin Gerri's maternal grandmother, a psychic who lived in the housing projects in North Bergen. Mrs. McGuire told my mother she would give birth to a girl, that I would stay in the hospital ten days, and that she should write this number down: 507. Mrs. McGuire wasn't sure if it was the number of the hospital room my mother would be in or my birth weight.

After my mother went into labor, Ash Wednesday, 1965, the whole family, with the smudge of ashes on their foreheads, called Uncle Henry to place their bets. I weighed in at 5 pounds, 7 ounces—a good bet and a favorite to win. Most relatives played 507, straight and boxed. But my father's sister Terri played 057. Straight. She felt that 5 pounds, 7 ounces translated into 057, not 507. Terri, the only Stapinski sister to move out of Hudson County, liked to do things her way.

The day after I was born, my aunts and uncles ran to get the *Daily News* at the Palace drugstore. And there, on page 72, at the bottom of the Gulfstream Charts were the last three digits of the total mutuel handle: 057.

Everybody hit the number, since they'd played it straight and boxed. But Aunt Terri hit it big-time. For her 25-cent wager, she was rewarded $125, not bad by 1965 standards. To show her gratitude, Terri bought me a $65 red snowsuit with white fur trim.

Since I was so small, it took a while to grow into. At only 5 pounds, 7 ounces, I was kept in an incubator for ten days, just as Mrs. McGuire had predicted. I was skinny and sickly, but I was considered a lucky kid. By everybody except Uncle Henry, of course, who lost a small fortune.

Jersey City and I shared the same birthplace, a small coincidence, considering the city is 14.9 square miles. The Dutch West India Company acquired the first tracts of land in Jersey City, those at the edge of the Hudson River in Paulus Hook, the downtown neighborhood where OLC was and where I spent my infant and toddler years. The neighborhood, named after Michael Paulaz, a Dutch West India Company agent, was 4,400 feet from Manhattan, on the Hudson River's west bank. OLC Church, with its sturdy stone façade, was Dutch Protestant before the Polish Catholics took it over. The Dutch also built my first house, on Sussex Street.

They referred to the area as Gammontown—from the Dutch word *gemeen,* which means "abject," "abandoned," "low," or "vile." Since the neighborhood was close to the water, it was often invaded by rats. Not the most desirable place to live. Even three hundred years later, longtime residents called it Gammontown, never Paulus Hook, a name reserved for real estate brokers and historians.

From history books, I learned that Manhattan's founders bought their land from the Native Americans at a discounted price of $600, but Jersey City's Dutch waged an unnecessary battle against the same friendly tribes. Why pay when you could steal? That was Jersey City's motto. In 1643, Dutch governor William Kieft, known as William the Testy, ordered the massacre of the peaceful Lenni Lenape tribe. His attack caused all the warring tribes to band together and destroy the Hudson County colony. In the early 1700s, once the tensions with the Indians dissolved and the colony was rebuilt, settlers in Hudson County erected fences around common lands, laying claim to property that was not theirs.

During the American Revolution, Jersey City's residents sided with the British, establishing a passive Tory community that was regularly raided by both sides for food, horses, and clothing. Woollen petticoats of the Dutch women were taken and used for blankets in the long winters. When you weren't picking on someone else in Jersey City, you were the one getting picked on. It was wise to strike first, and strike fast.

Once the war was over, Hudson County became a refuge for the losers on the burgeoning American political scene. Alexander Hamilton, driven from Manhattan and from office by the Democratic Republicans, moved to Hudson in the hope of building a rival city. Jersey City, under his Federalist guidance, would become a thriving metropolis, wonderful enough to compete with the one just across the river. But before Hamilton could make his plans, he was shot and killed by Aaron Burr in a duel just a few blocks from what would later be the site of my first bachelorette apartment.

In the late 1700s, New York had a population of 60,000, but Gammontown contained an unlucky thirteen residents, who watched the important people come and go from the Grand Street ferry landing. Stagecoaches left for Philadelphia from that spot, and the ferry took everybody who was anybody over the Hudson.

Gammontown was taken over in the 1800s by an immigrant wave of Eastern Europeans, a notoriously clean people. The Stapinskis were among them. The Stapinski, or Stapienski, family (depending on who was wielding the pen when they came through Ellis Island) emigrated from the rural village of Powiat, outside the Polish city of Rzcszów, near the Ukrainian border, a dreary part of the world that must have made Jersey City look like the emerald city.

Most of my father's family lived in Gammontown, right on Sussex Street, at one time or another. There was Uncle Henry, of course, and Aunt Terri, Uncle Joe, Uncle Mickey, Uncle Tommy, who lived there before moving to Meadowview, and Aunt Stella, whom we called Cioci, Polish for "aunt," because she was the oldest and seemed the most Polish. Babci, my Polish grandmother, lived on Sussex Street as well, though I never met her. She died the month before my mother became pregnant with me. I came out looking just like her, my squinty eyes and large nose proof that Babci had been reincarnated.

By the 1960s, when I arrived, Gammontown no longer had a rat problem. It was the city's prettiest neighborhood, with rows of historic brownstones and the scent of Colgate soap in the air. With a nearly unobstructed view of the Manhattan skyline and an open feel because of its nearness to the river, Gammontown had a light, and a lightness, that was missing from the rest of Jersey City.

Warren Street, just half a block away, provided a full view of the actual Statue of Liberty, even if her back was turned to us. It seemed she couldn't stand to look at Jersey City. When kids misbehaved in school, teachers would often tell them that Miss Liberty was so mad she had turned her back on them. How's that for a guilt trip? You were so bad that you'd caused a 225-ton green copper behemoth—the symbol for hope in the New World—to turn around and ignore you.

In Gammontown, the only thing standing in the way of the Manhattan view was the Colgate factory, most famous for its giant, red-lit clock, visible from across the river. Some New Yorkers even set their watches to it. But it was backward to us. From our side, Colgate was best known for its two enclosed white steam containers, which looked like giant Q-Tips and added to the clean, fresh feeling around you. The Q-Tips were there to catch the steam released from the factory's furnace.

Because of Colgate and its giant Q-Tips, the air quality in Gammontown seemed a little better than in the rest of Jersey City. People who worked at the soap factory were the freshest-smelling residents of the city. When my brother got a job there, my mother learned the hard way not to sprinkle laundry detergent on his clothes: His shirt and pants were already so filled with soap that suds overflowed from the washing machine, like something out of an episode of *I Love Lucy*.

Noise pollution was also absent in Gammontown. Sussex Street was quiet because of the overwhelming hush of OLC Church, which was like a big quilt thrown over a block square, muffling any unpleasant sounds. I never once heard loud music blare out of car windows. Motorcycles never roared past, and drug dealers didn't loiter on its corners. The block was stuck in a time warp. Men at OLC still wore fedoras and slicked-back hair long after the fashions changed. And women, including many of my aunts, paraded around with tall, dyed bouffants, wispy and full of air, like puffs of cotton candy. The neighborhood stayed quiet and conservative because it was home to two churches: OLC was back-to-back with the Russian Orthodox church Saints Peter and Paul. Their steeples were geometric opposites. OLC's Gothic triangle didn't mix well with the onion-shaped domes of Peter and Paul. In some ways, they were a continent apart. The Russians never bothered with the Poles. And the Poles never bothered with the Russians. At least until my family came along.

Though I was much too young to realize what it was, a heaviness always hung over Saints Peter and Paul, oozing its way over OLC's copper roof and stone walls. At first I thought the bad feeling came from the unfriendly Russians who attended mass at Saints Peter and Paul. Or maybe it was from the mass itself—a three-hour ordeal that made me thank God I was Catholic. Whatever it was, that dark, mysterious cloud always threatened to ruin my sunny first impressions of Gammontown, the place where a lucky kid could at least get a glimpse of the Statue of Liberty.

3

NO SOUP FOR SUPPER

When I was two years old, my parents moved us from our cramped Gammontown home to the more spacious apartment over the Majestic Tavern. Whenever we traveled back for church or a family gathering, I was like a pilgrim visiting the Holy Land. It wasn't just because of the clean air, the brownstones, OLC Church, or the Stapinski side of the family. Gammontown was where Grandma Pauline grew up. She was raised on the same street as Saints Peter and Paul, the church where she was baptized, her head round and new, with clean holy water poured on to cleanse any Original Sin that had settled there. Grandma was pure good, the angel to Grandpa's devil. To me, Gammontown was the fresh beginning, the Eden before the knowledge of all worldly things intruded.

Since I don't remember Grandma very well, she was never a real person to me, with a real personality. She was more of a force—or a light—in my life. No one ever spoke badly of her. She was a clean slate upon which many of the horrible family stories were written. I thought it was no coincidence that Grandma had died on an Ash Wednesday and that Ma had also had ashes on her forehead when she gave birth to me. I felt like the ashes were Grandma's silent signal that she would watch over me and make sure nothing bad ever happened. Every Ash Wednesday, we were told at OLC that ashes were associated with purification. They looked like dirt, but they were sprinkled on the altar in a ritual to clean the church. They were also a reminder that we were simply dust. And to dust we would return, like Grandma had. God used the same dust to mix with water to make the clay to make Adam, the first man, whose name meant "Earth." Ashes weren't the end, the priest said, but a fresh, new beginning.

In those first pictures implanted somehow in my brain, Grandma, her hair white and soft, holds me close to her. She baby-sat for me in the two-bedroom apartment on Sussex Street, which was too small to contain three rambunctious children. I imagine myself rubbing up against her as a toddler, trying to inhale her goodness and take it with me when we moved over the Majestic. Her goodness would brace me for the evil of Grandpa to come.

I thought Stanley and Paula were luckier than I was because they had grown up in Gammontown, with real memories of Grandma. I remembered isolated moments, abbreviated and colorful like dreams, which were recorded before full memory kicked in. Grandma taught me to play cards—games like War, Go Fish, and, for when I was without her, Solitaire. The thing I remember best is that Grandma never got mad and never yelled, even when I sliced open one of her vinyl kitchen chairs with a toy plastic saw.

Stanley and Paula remembered what Grandma's house smelled like, its walls infused with the aroma of the sauce she cooked for Grandpa and the chicken soup, with soft carrots and broad noodles, that she made for their children and grandchildren. I settled for the pleasant smells in my mother's kitchen, the recipes having been passed down over time.

My brother and sister told me stories about how on snow days they could build igloos in the middle of Sussex Street, since there was hardly any traffic. The snow stayed white, with no car exhaust and very few footprints to ruin it. Gammontown seemed like paradise to me. By age three, living over the Majestic, I was already nostalgic for the good old days, for the place where I had learned to take my first steps. When

I dreamed of home, I dreamed of Gammontown, not the Majestic. Grandma had been raised there, with books on the shelves, a sturdy brownstone roof over her head, and pots boiling on the stove. Before I was even old enough to reason, I wondered why she would marry a guy like Grandpa. How and why had good and evil collided?

I got my answer in a parable that sounded too bad to be true, like most of my family's history.

Grandma's mother, my great-grandmother Irene, was the illegitimate daughter of a Russian Orthodox priest and a Hungarian cleaning lady, a crime in itself in most social circles. She was a beautiful woman, with a shock of black hair, a smooth complexion, and a love for dancing— all passed down to my mother, who is named after her.

We have no photographs of Irene Kaminsky, only my mother's face and the stories handed down, like genetic code, over the past century. My grandmother did have a picture of her mother. It hung on the wall of the living room, but Grandpa, in one of his fits of rage, took it down and destroyed it by sticking his foot through it.

Because Irene was called Gypsy by her friends and family, I pictured her with hoop earrings and a tambourine decorated with colored ribbons. She was filled with Hungarian blood, energy, and life. If anyone could eventually escape from Jersey City, Irene could. She was pure fire and spirit.

Because of her poor social standing, Irene came to the United States in 1893, promised to a man named Peter. It was the year after Ellis Island opened its doors. The Statue of Liberty was new, shining bright in the harbor, causing a distraction from the dense Manhattan skyline. As Irene sailed into the harbor, she likely rushed onto the deck from steerage to get a glimpse of that skyline. Office buildings had only just begun to scrape the sky in Manhattan. The steel skeleton–framed Manhattan Life building was going up, not far from the Tower and World buildings on Park Row.

The skyline was noticeably smaller, a prepubescent version of the one I would come to know from the riverbank of New Jersey. But the city was amazing, young, and vital, just like fifteen-year-old Irene. With all the excitement of seeing New York, Irene probably never noticed Jersey City creeping up on her, a dwarfed, dirty industrial afterthought, like a midget with soot on its face.

Irene never really made it to New York. She probably visited. But she settled in Jersey City, the railroad link for the rest of the country. Immigrants would initially land at Ellis Island, but they would continue their journey into the New World from Jersey City. Two thirds of all Ellis Island immigrants—an estimated 8 million—passed through the Central Railroad of New Jersey terminal, pulling up into one of three wooden ferry slips. From the time its first terminal was built in 1864, Jersey City was the departure point for hundreds of thousands of Poles headed to Chicago, Norwegians with cousins in Minnesota, and truly adventurous souls on their way to the wilds of California and the Pacific Northwest. All aboard in Jersey City.

The crowds passing through, past my relatives, were so thick that the wooden station was rebuilt with red brick in 1889 and expanded in 1914, its tall, pointed tower and large white clock almost as much a beacon as the round domes of Ellis Island. By the turn of the century, the terminal handled between 30,000 and 50,000 arrivals each day, coordinating 128 ferry runs with 300 trains. Thousands upon thousands visited the waiting room that is Jersey City, just long enough to catch a train to a better life.

Some lingered awhile longer—resting on their baggage, or maybe moving into town while a generation passed. It's not uncommon for people, particularly on the East Coast, to have a relative who once lived in Jersey City. Like a modern-day Mesopotamia, it was a beginning for many people. But eventually they got it together and moved on.

Amid the thick black smoke and screeching, oily locomotives, the crowds of immigrants were herded through the north baggage tunnel of the three-story station to tracks 1 and 2, set aside especially for them. The powers-that-be made sure the passengers from steerage did not mingle with the first-class ticket buyers inside the French château–style headhouse, complete with a chandeliered restaurant, a newsstand, bar, post office, and barbershop.

Whether you had the luxury of the metal starbursts and iron balconies of the station proper or the cramped view of the baggage tun-

nel's wooden ceiling, the view of the railroad tracks at the other end
was the same for everyone: a dozen shining steel paths headed westward, with a shed supported by a forest of Corinthian columns.

Of the hundreds of trains that left from those tracks—from the
Central lines and the B&O and the Reading—a handful were local.
With the New York skyline at their back, some immigrants took the
train to Bayonne or to the Jersey shore. Some rode trains just a stop or
two away to prettier parts of Jersey City, to the West Side Avenue station, the Greenville station, Communipaw, Jackson Avenue, or Arlington Avenue.

Irene didn't even get that far. She hopped a trolley to Gammontown. I imagine her being so tired from the boat ride that she simply
gave up in Jersey City and surrendered to Peter, her mail-order husband. Perhaps she had schemed to board a train going farther west, but
he was there waiting for her at the station.

Peter was not a pretty sight. He was an albino, with hair so blond it
was white and eyes so light blue they were nearly colorless. He was
shorter than she was, five-foot-two to her five-foot-four. Looks weren't
everything, of course. But Peter wasn't even kind. He was wealthy—at
least by Jersey City standards—but he was a cheap bastard.

Irene grudgingly put her bags down on that Gammontown soil and
called it home.

Wherever she looked, east toward the tiara of the New York skyline
or west toward that great big bulge she couldn't conquer, Irene probably felt a little cheated. I know I would have. Jersey City was—and is—
an ugly place.

Other industrial towns nearby had their bright spots. Paterson,
founded by Alexander Hamilton before he caught that piece of lead,
had its falls. The 77-foot-high, 280-foot-wide waterfall laid claim to
being the second-largest, by volume, east of the Mississippi. So it
wasn't the largest, but it was easy on your eyes while you worked yourself to death in a silk mill.

When Irene arrived downtown, there were acres of rail yards, littered vacant lots plagued with sickly weeds, and miles of dirty streets,
which back then were clogged not with cars but with piles of horse
manure. The local pencil factories and canneries were just beginning

to belch the black smoke that would scar the city's buildings and residents—my family—for life. There were no waterfalls. No tall buildings. Coming to America through downtown Jersey City was like entering a big, beautiful restaurant through the service entrance. You passed the garbage and the stockroom along the way. You were ignored, and if you were lucky, you got to sneak a few scraps from the kitchen before your shift was through.

Even the city's name contained no poetry, no mystery to be unraveled. There were no Indian cadences, as in *Weehawken* or *Hoboken*. The name was the butt of a joke, worse than the punch line "Jersey" alone, with the image of urban squalor added on, like insult to injury.

Jersey. City. As simple and as ugly as that.

Those who, like my great-grandparents, came to the Hudson's west bank did not settle in Jersey City. They settled *for* Jersey City. They were settlers of a different kind, the kind who always feel cheated, because they settled for less.

In Irene's case, she settled for Peter, a Russian albino a decade older than she was. He had emigrated just six years earlier from Galicia, a place that was in either Poland or Austria, depending on what year you looked at a map. By language and religion, the family was Russian. Irene had no siblings. Except for her husband, she was alone in Jersey City—a strange and ugly land. Perhaps not as ugly as Galicia, but a tough place nonetheless.

Gammontown lived up to its nasty Dutch name. The railroads—with control of the legislature—filled in beyond the shoreline, extending the city out to the water's edge. The fill, comprised mostly of New York's garbage, started New Jersey's long and continuing reputation for smelling bad.

By then, Hudson County had its first convicted politician—William Bumstead, a builder and member of the board of aldermen. A list of indictments had come down in the Bumstead Ring scandal in the 1870s, but only the alderman was found guilty of tipping off a realtor about land to be purchased for a Jersey City reservoir, lending the guy money to buy it, then reselling it to the city for a profit. Soon after, city treasurer Alexander Hamilton (no relation) ran away to Mexico with $87,000 in bonds. Then, after the 1889 election, sixty-six election officials were convicted when seven thousand phony ballots surfaced. But they were all eventually pardoned and given new political jobs.

An even bigger scandal broke four years after Irene arrived. One of the nation's biggest jury-riggers had been making frequent visits to the Hudson County prosecutor's office until, finally, two officials were indicted. They were charged with taking bribes to let prisoners go free. Not surprisingly, the case ended in a hung jury.

In this less-than-perfect place she called home, Irene bore six children—three boys and three girls—two of whom, William and Mariana, died of cholera while they were still infants. After Mariana died, Irene had no more children. My grandmother Pauline, the youngest, stayed the youngest. Grandma was named after Peter's much kinder twin brother, Paul, who lived with the family on and off for several years, traveling between the Old Country and Jersey City at least three times in steerage. In 1913, he arrived with $25 in his pocket. The rest of his money was hidden in the soles of his shoes.

When I was young, I thought their church, Saints Peter and Paul, was named after Great-Grandpa and his twin. With brown hair and blue eyes, Paul was more handsome than his fraternal twin, and taller, meeting Irene's gaze at five-foot-four. Unlike Peter, Paul couldn't read or write, but he had lots of spunk. Some say he left Jersey City and returned to Russia to fight in the revolution. Another family story has him moving to Pennsylvania.

I often wonder if Irene slept with Paul in those last hours before he left for St. Petersburg—or Pittsburgh—to conceive my grandmother. Paul's name—not Peter's—has been carried through the generations, to my sister, Paula, and to her son, Paul. We have no Peters in our family.

The Kaminskys were well-off for a Jersey City family, since Peter owned their house and the attached row of brownstones on Grand Street. Irene thrived in the Gammontown soil, making the best of what she had. She kept a garden in the backyard, behind a high wooden fence that separated her from the neighbors. Each day she would shovel horse manure from the cobblestone street out front to use as fertilizer. It embarrassed my grandmother. But Irene didn't care who saw her shoveling shit. She kept an immaculately clean house. Because of the soap dust filtering out of the Colgate factory, housewives in Gammontown only had to add water to their rags to clean their windows. I can see Irene sticking her proud, bun-topped head outside her sparkling windows, breathing in that fresh, sanitized breeze, or the stench coming from the waterfront fill, depending which way the air was blowing that day. From the front of the house, she could watch the kids gather across the street at the Whittier House, an extra-wide brownstone that had been converted into a boys' club. From the rear window, Irene could glimpse her flowers, the small shed near the back fence, and, farther in the distance, the Morris Canal basin.

Along the canal, flat-bottomed boats carried coal from the anthracite mines of Phillipsburg, Pennsylvania, to homes and factories in New York City, bypassing Jersey City residents. Once the canal was closed and the railroads took over, local kids often raided the coal cars and took as much as they could cart away.

To Irene, the coal canal was likely a pretty sight from high up, a bit of country in an industrial area. But up close it was polluted. When kids went swimming in the canal, they came out looking as if they'd been dipped in tar.

Irene's son Sam swam in the Morris Canal as a child. While diving into the shallow waterway one afternoon, he got his head stuck in the mud and muck at its bottom. He was an excellent swimmer, but when he didn't come up for air after a minute or so, his friends jumped in and rescued him. Sam went home shaken, his hair a dark, cruddy mess. He probably got a beating from his mother. Or, more likely, his father. Peter was strict, sometimes to a fault. When his son John was arrested for some minor infraction years later, Peter left him in jail overnight. Uncle John cried and carried on but supposedly learned his lesson.

Whenever the potential for mischief arose, Irene and Peter were there, waving fists at their young sons and keeping them in line. On a Sunday morning in the summer of 1916, a Jersey City pier storing munitions headed for the European Allies caught fire, causing an explosion that rocked the metropolitan area for twenty-five miles around. The Black Tom explosion occurred at 2:10 A.M.; the city was sure of it, since the force of the blast stopped the clock atop the *Jersey Journal* building.

When it blew, Black Tom was the single most dramatic event in my family's history up until that moment. The blast was so strong that babies were thrown from their cribs and patients at St. Francis Hospital were knocked clear out of bed. The stage doors on the Majestic Theatre, down the street from the tavern, were pulled off their hinges. Yelling that the world was coming to an end, mothers, their babies in their arms, ran into the middle of city streets. Crowds of people whose homes had caved in gathered on the grass at City Hall Park and camped out all night around the tired statue. Inside, politicians inspected the cracks in the walls and the damaged floors and worried that City Hall might collapse, too. The blast broke hundreds of stained-glass windows in the city's churches, their images of Jesus and Mary falling into shimmering piles of red and blue glass. Shop windows came crashing down in a crystal hail.

In the early-morning blackness, hundreds of Poles from the neighborhood swarmed outside the wooden doors of OLC Church, trying to push their way in. But the doors were locked tight. The crowd grew hysterical until a brawny Polish guy—possibly one of my relatives—busted the door down. The parishioners rushed in and got down on their knees and started praying.

When their own house shook, my teenage uncles Sam and John jumped out of bed and pulled on their pants. They had no plans to go to Saints Peter and Paul and pray. They had some window-shopping to do. With the city's store windows gone, looters were out in force. Sam and John planned to join them. But Peter stopped his sons from meeting their hoodlum friends.

Neighborhood looting was kept under control, not so much by parents or police, whose billy clubs were knocked out of their hands by the force of the blast, but by the merchants. They made a run on hardware stores and lumberyards and nailed boards and wire netting across the gaping shop windows as soon as they could.

Only one looting incident was reported, and it didn't involve my family. Two hours after the blast, a young man carrying two typewriters was spotted by a cop on the beat near City Hall. "This is a kind of strange hour for a young literary man to be meandering around with his typewriters," said *The Jersey Journal*, getting inside the cop's head. When the cop asked him where he got the typewriters, the kid was "so disconcerted by the effects of the explosion that he couldn't remember," the paper said.

The young poet was escorted to the police station, which received a call five hours later from the receptionist at Jersey City Typewriter Exchange. Two typewriters were missing. The young poet was booked and fingerprinted.

The typewriters weren't the only things missing after the explosion. When they looked down Warren Street, residents thought the Statue of Liberty was gone, swiped by the blast. *The Jersey Journal* received calls all that night from people worried that she lay at the bottom of the Hudson, the target of German sabotage. Not to worry, the editors said. The dynamos lighting the statue were simply cut off, leaving the Lady standing in the dark. Her gown and skin were pockmarked with some shrapnel, but she was still there.

It wasn't until later that morning, after the sun rose, that the Lady reappeared. In the midmorning haze, many of the neighborhood kids went down to the Black Tom pier, where a thick cloud of smoke still hovered. They dove into the water naked, searching for souvenir shells. I imagine Uncle Sam was still too traumatized by the Morris Canal incident to participate. Maybe Peter locked his kids in the house, mistakenly thinking it would be safe inside 173 Grand Street.

Because 173 Grand was so near the canal and the river, the high water table would cause floods in the basement. Water filled the crawl space and would burst through the bricks. Neighbors called it a "tumultuous house." One plumber, who sidelined as a psychic, asked years later what on earth had happened there. He wasn't just talking about the water table. He claimed to have seen a spirit pass next door into the neighbors' basement. "Did someone die here?" he asked.

You could take or leave the psychic melodrama. But while doing construction on the house, the new owners ripped down the original backyard shed and found a human skull inside. Maybe it was an aborted baby or a lover of Irene's.

Despite his wealth and his good job as a railroad freight handler, Peter felt he didn't deserve Irene. By the 1920s, she spoke at least three languages—Polish, Russian, and English—and was a popular, independent woman who ran card games in the house and an employment agency in the basement, in addition to her job at a pencil factory.

Peter grew more and more jealous. Self-confident and headstrong, Irene often refused to have sex with him. To try and keep her in line, Peter beat Irene every now and then, just as he did the children. Wife battering was not uncommon in the 1920s. But one unseasonably warm autumn day—November 2, 1922—the mercury hitting 61 degrees, Irene refused to make Peter soup. Irene probably laughed at her husband, telling him, "It's much too warm for soup, you stupid albino bastard." Maybe she was too busy, with all her jobs, and told him to make it himself.

Peter and Irene got into one of their usual arguments. My grandmother, Pauline, only twelve years old, and her sister Helen, fifteen, were home that night and heard their mother's screams from the kitchen. They thought nothing of it, since their parents fought all the time. But that night was worse than other nights; Peter beat Irene viciously.

Despite severe head injuries, Irene continued her "housewifely duties," according to a story in *The Jersey Journal* the next day. I guess that means she gave in to Peter's demands—groggily filled a pot with water, threw in a few carrots and a chicken, then boiled some egg noodles before lying down and bleeding onto her bedroom pillow.

That morning, with their father at work, the girls found their mother unconscious in bed. My aunt Helen heard the death rattle in her mother's throat, threw open the carved, wooden front doors, leapt onto the wide stoop, down its nine stone steps, and out onto Grand Street, screaming to anyone who would listen that her father had killed her mother. A neighbor, Mrs. Phillips, calmed the hysterical girls and had Irene taken to the city hospital. She was pronounced dead at the age of forty-four.

Noticing a bruise on her head, a doctor notified police, who launched an investigation. Peter denied hitting Irene. But according to the second-to-last line in the news story, "The daughters say that it was no unusual thing for their father to beat their mother."

NO SOUP FOR SUPPER, SAY HE STRUCK WIFE FATAL BLOW was the

headline on November 3, 1922. My great-grandfather was charged with murder, but a week and a half later was acquitted. The family says that he paid off the corrupt Jersey City police officials and that because of his high profile as a landowner and railroad employee, he was let go. The charges were dropped.

Had my great-grandmother Irene died in any other city, or at another time in the city's history, my family might have given Peter the benefit of the doubt and said that, well, maybe he was innocent. But it was 1922, when Mayor Frank Hague was at the height of his long and powerful reign. Police corruption and cover-ups were so widespread that the FBI stopped accepting crime statistics from the Hague machine, because they were so unreliable. Nineteen twenty-two was also the year Hague was made New Jersey's national Democratic committeeman. And the year he started building the hospital maternity wing named after his mother, Margaret.

Peter was released in time for Irene's wake, which was held on the parlor floor of the brownstone. As far as we know, Irene was not buried in the backyard shed. Helen, emotionally wrecked, missed the funeral. Her father, probably haunted by her accusations, sent her away to a youth house for troubled children. That left Grandma Pauline alone with her murderous father. Her brothers were grown men by then, with wives and troubled homes of their own. For four years Grandma lived with her father in that brownstone, until he died, leaving her orphaned. Paul, her namesake, never came back to adopt her. I imagine her sitting in the front-parlor window, waiting for her handsome Russian uncle to come and rescue her on a white horse. But the family said he'd heard of the scandal and was too embarrassed to return.

Grandma inherited money from her father's real estate holdings, but at the age of sixteen, she failed to invest it wisely. She went to live with her brother John and his wife in Brooklyn for a few months. But she wound up back in Jersey City. Without her mother to give her guidance or her father to discipline her, Grandma started dating a good-looking Italian kid who hung out at the boys' club across the street.

His nickname was Beansie.

4

OFF THE TRUCK

––––––––

After Grandma died at what I considered the incredibly old age of sixty, I began asking my mother how old she was every few hours. Forty, she would say. Same as last time you asked. She questioned the pediatrician about it. The doctor said I was afraid Ma was going to go next— that she'd go from forty to sixty in a flash. And then die, like Grandma.

With Grandma gone, my mother attempted to enroll me in nursery school. Armed with my plastic Banana Splits lunch box, I went bravely into the playroom of Holy Rosary. The program was run by a nun so old that she barely had the energy to walk, never mind work a room of preschoolers. She tried in vain to get us to take long naps on the little cots she provided. And when that didn't work, she left us in front of a black-and-white television set. My schoolmates and I sat staring at the screen, watching Popeye scroll by. The nun didn't know how to fix the horizontal hold.

I missed my grandmother and the excitement at City Hall and was insulted that my parents would deposit me in such a boring place. To escape, I thought up a clever lie, the first lie of my life. I told my mother that the horrible nun was giving us vitamins. My mother was convinced she was drugging us to get us to sleep on the tiny cots, and immediately removed me from Holy Rosary.

My mother rarely left me with Stanley or Paula—not because she didn't trust them, but because she didn't want to burden them. Because her father was in jail and her mother was always working, she had been forced to watch her brothers and sister as a child. The only one she didn't have to keep an eye on was her older brother, Sonny, who kept an eye on her. But Sonny died when he was only fourteen, killed in a truck accident that left Ma the oldest in her family.

She knew how much she resented those long days of being the little grown-up, having to tell her siblings what to do. And she didn't want Stanley and Paula to have to go through the same thing with me. Besides, one of the few times my brother did watch me, we got into trouble. It wasn't his fault. I take full responsibility, though I think I blamed it on him at the time.

Stanley was my first hero, and my scapegoat, protecting me at all costs. He was skinny and dark-haired like me, but had hazel eyes and a crooked, uncertain smile that I would later inherit from years of living in Jersey City. It was part smirk, part fear of letting anyone catch you smile, and it shows up in decades of family photos.

While my mother was at work at the DMV, Stanley and I played a game of soccer. I kicked the hard plastic ball, the kind sold in large bins at the ShopRite supermarket, and hit the living room light fixture, a glass bowl hanging a few inches from the ceiling. It didn't break right away, but it came falling down toward the round coffee table in the middle of the room. It smashed into hundreds of pieces, creating a glass minefield all around us. We carefully tiptoed to the kitchen and called my mother to break the bad news. She came running home, more worried we were hurt than mad at us. Ma quit her job soon after that.

On the days indoors with Ma, I would place my father's dusty polka 45's on my Close 'N Play phonograph and fly through the rooms to the clarinet and accordion until I was exhausted. It sometimes took all day. When I needed a rest, I'd listen to my favorite 45, an old Jerry Lewis song that went, "Put something on the bar besides your elbow. Something like an old ten-dollar bill . . . They can't ring up your elbow in the till." When the song was over, I'd lift the needle and place it back at the beginning. I thought Jerry Lewis was hysterical, though I'm sure my mother couldn't stand to hear that whining, off-key voice sing the same stupid song over and over again.

But Ma never complained about the noise. Neither did our upstairs neighbor, Ducky, the guy who had tipped us off to Grandpa's plan to shoot us. Ducky often let me play with his Siberian husky, Keno, named after his master's favorite casino board game. Like Ducky, the drunks downstairs never complained about my noise, either. I was allowed to sing Jerry Lewis songs and run free in our three-bedroom apartment above the Majestic.

Depending on the season, Stanley and I would play Nerf football, basketball, or baseball, the home-run zone the space behind my father's vinyl recliner. After the incident with the light fixture, plastic balls were no longer allowed. And soccer season was eternally suspended.

One summer, Stanley and I ate dozens of Popsicles and used the sticks to build a miniature of the Twin Towers of the World Trade Center, which were growing at a much faster rate than I was. Stanley and I watched it rise floor by floor from across the river. First the steel girders were laid down, one atop the other. Then the vertical holes were filled in with concrete, metal, and glass.

Every day I would beg Stanley to play house, and he would grudgingly agree. "Pretend I'm your husband and I'm at home sick," he'd say, turning on the television and lying down on the couch, smiling that crooked smile.

To pass the time between my favorite TV shows and the City Hall excitement, my mother would read to me. My favorite book was a children's biography of Christopher Columbus, which she read in a mock Italian accent, imitating her own grandmother. She would improvise passages: "And then, his-a mama said, 'Christopher, whatsamatta for you? You don't like-a my meatballs?' " My mother and her siblings all had a sense of humor, which was how they survived Grandpa all those years.

When things were calm outside, I would go downstairs and place my feet in the stream of cool hydrant water that flowed down Mercer Street. The hydrant was turned on by the Puerto Rican kids down the block. I envied them, because their parents let them play out in the street on those hot summer days, letting them run in and out of the hydrant's spray. I could see them in the distance doing their awkward hydrant dances, arms flailing, bare feet kicking. Beyond the high, cold spray, and a block or two past the low-rise homes and boarded-up city buildings, stood a few trees. I wondered if that's where "the country" was and if someday I might be able to walk there. For the time being, I was confined to the curb, the small brook washing over my tanned feet, my only entertainment an occasional cigarette butt or a much-needed Popsicle stick floating past.

I had seen the dark side of playing in the street, so I knew my mother was right to confine me to the curb. Every summer, souped-up Chevys and Caddys without mufflers sped past, and each year kids were run down. Parents had petitioned for a traffic light at the corner of Mercer and Grove, but because the poor neighborhood had no pull at nearby City Hall, a traffic light was never installed.

At a very early age, I got used to the drill. The screech of tires was followed by a thud and a scream, my mother's signal to run downstairs with blankets and bandages. The smaller the kid was, the more likely it was that he would die, because his head would be about even with the car grille.

To get me out of the neighborhood, my parents took me everywhere with them. Some parents in Jersey City just left their kids at home while they went to work. Once in a while, there'd be a story in the paper about a kid discovered handcuffed to a radiator while his parents went out on the town. Most mothers stayed at home with their kids, ignoring them and providing very little entertainment. But I was constantly amused. My parents held me close, but they rarely sheltered me.

Daddy liked taking me to the movies, particularly to Journal Square, to the Loew's or Stanley Theatres, the only bright spots in that part of the city. Journal Square was a mini-Calcutta, filled with crippled pencil sellers in wheelchairs, midgets who hawked the evening *Jersey Journal*, deranged people with growths and tumors, and mumblers who walked the streets talking to themselves. Chief among the mumblers was a defrocked priest who still wore his frock and paced up and down the sidewalk delivering private sermons.

The deformed and disabled liked to congregate on Journal Square. One woman had a goiter on her neck the size of a baby's head. There was a bowlegged dwarf with an underbite named Helenka, who always wore a housedress. The local guys would tease Helenka by picking her up by the ankles and shaking her. Back in the old days, there was a man with no legs who came around begging on a little board with skate wheels, singing songs like "My Time Is Your Time" through a megaphone. He had a beautiful voice. People would lean out their windows and throw down two or three cents wrapped in a small piece of paper torn from *The Jersey Journal*.

Wandering the streets was a grown-up mongoloid named Rachel. She wore several dresses and coats but would take the top layers off to turn rope for the kids in the street, her strong, long arm throwing the jump rope into a high arc. There was also a guy who would step up onto the curb and then back down, over and over again, then march in place. He was probably a war veteran, but no one ever got up the courage to question him. Sometimes out-of-towners unfamiliar with the curb guy would wind up walking behind him and get stuck at the curb until they realized he was crazy and that they should walk around him.

Because of the Journal Square bus and PATH station, the area also attracted the homeless, who back then were called bums. My favorite was a woman named Mary, who never spoke but always ran around in a rush, dressed in a raincoat and worn black loafers. I wondered where she was off to in such a hurry.

The Loew's—mispronounced *Low-ees*—was just about the only pretty thing left on Journal Square and was as magical to a five-year-old as visiting Disney World. More than pretty, the Loew's was beautiful. Or as Jersey Citizens pronounced it, *beauty-ful*.

The place was ornate and over the top, with a huge white, lighted marquee, a tall tower, and a clock that featured St. George slaying the dragon. The façade was made of textured terra-cotta blocks, encrusted with dirt from years of Journal Square traffic pollution. What made the Loew's beauty-ful were the fantasies and, later, the memories everyone attached to it.

Once in the lobby, I would let go of Daddy's hand and run up the red-carpeted stairs. Not bothering to hold on to the bronze railing and the lion's-head banisters, I'd head straight to the red velvet–trimmed balcony, where I would stand overlooking the rococo lobby and wave to my adoring fans, Daddy in particular. He would wave back, smiling his toothless smile. There were golden mosaic tile alcoves and red-and-gold tapestries along the walls. The ladies' room had a marble mantelpiece and four big, mirrored vanities, which made me feel like a movie star. Daddy would wait for me outside the bathroom near the shell-shaped blue-tiled fountain, where goldfish swam. Hanging over everything was a Czechoslovakian-crystal chandelier that cost $60,000 back in 1929, the year the theater was built, just a month before the stock market crash.

Whatever decade it was, when you went to the Loew's, you felt special. It inspired you, unlike any other place in Jersey City. It was where a young guy named Sinatra took his date to see Bing Crosby sing in 1933 and decided he could do better than that. And better than Hudson County.

It was where a giant Wonder Morton organ piped out *Phantom of the Opera*–like chords that rattled your insides and made you think God lived inside the theater.

In 1960, with John F. Kennedy on his way to visit Journal Square during his campaign, local politicians held a rally outside the theater. The loudspeakers and music were so loud that they bled into the theater. The manager asked them to turn it down, to preserve the quiet inside and the illusion that the theatergoers were royalty. When the Democrats refused to turn down the volume, the manager threatened to shut down the marquee that night—which would have left JFK in darkness. The young Democrats bowed to the Loew's and piped down.

One of its architects commented that the Loew's was "where the rich rub elbows with the poor, and we are the better for it." Even in the 1970s, when vandalism on Journal Square was at all-time high, graffiti never touched its walls. Young vandals knew the theater was special.

As if to make up for all the ugliness in Jersey City, Journal Square had two movie palaces. The Stanley Theatre, which I used to think was named after my brother, was a block away and was almost as gaudy as the Loew's. Built in 1928, it had a vestibule made of Italian marble and stained glass and lighted by a colorful chandelier hung with crystal fruit baubles. In the main lobby hung a Grand Crystal chandelier taken from the old Waldorf-Astoria, which was knocked down to make way for the Empire State Building. The chandelier was 13 feet high and 10 feet wide and shimmered with 144 lights and 4,500 pieces of crystal.

The ceiling was painted sky blue, with wisps of white cloud sailing across. Brass rails ran along the staircases, and at the top hung small lanterns. A woollen shepherd tapestry, an antelope mosaic, and a tiled fountain with a lion spitting water decorated the upstairs lobby. The Stanley, with its stylized animals, was as close as Jersey City came to having its own zoo.

My favorite part about it, though, was the auditorium. The huge room held 4,300 people and was decorated like a Venetian courtyard, with painted urns and flowers. There were no real flowers in Jersey City. Spring was marked not by the first tulip or crocus but by the first floater, or dead body, to wash ashore in the Hudson River, its arrival always recorded in *The Jersey Journal*.

At the Stanley, terra-cotta buildings with red-tile roofs surrounded you, and the Rialto bridge stretched over the wide screen in front of you. The only dead bodies inside the Stanley were the ones that turned up on its extra-wide movie screen.

Overhead, stars twinkled and clouds actually floated past, thanks to the Stanley's mysterious cloud machine. Because of its ceiling and because it was named after my brother, the Stanley was my favorite place in Jersey City, and for years, my favorite place on earth, long before I knew there was an actual place called Venice or real courtyards with flowers and stars.

My mother saw her first movie at the Stanley when she was twelve years old, with her brother Sonny. When he noticed the stars, he got scared and told her they had to get home. "Sissy," he said. "It's late. Look. It's already dark out. Mama's gonna be mad." It was always a shock, even twenty-five years later, to emerge from the Stanley and be greeted by daylight and the reality that was Jersey City.

To escape reality, my parents had gone to the Stanley on hundreds of dates, the most memorable in 1953, when they went to see *The Moon Is Blue*, an Otto Preminger film starring William Holden and David Niven.

The movie wasn't very racy, but the dialogue included the words *virgin, sex,* and *tramp.* Local priests objected to the theater showing it, but the Stanley's management showed it anyway. My parents, who hadn't heard yet of the controversy, sat upstairs in the loge, where they always sat, so that my father could smoke and my mother could watch the stars twinkle and the clouds drift. Each in their own way, they waited for the movie to begin. But it never did.

The house lights came up and an announcement was made that everyone in the theater had to leave: *The Moon Is Blue* was no longer being shown. My parents left their seats and walked down the long, grand staircase in the lobby, that Waldorf chandelier blazing overhead. Like Norma Desmond in *Sunset Boulevard,* my mother slowly descended, with newsreel cameras and photographers' flashbulbs going off at the foot of the stairs. It turned out that Jersey City's public safety commissioner, Bernard Berry, had had the theater's manager arrested. It was big news, making national headlines. Once he became mayor, Berry continued to boycott the Stanley, banning the movie *Blackboard Jungle.* Berry and Jersey City became synonymous with small-town, narrow-minded thinking. It was already considered too corrupt a place to be thought of as puritanical.

While still a preschooler, I could never tell the difference between a trip to Journal Square and a trip to Manhattan. From downtown Jersey City, we had to take the underground PATH train—called the Hudson Tubes—to both places. There were trips to Macy's in New York, where Mom would let me play with the toys and ride the bicycles around the showroom floor, and excursions to the Battery, the place where the boat left for the Statue of Liberty. We would feed Cracker Jacks to the pigeons and watch the tourists line up for ferry tickets. Mom gave me dimes for the viewing machines in the park, which were meant for looking at the statue and Ellis Island. But I would focus my sights on Jersey City, searching for the Majestic and for Vince sweeping the gutter. In the summer, we'd go to Greenwich Village, to check out the hippies in Washington Square Park or the annual outdoor art exhibit.

But more fun, and more frequent, were the trips to the funeral parlor. My mother attended hundreds of funerals with me in tow.

To my mother, there was no concept more depressing than dying and having no one come to view your body. Funerals were my first lesson in what-goes-around-comes-around. If there were three or four people at a wake, it was obvious the person in the casket had not made many friends and had not gone out of his or her way to help others. The more people at the wake, the kinder the person was in life. It was a true, and final, test of character.

Heaven wasn't so much the goal after death. A crowded funeral parlor was.

Since my mother had lots of friends and knew practically everybody in the city because of the DMV, she attended everyone's wake. My grandmother's wake is the first one I can remember, though not the first I attended. Grandma was dressed in a powder blue gown that matched her eyes, which were now forever closed, and rosary beads were weaved between her fingers. I was so blasé, I leaned my coloring book on the kneeler in front of the casket and broke out the Crayolas. Dead bodies didn't faze me in the least. As a preschooler, I was an expert in public grief.

At other families' wakes, I knew the right moment to approach the relatives of the deceased, when to cut off conversation and kneel in front of the coffin, how long to pretend to pray and gaze longingly at the stiff inside, and how much the mass cards and flower arrangements cost. By the time my best friend's grandmother died, I was a pro. Still a child, I took Liz's freckled hand and bravely escorted her up to the casket, the stuffed body inside and the gardenias surrounding it. My mother was so proud.

Wakes were important, because that's where many of the family stories were retold. Funeral masses were better than wakes, because they were followed by the burial and a full meal at a local restaurant. The burial was key, because it guaranteed a romp on some of the only green grass in the county. There were trees and grass and freshly cut flowers thrown on the coffin at Holy Name Cemetery, signs of nature I was otherwise deprived of. It made no sense to me that the dead got all the green space in Jersey City. They certainly couldn't enjoy it.

While the casket was lowered into the freshly dug grave, I was off running and jumping on the grass between the other, older graves. I never stepped directly on them, avoiding them like I sometimes avoided stepping on the cracks in the sidewalk. Ma said stepping on a grave was sacrilegious.

The reward for attending the burial was the meal afterward. If the deceased was a close enough relative, we'd get to ride in a limo to the cemetery and restaurant. Otherwise, we'd have to bum a ride off someone in the funeral procession. Ma didn't drive; neither did Daddy or their parents or most of the Stapinskis. For forty-one years, my father got a ride to work from a friend. He and my mother took a bus to her senior prom. In the snow. (She graduated in the winter semester.)

After a burial, we'd hitch a ride with an old friend of my mother's to a place like the Hi Hat, a big banquet hall in Bayonne, the town to the south of Jersey City, where some of my Polish cousins lived. The Hi Hat specialized in funeral meals. A good funeral meal was something you never passed up.

Eating was the most important form of entertainment in my family—better than the movies, better than polka music. We were taught at a very young age never to waste food or turn your nose up at it or disrespect it in any way. I cringed when I saw other kids in nursery school throw their peanut butter and jelly sandwiches in the garbage or, worse, throw them at each other.

It was a sin to throw God's food on the floor. Though our family had plenty of food, we treated each supper as if it might be our last. Both my parents were born during the Depression, so they never took basic things like food or heating oil for granted.

As a child, my mother and her brothers and sister stole K rations from the Armour yards and coal from the railroads to keep warm. Always on the lookout for "the bull"—the railroad detective—they would steal loads of the dark black fuel and drop it down to their accomplices stationed under the trestles. My father and his brothers did the same. Well, most of them.

My uncle Eddie, Daddy's brother, didn't like to get his hands dirty and usually stayed away from the shoots, the coal cars down on the tracks. But on one occasion, Daddy and his brothers brought Uncle Eddie along to be their lookout. "You stay here," they said to Eddie, "and watch for the bull." But they never told Eddie that *bull* was slang for "detective." So there Uncle Eddie stood with a big red wagon, waiting for a bull to come running down the tracks.

It wasn't such a dumb mistake. The rails were often filled with cattle and other animals, mooing on their way to slaughter at the Armour stockyards. My mother and her friends saw a dead lamb one morning in the street, which had fallen from a train car stopped on the Seventh Street trestle. Another time, a bull actually got loose. My mother was wearing a red coat that day, and ducked into a hallway to avoid the charge.

So it was no surprise when one of Uncle Eddie's brothers yelled, "Cheese it! The bull!"—code for "Get going! The cops are coming!"— and Eddie hung around to get a glimpse of the animal. Wildlife was rare in Jersey City, save for the doomed livestock, a few pigeons, rats, and the ornamentation at the Stanley. A chance to see a bull charging down the railroad tracks would not be missed by young Eddie.

But there was no bull. Just the railroad detective, who caught Eddie red-handed with the red wagon. "Who sent you here?" the cop demanded. Not knowing what to answer, Eddie stupidly said, "My mother."

Eddie was escorted to the police precinct for a good scare, then home in a big car. He was sure he was being taken to jail. He probably would have been better off. The police reprimanded Babci, and after they left, she reprimanded Eddie, giving him a beating like he'd never known. His brothers never took him to the shoots again.

Poor epileptic Uncle Tommy even got in on the action and was caught stealing oranges at a fruit-and-vegetable stand in the neighborhood. The police brought him home and yelled at Babci again for not keeping a better eye on Tommy. Daddy got into trouble, because Tommy was usually his responsibility. Uncle Tommy was held back in school two years so that he and Daddy would be in the same class. That way Daddy could keep an eye on him. It was like asking one inmate to keep an eye on another.

Stealing food outright from stores and delis was never condoned— not when my father was little and not when I was growing up. But my father, a Teamster, fed us with the merchandise that fell off the truck at work. At the Union Terminal Cold Storage he was a warehouse checker, which meant he had to make sure everything they said was on the truck got into the warehouse, and vice versa. There were meat and fish trucks on their way to butcher shops and fish stores, sausage that was delivered to the feasts in Little Italy, and more exotic food—like snake, venison, and bear—on its way to the swankiest restaurants in Manhattan. Everything stopped at Daddy's place before going on to Tavern on the Green and Sparks.

At least once a week, a crate of Steak-umms or prepackaged Chicken Cordon Bleu would fall off the refrigerated truck and into our own freezer at home. Mom insisted Daddy never stole a morsel, that the boxes were gifts from the truck drivers for whom he did favors. As if it was theirs to give away.

Thanks to the drivers who Daddy let cut in line to unload their hauls, we always had a big bag of frozen french fries on hand for late-night snacks. Daddy would come home half-crocked from the Majestic and cook them up for us in a pot of oil, the flames licking the ceiling.

My mother resourcefully used everything he brought home, which usually came in large quantities originally intended for restaurant delivery: A big box of clams was made into a big pot of clam chowder. A huge hunk of Muenster cheese was melted over macaroni. A giant bag of oranges was sliced up and placed on a ham Daddy had brought home a few days earlier. Our family never once bought a turkey for Thanksgiving. It was part of the unofficial Teamsters' benefits package: major medical, dental, and swag—the extra box that just happened to fall off the back of the truck.

Because of my father's daily packages, tied in brown paper and carried under his arm, I was the only kid on my block who knew how to peel a lobster tail from its curled shell and who could tell the difference between a sirloin and filet mignon. For a while, I thought lobster and steak were staples in all working-class homes. But my father knew it was special. When the timing was precise and the right boxes fell off the truck at the right moment, my father would treat us all to surf and turf, with a shrimp-cocktail appetizer served on a bed of iceberg lettuce to start. His cocktail sauce was a sinus-searing light pink mixture of six parts fresh horseradish to one part ketchup. My mother wasn't allowed to cook the lobster or steak. That was Daddy's job. He would place the orange-black shells in the broiler with love, and join the lemon and butter in a small saucepan. With tenderness, he would trim the fat from the steaks, leaving just enough gristle to give the meat its sweet, juicy flavor. My mother complained that my father had missed another of his many callings: He should have been a butcher. He handled that meat more gently than he handled her. The steaks—the love of his life—were then grilled to perfection.

It was because of meals like these that my cousins were always sleeping over at our house. Gerri started having a weight problem because of my father's hot roast beef sandwiches. My father loved Gerri, because she had such a good appetite. And she loved him. Uncle Babe's cooking was always the best in the family, she said, even better than my mother's sauce or my aunt Millie's meatballs. And each day we destroyed the evidence, our insides digesting the buttery fingerprints Daddy left.

There was no money saved for college, since most of my father's cash went to Uncle Henry and to Nicky, in the Majestic, for gambling and booze. But we always had plenty of food. And we always had a block of dry ice that Daddy would bring home from work on Halloween to place in a bowl of water to make bubble and smoke for my astonished party guests. We couldn't go trick-or-treating, since the neighborhood was dangerous, so my mother invited all the kids over to bob for apples.

Thanks to Daddy, I was never at a loss when ordering in a fancy restaurant. Whenever he hit the number, Daddy would don his suit and star-sapphire pinkie ring and take us all out to eat. He loved food so much that he couldn't confine himself to the kitchen. It was at places like the King's Court, a Jersey City restaurant with its own coat of arms, and the Top of the Meadows, a swellegant spot atop the North Bergen Holiday Inn, with a view of the swampy meadowlands, that my father and I learned lessons in fine dining.

By the age of six, I knew the menus by heart, the difference between a scallop and scrod, between Chateaubriand and porterhouse, the maître d' and the waiter, all thanks to Daddy. Because he brought home high-quality frozen cakes, the kind restaurants use, I could tell

whether a restaurant had a bakery on the premises or not. I could identify the culprits: seemingly homemade but actually mass-produced
wheels of cheesecake, or Black Forest chocolate cake that we had in
our freezer at home.

Sara Lee cupcakes were a favorite commodity at Daddy's warehouse, and they sat piled high atop our refrigerator, each box missing
its chocolate cupcake first, its strawberry next, the coconut and lemon
left for desperate midnight raids. Sometimes you'd have to search
through six boxes before getting to the cupcake you wanted, hidden at
the bottom.

Whenever there was a parish event at Our Lady of Czestochowa—
a card party or a Chinese auction—my father provided the dessert free
of charge. And any Pepperidge Farm chocolate layer cakes that were
left over, the Polish nuns took back to the convent with them. As far as
I know, they were never charged with receiving stolen property. Like
us, the nuns ate the evidence.

At one card party, a woman named Lillian tried to steal the cake
that was left over, stashing it under the table. "Imagine the nerve?" my
mother complained. Stealing stolen chocolate cake from the mouths of
nuns? Lillian was destined for the fires of hell.

Bake sales at school were easy for my mother, even though she
didn't know how to bake. She would simply show up with an armful of
Daddy's swag from the Cold Storage. That cake was the first to go at
the sale, before Mrs. Romanski's cupcakes or my aunt Julie's cream
puffs. It wasn't exactly in the bake-sale spirit of things, but this was Jersey City. Swag was just part of everyday life.

Swag wasn't the same thing as out-and-out stealing. It was an un-
written rule in Jersey City—and all of Hudson County—that you
could take as much merchandise as you could carry from your job. The
politicians skimmed off the top, so why shouldn't the little people?

As far as I know, my father never got into trouble for taking all that
cake and lobster. His hauls paled in comparison to the other stuff going
on at the Union Terminal. In the 1970s, vast numbers of canned hams
started to disappear from the warehouse. It turned out that a night
crew was pulling a truck up during the lobster shift (which I thought
was named for the lobster crates that came in around midnight) and

piling on the canned hams. One night, when they were almost caught, the crew threw the canned hams in the freezer to hide them. Canned hams are never frozen, merely refrigerated. So when the bosses found dozens of canned hams in the wrong place, they launched an investigation. Fingerprints were lifted from the frozen hams and about twenty-five guys were collared.

Things got worse over time. A new foreman affiliated with the Gambino crime family was brought in, because the Bonanno family was hijacking trucks. As long as the swag didn't exceed daily needs, bosses in Jersey City looked the other way when employees walked away with a paper bag or two of merchandise. Some companies even gave the merchandise away in small quantities, to discourage grand theft. Excessive greed was to be avoided. In 1943, for instance, three men were arrested for stealing $23,000 in toothpaste from Colgate. For months, they had been pulling a truck up to one of the loading docks and taking boxes of the stuff, selling it as part of a fencing ring in New York City. As long as you stayed modest, you were safe.

When I was growing up, because we had friends and relatives at Colgate, we were never in need of toothpaste or toothbrushes. It was ironic that the Polish side of the family, which lived closest to Colgate, always had such bad teeth. Our Colgate connection also provided us with a steady stream of shaving cream and soap. We had all the Irish Spring we needed. When a new product line debuted, like the Colgate pump, we were the first in the state to try it.

Though he was the biggest swagster in our family, Daddy was certainly not alone. When she was in high school, my mother worked at the General Pencil factory. Half her class seemed to work in the same building. Her job was to polish—or paint—the pencils yellow in the second-floor "dip room." The more important your job, the higher the floor you worked on. Downstairs, black workers were busy putting lead in the pencils, exposing themselves to lead poisoning. Erasers were placed on the pencils on the third floor. So the pencils my mother and her classmates stole for school never had erasers on them. It made her a more careful person, never able to erase her mistakes.

My mother and her friends would also go down to the Old Gold cigarette factory and yell up to their friends working inside, who would throw down loosies. Old Gold was my mother's first smoke.

All the books on our shelves were swag, either from Grandpa from the *free* public library or from my aunt Mary Ann, who worked at the American Book Binding Company. They weren't crummy little paperbacks or galley proofs. These were serious hardcover books, which, over the years, grew into an impressive library.

The first book I ever read—*A Mystery for Meg,* a sort of Nancy Drew knockoff—came free of charge from Aunt Mary Ann. My adolescent fantasies ran wild thanks to the collection of Daphne du Maurier novels that she brought home. Like Rebecca, I pined for Manderley. My favorites, though, were the leather- and clothbound series of half-size classics. Aunt Mary Ann transported them in her oversize girdle, worn intentionally to place the whole collection—nineteen books in all—around her midriff. When a coworker jokingly grabbed Aunt Mary Ann one afternoon and swung her around, he commented that she'd gained a little weight.

I loved to flip through the books and smell their yellowing pages, thinking that Aunt Mary Ann had taken them just for me. *The Collector's Edition Book of Quotations* and *The Pocket Book of Greek Art,* with photos of statues missing their arms, were my favorites from that series. I looked at those pictures for hours and wondered if someone had stolen the arms. What could they want with arms?

Aunt Mary Ann didn't limit her talents to books alone. While working at the Jersey City Medical Center, where she landed a job sterilizing instruments for the operating room, Aunt Mary Ann brought home the occasional unnecessary tool. We had a stainless-steel funnel, which my mother used for cooking, and a surgical clamp, which helped us change the channel on a small black-and-white TV long after the knob had fallen off.

Aunt Mary Ann was my idol—not only because she loved books, but because she was the first person in my mother's family to move far away, to the wilds of Miami. We visited her there three times when I was a child, and just a taste of life outside Jersey City—the coconuts and palm trees, the white sand and surf—made me dizzy with happiness. Back in New Jersey, I took to wearing suntan lotion just so I could smell like Florida, and Aunt Mary Ann.

My new favorite 45 immediately became a Harry Belafonte calypso number called "Marianne." Jerry Lewis was knocked off the charts.

The song went something like this: "All day, all night, Marianne. Down by the seashore sifting sand. All the little children join in the band." I believed it was written for my aunt. And I loved her deeply, though I hardly knew her.

All I knew was that Aunt Mary Ann was everything my mother was not: bleached-blond, sarcastic, and cynical. For years she swore she'd never get married, and even when she did, at the old age of thirty-six, she stayed independent and sexy. She never had kids, and she wore a purple velvet bikini even after she married Uncle Ray. Their apartment had modern orange furniture. They were cool.

Just the mention of her name conjured thoughts of the mystical. Whenever my mother cursed, she would shout, "Jesus, Mary, and Joseph," which I misheard as "Jesus, Mary ANN, Joseph." I thought Aunt Mary Ann was a member of the Holy Family. The outlaw member.

Moving out of Jersey City didn't destroy Aunt Mary Ann's talent for swag. She was the family's only test case that showed swag was in your bones, not a viral infection floating through the Hudson County air. As a dental hygienist in Dade County, Florida, Aunt Mary Ann compiled an impressive stockpile of toothbrushes and dental floss in her pantry at home. We even had a small chrome dental mirror, which kept me occupied for hours as I checked my incoming molars.

Aunt Mary Ann rarely stole for herself. Like Robin Hood, whom I had seen at the Loew's in an animated Disney film, Aunt Mary Ann selflessly took from the rich to give to us. There was the story about the lamp on the wall in a fancy restaurant in Florida that someone had admired during dinner. Aunt Mary Ann unscrewed it and placed it in her large pocketbook. She was brave, ballsy, and wonderful. She was the outsider. And in a campaign to be more like her, I began to swipe restaurant ashtrays, smudging my rigid, childish concept of good and evil.

5

THE MACHINE

For as long as I can remember, the time after supper was reserved for reading in our house. Whether we ate lobster tails or macaroni and cheese, we'd retire to the living room afterward and unfold a newspaper or crack open one of the books Aunt Mary Ann had brought home in her girdle. Daddy brought a pile of newspapers home with him every night folded under his arm, next to the frozen food of the day.

Reading time was one of the few times my parents ignored me, their faces buried deep in the *New York Post,* the *Daily News, The Jersey Journal,* and the other local paper, the *Hudson Dispatch.* Before I could even read, I looked at those headlines and traced the letters with my fingers. It seemed that every day the local papers carried a story about some politician under investigation or accused of wrongdoing. I assumed all cities were filled with such sleazy city workers.

In Jersey City, the dirt ran deep. Corruption was so ingrained over the decades that adults thought, as I did, that every place was the same and that you couldn't escape it—that you might as well vote for the person who could help you or your relatives get a job on the city payroll.

Though there was no escape, there was a reason the world—our world—was the way it was. The reason was Hague.

I can't remember the first time I heard his name mentioned. For kids in Jersey City, it was a syllable—like *God* or *Ma*—that had always been in our vocabulary.

Hague. Omnipotent and ever-present.

He ruled for three decades—from 1917 to 1947—though his control and influence bled over into later years. Dozens of county politicians who came after Hague used him as a model for robbing their cities blind. Beating suspects like Grandpa to a pulp, taking kickbacks, doling out no-show jobs to political supporters, getting the votes of the dead and buried, demanding tribute money—it was all synonymous with the name Hague. Though he wasn't the first crooked politician to come out of Jersey City—and certainly not the last—Hague raised corruption to an art form.

Like Grandpa, Frank Hague was born in the Horseshoe section of downtown, so named because the Republican-controlled state legislature tried to cram all the Democratic voters into one U-shaped assembly district in 1871. Grandpa was born on Bay Street, on a block that's still one of the shabbiest in the city; Hague was born on Cork Row, an Irish enclave located where the approach to the Holland Tunnel is now.

Both Hague and Grandpa were afraid of germs. Growing up in squalor will do that to a person. Grandpa spent his early years in a seedy tenement called the Bay View. There was no bay, and not much of a view. Hague was raised in a tenement called the Ark, because it seemed adrift on a large pool of smelly water that often collected outside its wooden door after a heavy rain.

Hague, like Grandpa, was the fourth child in a large family. Their mothers were strong and domineering. Their fathers were quiet working-class guys: Hague's father was a watchman at the Beehive Bank; Grandpa's father was a barber.

Both Hague and Grandpa left school in their early teens. Grandpa quit when he was thirteen; he was in third grade. By then he already had a few tattoos, and sat with his sleeves rolled up beside children half his size. When his teacher saw the tattoos, she covered her mouth and exclaimed, "Oh, you poor child!" Grandpa probably told her to go to hell.

Hague was expelled at fourteen from grade six, too early to learn proper grammar, a problem which made him an easy target in national circles—especially after he delivered a speech or testified before an investigative committee.

On paper, he and Grandpa were physical opposites. Hague was a tall Irish redhead, and Grandpa a short, dark Italian. But there was something about their stern faces, bald heads, and hand gestures that linked them in my mind. I had never seen Hague in action, but I had seen pictures, particularly one in which he's banging his fist, just like Grandpa did on our kitchen table.

I liked to think of Hague and Grandpa as opposite sides of the same stolen coin. They both had an aversion to physical labor. My grandfather refused to hold down a job and would go to great lengths to find money from other sources—other people's pockets. He once took a train to Indiana, then a cab to his son Robby's military base, just to ask him for a loan. Grandpa had no other business in Indiana.

Hague was a bit more inventive when it came to finding cash. He had only to work one menial labor job—on the Erie railroad, as a boilermaker—to know that the blue-collar life was not for him. While he was a teenager, Hague managed a Brooklyn boxer named Joseph Craig. Soon after, he entered the world of politics.

In 1896, a local saloonkeeper named Ned Kenny, known as the Mayor of Cork Row, gave Hague $75 to run for constable in the second ward. Hague parlayed that job into deputy sheriff, then precinct leader, ward leader, and custodian at City Hall—a job that helped him develop his talent for patronage: There was always room for one more maintenance man on the payroll.

One of the things Hague liked most about politics was dressing for the job. Like Grandpa, Hague appreciated fine clothes. Grandpa had his fedora cleaned and blocked once a week and made his kids get down on their hands and knees to spit-shine his shoes. Grandpa often urged his son, a clerk at Zampella's clothing store, to steal merchandise for him.

Hague, even with his $100-a-month job as ward constable, could buy his own tailor-made double-breasted suits and derby hats, his pearl-headed stickpins and silk underwear, and his high, white Belmont collars, which he wore to keep drafts away from his throat. He was deathly afraid of drafts. One legendary story had an eight-year-old Hague nailing shut all the windows in his house to keep out those nasty breezes. Later in life, he would keep the windows of his limousine rolled up to the top, even on the hottest days, though every now and then he'd have his driver pull over so that he could roll the windows down and lead his entourage in breathing exercises. The first thing Hague did when he awoke in the morning was take his own pulse.

Because he was such a stickler for hygiene, Hague kept an office—used as his main office—at the state-of-the-art, multimillion-dollar hospital he built.

Grandpa didn't have the pull to build institutions, but he did wash his feet three times a day, a textbook example of obsessive-compulsive behavior.

Before he became mayor, Hague staked his claim as commissioner of the Department of Public Safety, heading up the city's police and fire departments. His goal was to abolish police drunkenness and extortion, and through a series of trials, he cleaned up the force. "Jersey City," he declared ungrammatically, "is the most moralest city in America."

He created an elite squad of plainclothes police known as zeppelins, or zepps, who were there to do his bidding. They came down on anyone loitering, causing trouble, or bad-mouthing Hague. Through his zepps, Hague established a strong police presence that he would use for his own devices when he was elected mayor four years later.

Because of Hague, Jersey City became a safe place, with a cop on every corner—unless, of course, you rankled the cops or the powers-that-be. Then it was an unsafe place and you got your head broken, sometimes in several places. "I am the law," Hague once said. And he was. He created his own rules. One story had it that Hague's zepps killed a tavern owner, then let the man's widow run the tavern, just to shut her up, even though it was illegal for women to work behind the bar.

But if you could point to one single event that made Hague what he was, this was the one: The story illustrated the hatred between the Irish and the Italians, who had banded together against the Puerto Ricans and blacks in Jersey City by the time I was born. But back when Grandpa was coming of age, the Italians were considered to be the scum of the city. They were the bad guys in Hague's moral universe, a place where nobody but he and his Irish friends prospered.

During Holy Week in 1916, while residents of other cities were busy Easter-egg rolling and bonnet shopping, Jersey Citizens were embroiled in a murder mystery. The victim was the son of Ned Kenny, the Mayor of Cork Row, the man who had given Hague his start in politics.

On Good Friday, twenty-six-year-old Frank Kenny and his new wife were strolling along West Side Avenue on their way home from church at St. Aloysius, the same parish where I would attend high school years later. The West Side was below Journal Square, on a slope near the meadowlands, part of the Greenville ward. The West Side overlooked Newark Bay, so polluted with spilled oil, it was brown. I mistook the bay once for a large parcel of undeveloped land. Back in 1916, before it became nasty-looking, people with money lived in Greenville, in big, beautiful houses not yet ruined by aluminum siding.

On that Good Friday, Kenny went into a bakery on Union Street for a bag of rolls, and for some reason, left his wife standing outside. Maybe he wanted to surprise her with an especially large coffee cake or a dozen hot cross buns—who knows?

While she waited for her husband, Mrs. Kenny was accosted by an Italian immigrant. Witnesses later said they noticed the Italian guy cat-calling as women went by. In Mrs. Kenny, he chose the wrong cat. And the wrong call.

"Hello, chicken," he said to her. *Chicken* was a term of endearment back then, maybe a precursor to the more modern but just as annoying *chick*. Or maybe Mrs. Kenny simply looked like a chicken. Insulted, and in an effort to avoid the Italian, Mrs. Kenny walked quickly down the street toward her house, the creep following close behind.

When Frank Kenny came out of the bakery, he saw his beloved chicken and the Italian up ahead and ran to catch up with them. Kenny insisted that the man apologize to his wife and, depending on whose version of events you believe, probably used a few choice racial slurs to get his point across.

The pro-Kenny version was the tame "You apologize to my wife or I'll turn you inside out." Nice dialogue, but highly unlikely in Jersey City, where practically everybody had a dirty mouth, even my mother.

The Italian said Kenny called him a dago and a wop and then smashed him in the face. Either way, provoked or not, the Italian pulled a revolver from his breast pocket and shot Kenny, point-blank, in the chest. With a bullet to the heart, Kenny died on the spot, right outside his house, the rolls still warm in their bag.

The murderer escaped into the meadowlands, losing his hat, a dark-blue felt number with a green velvet band and the name of the hat store written inside. Jersey City police, under the direction of commissioner Frank Hague, traced the hat to twenty-nine-year-old Michael Rombolo, a strikebreaker at the Ryerson steel plant.

The search for Kenny's killer began, with mobs of angry Irishmen shaking down every Italian who fit Rombolo's description: five-foot-six, 130 pounds, with a stubby black mustache and a big diamond ring on the second finger of his left hand. Every Italian in Jersey City fit that description, even some of the women.

Italo-Irish relations reached an all-time low. Suddenly, the Irish who ruled the city had a very good reason to hate the Italians, not that they really needed one. They were in charge, so they could hate whomever they pleased. Their plan, once they caught the murderer, was to string him up from the nearest telegraph pole. The police began a systematic "cleanup" of the Italian and Polish sections of the city, raiding saloons and conducting random searches, harassing as many immigrants as they could find.

A week after the murder, Hague and his henchmen traced Rombolo to a boardinghouse in Newark. Hague said he found the man in a local grocery store. As soon as he saw Hague, Rombolo ran out the back door, almost into the arms of a waiting Newark detective. But Rombolo made a break for it, sprinting down an alley to a playground two blocks away. Hague was close behind.

Rombolo hid behind a public rest room, but Hague came around the other end of the building to find him crouched down on one knee, his gun drawn, waiting for Hague to come into view. Hague jumped on top of Rombolo's back and wrestled him to the pavement. During the struggle, Rombolo slipped his revolver into his coat pocket. But a Newark detective frisked him while Hague held him down, pulling out the revolver and a knife.

Italians from the neighborhood poured out into the street to watch the drama, and to try and get in between Hague and his waiting car. Hague half carried and half dragged Rombolo to the car, knocking the other Italians out of the way. All the while, Rombolo threatened to kill him.

Hague drove Rombolo back to Jersey City in his own car to prove he was the one who had made the collar. The soon-to-be-mayor was greeted by a crowd of zepps and Jersey Citizens, including twenty-three-year-old John V. Kenny, the young brother of the murder victim.

When they arrived at police headquarters, Hague asked John V. if he wanted to take a few potshots at his brother's killer. When John declined, Hague did the honors, swinging his polished shoe back and smashing Rombolo in the ribs. Rombolo confessed to the murder later that night and was eventually sentenced to the electric chair.

That night, the Friday after Easter, *The Jersey Journal* wrote a glowing editorial about the commissioner of public safety, pushing the start button on the Hague machine.

It was partly due to Hague's success that my grandfather was such a failure. Beansie could never get a break under the Hague regime because his name, like Rombolo's, ended in a vowel. Even when he cooperated, he got screwed. Once, the local cops asked Grandpa to round up some gamblers for a floating crap game. The plan was that the cops would raid the game, then take all the money and give Grandpa a cut. But when the raid was over, the cops left Grandpa empty-handed. They threatened to arrest him if he complained.

Because he was not a yes-man, Grandpa was arrested and beaten down time and again. When the police captain shouted, "Round up the usual suspects," Grandpa was always on his list. I wouldn't be surprised if he was hauled in for a lineup in the Kenny murder. Grandpa was only nine years old at the time, but he got off to a bad start early in life.

Grandpa was hit by an ice truck when he was a kid. The accident apparently knocked something loose in his head. "Pazzo," my relatives would say, making circles near their ears. My mother was convinced Grandpa's problem was that he was once locked in the closet when he was a kid. He was extremely claustrophobic and couldn't stand to even ride on a train through a tunnel. Some nights he woke up in bed screaming, my grandmother consoling him in the darkness. We weren't sure what had happened to Grandpa early in life, but whatever it was, Hague only made it worse.

When one of his brothers did something wrong, Grandpa was often arrested for it, because they all looked so much alike. In the 1940s, my uncle Bicky broke a guy's nose at the Sunflower diner for picking on their brother Frankie. That night, the cops were out looking for Beansie.

Like Grandpa, Hague was a bully and would think nothing of hauling off and punching you in the nose. One of the most famous stories about him was the time he called for an ambulance in the middle of the night and, when the driver got there late, the mayor lost his temper. While the man was explaining that it had taken him a while to get dressed, Hague punched him in the face.

"Justice at the end of a nightstick" was one of Hague's favorite slogans. And Grandpa's head, already damaged, was often on the other end of that stick.

Grandma had pictures of Grandpa with welts on his back from one of many rubber-hose beatings by Hague or his henchmen. They said they were going to do something about it, but then they threw the pictures away. You couldn't beat the machine. But it could beat you—whenever it liked.

The Irish ran the city, through a group of neighborhood wards and committeemen and -women, who were usually based out of local saloons. When I was growing up, the city was divided into six wards, a term that always reminded me of Meadowview: Wards were for crazy people.

In my family's case, it would be convenient to say the criminal insanity trickled down from the top, from Hague to Grandpa and to later generations. But considering our track record, that's just not true. It's more complicated.

What Hague and his criminal progeny did was establish a climate for the crimes and immoral acts my family committed. A justification. Because if the Boss was doing it, how illegal could it really be? It was more than just okay to steal; it was your birthright. It was all right to beat people up, since Hague's zepps did it all the time. That's just the way it was. Nobody could change it. Nobody.

Though he had ties to mobsters Longie Zwillman and Willie Moretti, Hague allowed no boss but himself to operate on his streets. Even the powerful Dutch Schultz, who liked to travel to Newark every night to play cards, had to get permission from the Boss to come through Jersey City. One night, after coming through the Holland Tunnel, Schultz was stopped by Hague's zepps, who were always on the lookout for troublemakers and those who didn't belong. Because Schultz hadn't gotten Hague's permission to pass through his little fiefdom, he was arrested for vagrancy.

In 1920, a group of Princeton students traveled to Jersey City to help ensure a fair election. They were met by a dozen Jersey City men—with names like Mud Miller and Piggie Wilbough—who kicked the shit out of them and sent them crying, with concussions, back to their ivy-covered walls. The incident led to the first full state investigation of Hague, which led nowhere because of the many judges and high-level politicians he had placed throughout the state. His greatest coup was appointing his son, Frank, Jr., who didn't have a law degree, to the Court of Errors and Appeals, the highest court in New Jersey.

During political campaigns, Hague's zepps took control of the streets. Jersey City, even when I was growing up, was still known for its political rallies and bonfires. Kids would beat each other up in school yards over which candidate their parents planned to vote for. Back in Hague's day, parades were held at night, with supporters carrying signs and oil-lit torches, not unlike the angry villagers in *Frankenstein*. Speeches were made from soapboxes and the backs of trucks, with clowns like Muggsy Haskins entertaining the crowd until the mayor arrived. Muggsy, with a bright red nose, matching tie, beat-up hat, and white suit, was abruptly knocked off the platform when Hague got there.

When a vote didn't go his way, Hague would have the paper ballots thrown into the river. At certain locations, Hague would hire "sluggers"—

groups of bat-wielding men, who would chase opponents away from the polls. Once, an eight-year-old girl was accidentally hit in the head by one of the sluggers and killed.

When voting machines were finally introduced, Hague taught his committeemen and -women a trick to ensure that the residents voted for the right man. One of those women was Beansie's sister Katie. Taught by Hague, the master, Aunt Katie would place ashes on the lever for the correct candidate and then shake the hand of the voter when he stepped from the voting booth. Katie needed only to look down at her hands to see if the person had voted for the right candidate. Depending on the outcome, either a pat on the back or a swift kick in the ass followed.

Hague knew at all times what was happening on his streets. Phones were tapped, mail was opened, and spies lurked at Bickford's, a popular Journal Square cafeteria. And, always, the traitors were punished. His critics would find their right to vote revoked or their tax assessments raised, and if they were especially feisty, they'd be beaten and then arrested for "sarcastic criticism of superiors."

Though many of its reporters were kept on Hague's payroll, *The Jersey Journal* would occasionally launch an attack on the mayor. In the early 1920s, when the paper criticized Hague's payroll-padding, its tax assessment was raised by $175,000. *Journal* delivery boys were found in violation of child labor laws, and Journal Square was renamed Veterans' Square, although the new name never stuck. Movie houses were bullied by City Hall into pulling their ads from the paper. Word on the street was: "If you want to know what movies are playing, call Mayor Hague."

Intimidation was not the only key to Hague's success. Making certain people feel like they were part of the machine also had a lot to do with it. Aunt Katie was one of those people. Carefully building his support one favor at a time, Hague worked his way up through the county political structure, using the railroads and big business as a foil and identifying with the working-class voters. It didn't take a lot to make people happy, especially during the Depression. In 1933 alone, Hague's people delivered more than fifteen thousand Christmas baskets to hungry families. A job here, a job there. Only Hague could get away with creating titles like "supervisor of sinks" and "foreman of vacuum cleaners" for friends. Even the clergy got in on the action: More than fifty priests, rabbis, and ministers were on the city payroll.

But the favors were returned. Through his deputy mayor, John "Needlenose" Malone, Hague collected his tribute. Each worker was required to turn over 3 percent of his or her salary to the Boss each month on what was called Rice Pudding Day.

In addition to their tribute, Jersey City residents paid the highest taxes in the nation—for very little in return. Streets were safe, but they were dirty and filled with potholes; open horse-drawn wagons still collected garbage long after trucks became the norm in other cities; gaslights lit the street corners years after Thomas Edison made his discovery. The sewer system was in rough shape, rats were rampant, public schools were in poor condition and overcrowded (but there were few complaints, since those with the power sent their kids to Catholic school), and there were no after-school recreational programs—despite the large Recreation Department payroll.

And no one complained, because practically everyone was guilty: There were policemen who were paid $8,000 to sing in the police quartet, two county-jail organists, workers in the City Clerk's office who were paid daily to repair the ballot boxes, and a special inspector of kosher meats.

Though his own salary was only $6,500 a year, Hague owned a $125,000 summer mansion on the Jersey shore, in what was called "the millionaires' colony"; a luxurious fourteen-room Jersey City duplex apartment; a place on Park Avenue; a villa in Biscayne Bay, Florida; and he spent the rest of his time vacationing in Paris.

When questioned about his finances, Hague told the authorities to mind their own effin' business. And because he made it a policy never to put anything in writing, his padded payrolls and kickback schemes could never be traced. It helped that Hague had practically everyone in his pocket.

Hague controlled not only Jersey City and its residents; as vice-chairman of the Democratic National Committee, he pulled in the vote for Franklin D. Roosevelt as his point man in the Northeast. In August 1932, Hague bused in over 100,000 Hudson County residents to Sea Girt, New Jersey—providing a free box lunch and a day "down the shore." It was one of the largest outdoor political rallies ever held. In Hudson County alone, Hague brought in 184,000 votes for FDR that year.

Roosevelt was warned about Hague's corrupt tactics and told by aides that the man was "a son of a bitch."

"Yeah, but he's our son of a bitch," replied FDR.

The relationship was a give-and-take. In return for Hague's loyalty, Roosevelt poured $47 million of WPA money into Hudson County. For Roosevelt Stadium alone, $3 million was given to the city. The playing field for the minor-league Jersey Giants was built in tribute to Hague's friend in Washington, next to a site that contained a million tons of toxic waste. Each season, Hague was there, ready to throw out the first ball. Guaranteed to be in the stands was his legion of no-show city workers—all required to purchase Giants' tickets. Hague loved sports, particularly baseball, and one of his favorite sayings was "Play ball with me and I'll make you rich."

Roosevelt often made a pilgrimage to Jersey City when an event was important enough to Hague. In 1936, for instance, the president laid the cornerstone of the Medical Building of the Jersey City Medical Center. My mother was there that day with the rest of the kids in her kindergarten class, waving a little American flag as Roosevelt drove by in an open car.

The Medical Center was a wonder. I was born there, as were my mother and most Jersey City residents, pulled kicking and screaming from their mothers and into the city. The Margaret Hague maternity hospital was one of seven Medical Center buildings that were the only distinguishable features of the city's skyline.

The hospital's stepped Art Deco buildings climbed into the overcast sky like some ancient stone ziggurat that an alien culture had plopped down on the Hudson River's western shore. The Medical Center looked lonely and abandoned from a distance. And up close, its twenty-three stories didn't fit in with the surrounding low-lying, dilapidated buildings.

The Medical Center was not just an architectural wonder but a Democratic one. The $30 million complex was Hague's experiment with socialized medicine, and for a while, the experiment worked. Medical Center surgeons saved my uncle Jerry's leg after an attack dog nearly chewed it off. Grandma was treated there for cervical cancer by one of the best gynecologists in the metropolitan area. She even got a job there, in the nursing school's dining room in Murdoch Hall.

But by the time I was born, the Medical Center was growing shabby and was headed for bankruptcy. The city was no longer known for its first-rate hospitals. When teenagers learned to drive in Jersey City, part of the instruction was to keep driving if you had an accident inside the Holland Tunnel so that you could pull up to a good hospital on the New York side.

The Medical Center's woes were often blamed on the politicians who came after Hague. But the truth was, Hague was partially responsible for the hospital's decline. Though the Medical Center did offer free services to the poor, it also offered those same services to people who had the money to pay. It was bad business. In Hague's day, there were so many no-show jobs at the hospital that the patient-to-staff ratio was said to be one to one. Janitors outnumbered nurses. Patient costs were double those at private hospitals. A French chef cooked all the staff meals.

Though the hospital and city finances were a mess, Hague was so powerful as to be beyond reproach. It wasn't until 1937—the year after FDR's visit—that Hague took things too far. That fall, forty members of the Committee on Industrial Organizations (CIO) came to Jersey City to hand out flyers and copies of the Bill of Rights. Thirteen members were arrested; the others were put on the ferry back to New York.

The following winter, *Life* magazine ran a seven-page spread on the Hague machine's union-busting activities, calling the mayor a dictator and comparing him to Hitler, saying he lacked the Führer's imagination and "rabble-rousing eloquence." Though the magazine was banned on Jersey City's streets, "Haguetown" became the laughingstock of the nation.

The CIO successfully sued, forcing Hague to take the stand for three days—ample time for him to put his ass-kicking foot in his ungrammatical mouth and denounce democracy. At one point, the mayor proposed deporting all of the country's rabble-rousers. Communists, he said, should be sent back to Europe where they came from. If the rabble-rousers were born here? "We ought to establish a camp in Alaska there and house them there away from the American people."

Roosevelt was embarrassed. And, eventually, so were Jersey City's residents. It was the first time they realized that the rest of the world wasn't quite like home. This was no land of the free. And what was this Bill of Rights everyone was talking about?

It wasn't long before Jersey City's young men found themselves defending democracy, sitting in foxholes with guys who teased them about their city's dictator, exposed in the pages of *Life*.

By the mid-1940s, Hague was losing his grip, because young veterans like Uncle Bicky had seen and experienced other places, and had walked down the Champs-Elysées. Even war-ravaged and blown to bits, most places were a lot better off. And a hell of a lot prettier. More important, the Depression, which had helped Hague keep his grip on poor and hungry Jersey Citizens, was finally over. Political reform seemed like it might be in the cards.

Sensing his loosening hold, Hague made one last indirect grasp at power, resigning midterm in 1947 and passing the mayoralty to his nephew, Frank Hague Eggers, a stubby man with none of his uncle's charisma. Though the resignation was made with great fanfare, including aerial bombs and a brass band, Hague planned to run the city by proxy, away from the heat. His exit was purely theatrical.

Resentful that Hague would choose a relative over a loyal soldier like himself, one popular ward leader began mounting a campaign to unseat Eggers. The ward leader was John V. Kenny, son of the Mayor of Cork Row and brother of Frank Kenny, whose murder had helped cement Hague's popularity with voters.

John V. Kenny had stood at Hague's side the night Rombolo was hauled into the precinct. That night, John V. had refused to kick a man when he was down. But since then John had grown up a bit. Like Aunt Katie, Grandpa, and most people in Jersey City, John V. had learned from the master.

6

CHECK YOUR
COAT AND HAT

———

The summer after I graduated from kindergarten, Jersey City's mayor
was convicted and thrown out of office. By first grade at Our Lady of
Czestochowa, I knew how to spell *indictment* and *subpoena*—two
tricky vocabulary words for a six-year-old. I also knew how to spell
Czestochowa, an even bigger feat. Pronouncing it was hard enough.
Grandpa jokingly called it "Our Lady of Check-Your-Coat-and-Hat."

In 1971, while I was learning to write, Mayor Thomas Whelan and
eleven other local politicians were part of the biggest corruption case
in Hudson County history. Known as the Hudson Twelve, they were
charged with taking $3.5 million in kickbacks for county construction
contracts.

To teach us right from wrong, all the nuns at OLC would have
needed to do was tell us about Whelan and his buddies. Every moral
lesson we needed to know was right there in front of us: Thou shalt not
steal. Thou shalt not bear false witness against thy neighbor. Thou
shalt not covet thy neighbor's goods. Instead, the lessons we learned at
OLC came from an occasional film strip on the life of Jesus or about
the evils of drugs, two things that seemed to have no bearing on my life

at age six. Every so often an overweight, dim-witted Jersey City cop called Officer Friendly would come to class and try and teach us about right and wrong. "Cross at the green, not in between," he said. "Cross at the red and you'll be dead." By first grade, I knew that life on Jersey City's streets was much more complicated than that.

I found it strange that no one mentioned Mayor Whelan at school or at church. He was never held up as a poor example of human conduct. The waterfront was nasty and abandoned and the parks were filled with garbage and broken glass because of politicians like Whelan. That's what they should have taught us—I could have related to that. But maybe Officer Friendly and the teachers were Whelan supporters.

One teacher did sit us down in front of the television to watch the Watergate hearings, though. Not that she understood what was going on. She never explained it to us. She just told us it was a historic moment. Really, it was a moment for her to ignore us and file her nails.

OLC functioned in its own bubble, stuck somewhere in the late 1950s or early 1960s, with bored housewives working more as babysitters than as teachers. The school was out of touch with the world around it. At OLC, there was an alarming number of boys with crewcuts, whose parents couldn't face the fact that it was the 1970s.

A cultural revolution was passing our parish by, and no one wanted to know about it. The Equal Rights Amendment was evil, one nun told us. Why would we want to share bathrooms with men? she shouted at us girls. For years I thought equal rights for women meant the right to use a urinal.

I had no idea that society at large, and even Catholic churches throughout the county and the country, were undergoing great changes. Girls were allowed to be altar "boys," and women deacons were even handing out Communion. One friend went to a church where they celebrated a folk mass, with guitars, tambourines, and songs written in the twentieth century.

At OLC, all the songs in church were played by an immaculate man named Matty, who knew a few chords on the organ and sang in a nasal monotone, like a fifteenth-century monk with a bad head cold. To imitate Matty, you had to hold your nose, then spit out the lyrics in one long gasp, chanting more than singing, one syllable a note higher than the others: Glory-be-to-the-father-and-TO-the-son-and-to-the-holy-SPIIIIrit. As-it-was-in-the-beginning-is-now-and-ever-SHALL-be. World-without-end-A-men." That was considered singing at OLC. We didn't have a real musical director, because Matty came cheap. He worked for nothing.

I longed for a folk mass. *Godspell* was my favorite Broadway cast album. And in my heart of hearts, I knew Jesus was a groovy guy who wouldn't mind long hair, rainbow suspenders, and the ERA. Jesus, from what I could tell, was a revolutionary.

I knew that even He would be bored by the sermons at OLC. Never once did I follow a sermon all the way through during a mass. At first I thought it was my fault, that I was intrinsically bad or that my powers of concentration were flawed. But then I attended mass at nearby St. Peter's and realized it was just our priests who were incredibly dull. They never bothered to write down interesting lessons drawn from everyday life that the parishioners could relate to. They'd just get up there and wing it. I wasn't sure if the parishioners stopped listening first or the priests stopped trying to make them listen first. Daddy stood at the back of church during mass so that when the priest got up to talk, he could sneak out and have a smoke. I wished I could go with him.

If OLC taught me one thing, it was that nothing was sacred in Jersey City, not even church. The truth was that most of the priests in my parish needed to hear a sermon themselves. At OLC, one oversexed priest chased my mother around the rectory one afternoon when she went in to buy a mass card for a funeral.

There were tales of Father Piasecki, whom we called Father Grab-It-All. Piasecki often took weekend trips to his house in Pennsylvania with the rectory housekeeper, Wanda, who always wore a plush fur coat, a gift from the generous pastor. My sister once asked my mother if Wanda was the pastor's wife. When Piasecki retired, letters were sent to parishioners asking them to come to his farewell party. People mailed him empty wallets and ripped-up dollar bills. Only the ass-kissers attended the gala.

At a very young age, I discovered that our parish was hardly hallowed ground.

Father Ziggy, who had emigrated from Poland, seemed more pious

than the other priests. But then again, how would we know? He spoke
no English. Ziggy came to our school once a month to hear our con-
fessions in the children's library. Ziggy and I sat on folding chairs, facing each other. No screen, no kneeler. With his face turned and his
eyes averted, Ziggy would listen and nod his head as my sins poured
out past the Nancy Drew mysteries and Encyclopedia Britannica.

Father Ziggy had no idea what I was saying. No matter what I confessed—whether I told him I had disobeyed my parents or I confessed
to killing Archduke Ferdinand—the penance was still the same, delivered in broken English: "One Our Father, two Hail Marys." It was the
only English Ziggy knew.

Every Friday during Lent we got into a double-file line and were
marched four blocks over to the parish church to go to confession
there and to recite the Stations of the Cross, fourteen vignettes that
traced Jesus' last, horrible day on earth: from being sentenced before
Pilate to meeting the Good Samaritan along the road to being cru-
cified. The stations were like a Top Ten countdown: Jesus' greatest
hits. We followed along with the graphic depictions along the church
walls.

Easter was considered the holiest time of the year, even holier than
Christmas. It was so holy that you had to do penance for forty days before it, to cleanse your soul in preparation. It all started on Ash
Wednesday, when you were expected to give something up for Lent.
Some people only went to church on Ash Wednesday and then, a few
weeks later, on Palm Sunday, the two days of the year they got something for free. The pastor called them A&P Catholics—for *ashes* and
palms. I thought maybe OLC should hand out little gifts every week,
then maybe more people would come, like on bat day at Yankee Stadium.

Mass could be painful. On Holy Thursday, three days before Easter
Sunday, a High Mass was held in the evening. The mass was penance
enough for the entire year. We had to wear our blue-and-white-
checked school uniforms and beanies. It was bad enough we had to
wear them day in and day out. Wearing them at night was especially
humiliating. The worst part, though, was parading around the church
carrying ten-pound lily pots. The lilies would poke me in the eye,

blocking my vision. If I was really unlucky, yellow dusty pollen from inside the flowers would get in my eyes or in my nose. I couldn't rub it out, since I was, after all, holding a ten-pound pot of lilies. By the last processional round, with my eyes and nose running, that pot grew mighty heavy. I tripped countless times at Holy Thursday mass but, miraculously, never fell.

The best part of the mass was when the priest pretended to be Jesus and washed the feet of a dozen pre-chosen male parishioners, who were seated on folding chairs up on the altar, playing the part of the Apostles. We watched in awe as the guys took their black shiny shoes off and rolled down their dress socks and Father Pastor, as we redundantly called him, actually washed their feet in a basin. The point of it all was to show that no man was better than another. But to us kids, there was a perverse excitement in seeing the naked feet of men from the neighborhood. In church no less. On the altar.

Every Holy Thursday—and at most Sunday masses, really—a crazy Polish lady in a babushka would get up and pray loudly to the statues in church. She would yell and gesticulate and make me really nervous, mostly because I feared the stone statues would come to life and yell back at her. One Holy Thursday, Father Pastor just couldn't take her ranting and raving anymore, and right in the middle of mass he stopped his boring sermon, turned to her, and yelled, "Shaddup." Everyone in church had always wanted to say it but couldn't get up the nerve.

On Holy Saturday, the day before Easter, my family would go to the church basement to have our Easter food blessed. There was a mound of butter shaped like a big Easter egg, which my father sculpted each year by rolling a pound of butter around in a bowl for a half hour or so. He placed a fuzzy sprig of parsley on top for garnish. Surrounding the butter on the fancy crystal plate was a ring of fresh kielbasa. Easter eggs that I had colored were placed around the outside of the kielbasa, beside a shot glass full of salt. On another plate was the babka, a soft and airy cakelike bread that I was always tempted to rest my head on, like a pillow, while we waited for the priest to finish his blessing.

Father Pastor would throw holy water on the food and on us, usually hitting me in the eye with a drop or two. Then we'd carefully carry the plate back home to our refrigerator, opening the door every now and then to peek longingly at the kielbasa until we could eat it the next day. It was so garlicky that it made everything in the fridge smell like it, even long after Easter was over.

Though the nuns and priests did their best to ruin my concept of religion, it was always beautiful inside OLC, with its tall stained-glass windows and Gothic glass-and-wrought-iron light fixtures strung from black chains. The most striking feature was the huge wooden crucifix above the altar, upon which a suffering, bleeding, life-size Christ was nailed. More than any parable or film strip, that cross convinced me what a great guy Jesus was. He looked so miserable up there. And He was doing it all for me. He would even wash my feet if I asked Him to.

As I gazed up at the cross, ignoring Father Pastor's sermon, I remembered what the nuns said: Jesus died for my sins. My sins didn't seem bad enough for anyone to die over, though. I never could understand how Jesus' dying wiped my slate clean, but I was grateful to Him. If only the nuns could follow His selfless example. For them, fear and intimidation were synonymous with "morality."

When something was stolen in the classroom, like the time Shawn swiped Anthony's race car after show-and-tell in second grade, the nuns resorted to Nazi tactics and would punish us all to try and rout out the perpetrator. Our principal hit everyone in my class with a paddle in the hopes that someone would rat out the evildoer or—far less likely—that the evildoer would confess.

It never worked. The evildoers would continue to do evil, unpunished. The girl who stole my pencil case in kindergarten wound up getting a job in city government.

Like the priests, the nuns were often on the wrong side of the moral lessons they were trying to teach us. They set a good example of what not to do to your friends and neighbors. Sister Isabelle was by far the most sinister. She told us in second grade that Noah's Ark had recently been found, which signaled that the end of the world was coming. It was prophesied, she said, that once the Ark was found, the end was near. She told us—we're talking seven-year-olds—that the Russians had a button they could push which would destroy us all. Any day now, she said.

I sat awake at night biting my nails, waiting to be blown up.

Sister Isabelle's greatest crime, though, was terrorizing my best friend, Liz, the only girl in school whose parents were divorced. Sister Isabelle embarrassed Liz in front of the whole class, singling her out and declaring divorce was a sin. As if it were Liz's fault that her parents had split up.

Every day at OLC crimes were committed, but none that the administration could be charged with. One teacher smoked in the classroom and swore us all to silence. Her bad habit was to be our little secret, she said. In third grade, Miss Linda, who wore miniskirts to show the eight-year-old boys what to expect in a few years, filled two blackboards with homework assignments one afternoon because, she said, we were bad. We copied it down, crying all the while, not knowing how we'd ever get all that work done in one night. As the dismissal bell rang, Miss Linda yelled, "April Fool!" She laughed as we all whimpered out of class, trying to catch our breath from crying so hard.

Instead of showing us Jesus film strips, our fourth-grade teacher, Mr. C., pulled down the shades and showed us slides of his honeymoon, complete with his wife sprawled out on a hotel bed. For science class, he had us melt chocolate eggs and crayons on a hot plate, then feed each other fish food.

In a burst of creativity, Mr. C. decided to prove how terrible it would be to be blind. He paired us off and blindfolded one person in each pair, then had the seeing-eye student lead the blind kid around the school. It was all fun and games until someone led her partner down a flight of stairs. The "blind" kid nearly lost an eye.

Though I had a great deal of fun, I learned absolutely nothing in fourth grade.

Thanks to two or three good teachers, I somehow learned to read and write. Geography was not considered an important subject: Jersey City was all you needed to know.

My favorite class was gym, because my brother was the teacher. He tended bar at the Majestic most nights, but he still had his afternoons free. He took the gym job to make a few extra bucks. Stanley lasted only one year, but I was so proud of him. He came to class in sweats and sneakers and made us do relay races and play actual games. OLC had no sports teams or after-school programs. But when Stanley arrived, he had us compete for the Presidential Physical Fitness Awards, a national program to try and slim down America's fast-food-gorged youth, which involved a series of sit-ups, pull-ups, and wind sprints.

Even when Stanley gave up the gig and got a job sweeping bubbles off the roof at Colgate, gym was still my favorite class. It was the one hour of the day when we were allowed to run without getting yelled at. I longed to roam free, and even considered running away from home. But I could never do that to my mother. I liked her too much to worry her.

Gym was held in Victory Hall, which was divided into Upper and Lower Victory Hall. Upper Victory Hall had a big stage and was mostly used for our lame school "productions" on the priests' feast days. We never put on plays or shows. OLC had no activities of any kind. On the afternoon of the given day—which fell on the feast day of the saint that the priest was named after—we were simply dragged onstage, class by class, to sing ditties like "Old MacDonald" or "The Wheels on the Bus." Parents were never invited. It was all for the amusement of the priests and nuns.

Victory Hall was connected to OLC via the boys' bathroom. To get to Victory Hall, teachers had to either drag the schoolchildren outside and around the corner, an undertaking that involved putting coats and hats on each kid, or simply escort them through the boys' bathroom. The teachers always took the easy way out. Whenever my schoolmates and I took the shortcut to Victory Hall, we made sure to hold our breath to avoid smelling the overwhelming stench coming from the urinals. The teacher would yell a warning before traipsing through with us, just in case a boy was still at the urinal doing his business. Inevitably, there was one boy who was still taking a piss, or at least pulling up his fly. The teacher told us girls to close our eyes, but I usually peeked, in the hopes of seeing what the big deal was. The urinals fascinated me, since they were the key to equal rights for women.

Lower Victory Hall was graced with a netless basketball hoop but little else. In the years before and after Stanley's short stint, our gym instructor was Sophie, the kindhearted but physically unfit cleaning lady. Sophie was the all-around school Mrs. Fix-It. When someone threw up, it was Sophie who came by with the sawdust to sprinkle over the mess. It was Sophie who heated our soft pretzels in the ovens of Lower Victory Hall for recess break, Sophie who, if you gave her a few bucks in the morning before classes began, ran out and got you pizza for lunch. Sophie was the pizza connection and everyone's stand-in mom. For gym class, the principal simply handed her a whistle. Sophie was not trained in physical-fitness education, so she just let us run wild and scream for a full hour or sometimes threw a dodge ball our way to let us fight it out.

The best gym activity was pretending to work in the old ticket booth and coat-check room located between Upper and Lower Victory Halls. Though they provided hours of entertainment, I wondered what the ticket counter and coat-check room were for, exactly. Certainly no one was purchasing tickets to Father Pastor's feast-day celebration.

Digging through my mother's dresser drawers one rainy afternoon, I realized the ticket and coat-check facilities were left over from the days when Victory Hall, like Jersey City, was a much more important place. In its prime, Victory Hall had been ground zero for the Polish community, a place for polka dances and parties, where group pictures were taken of the whole crowd, hundreds of people decked out in fancy dresses and suits, sitting at long tables. I found a few of those big black-and-white photos among my mother's things and spent hours searching out Ma, Daddy, and all my Polish relatives. The focus was deep, so even the tiny heads at the back of Victory Hall were clear, their features recognizable.

The two-tiered Victory Hall was where my parents' wedding reception was held and where the Dudley Club held many a polka night. During one of those dances, in 1949, John V. Kenny made a campaign stop on his hand-shaking/baby-kissing rounds to unseat Frank Hague Eggers. Kenny's campaign was called the Freedom Ticket and worked off the momentum of World War II. Wherever they went, his supporters flashed the V made popular by Winston Churchill. V for victory and for John V.

Victory Hall was an obvious campaign stop for John V.

Though Kenny was an Irishman through and through, he was concerned with pleasing all the ethnic groups in Jersey City. He wanted the Poles—a strong Jersey City voting block—on his side. And the night he visited my father's Dudley polka dance at Victory Hall, he got them.

It was a warm spring night. A polka band was playing downstairs behind the basketball hoop, and an American band was on the stage upstairs. There were two bars—one set up on a long card table on the upper level and one built-in wooden bar on the lower level, complete with stainless-steel sinks and brushes, just like in the Majestic. So many people attended the dances at Victory Hall back then that they worried the upper floor would cave in and the revelers would come crashing down on the lower-floor dancers.

Kenny, dressed in a dark suit, his graying hair slicked back, walked into Upper Victory Hall, the crowd swarming around him, the air close with cigarette smoke and the musty smell of tap beer. Word must have traveled upstairs quicker than Kenny himself, past the coat-check room and ticket booth, because when he made that grand entrance, the American band was already playing his campaign song, "Now Is the Hour."

"Now is the hour when we must say good-bye," the song went, a direct jab at Hague.

Since this was indeed a dance, Kenny decided to get out on the floor. He probably wasn't a very good polka dancer, being Irish and all. The American band was much more his speed. And they were playing his song.

Of the hundreds of women in the crowd, my mother was the one Kenny grabbed and swept onto the dance floor for a waltz. Kenny, who was only slightly taller than my mother, picked her because she was petite and pretty. Little did Kenny know that she was a great dancer, too. It was the Russian blood in her veins, Great-Grandma Irene's. Russians were great dancers, I thought, because they had to move around a lot to stay warm in the old country.

My mother was happiest when she danced. She could do it all: the polka, the jitterbug, the lindy hop, the Montclair. She even made the hokeypokey look graceful. Whenever she was out there, she glowed, and could make any guy look good on the dance floor. She could lead without letting on and embarrassing the guy. When my father danced with her, he barely had to shuffle his feet. My energetic mother twirled and bounced enough for the both of them.

So Kenny had picked the right woman. She and Kenny spun around, my mother's dress twirling in the humid Victory Hall air and making short, unattractive Kenny look like Gene Kelly, graceful and handsome and the center of attention. The other women looked on in awe as my mother enjoyed several minutes of local fame. Everyone loved Kenny. And she was the one to dance with him. The only one.

My father, never a jealous man, was so proud of his beautiful girl: This was his dance, and that was Jersey City's future mayor dancing with his girl. He sipped his Scotch and flashed a wide, white smile. It was 1949, so he hadn't yet lost his front teeth.

After the Victory Hall dance, every piece of the campaign puzzle fell into place for Kenny. The candidates were made to draw for their positions on the ballot. Eggers and his running mates drew the coveted first four spots. Kenny drew spots seven to eleven, but brilliantly used the numbers to his advantage. Every gambler and bookie in Jersey City could identify with the 7–11 craps reference. "A natural," was Kenny's slogan. The numbers were an omen and Kenny's secret sign that illegal gambling would not only be tolerated under his administration but that it would flourish.

Kenny had been a ward leader for thirty-five years and knew the inner workings of the system. Some say he had been planning his attack on Hague since 1929. It took him two decades to get up the gumption. In 1936, Hague got wind of Kenny's plot to overthrow the local government, called him down to the mayor's office, punched him in the face, and then made him pledge publicly, "All I am and all I ever will be, I owe to my dear friend Frank Hague."

But by 1949, everyone was sick and tired of being beaten down by Hague, even Aunt Katie. She became one of Kenny's biggest supporters. When Hague came downtown to campaign for his nephew, Katie made sure he was not greeted warmly. While delivering a speech outside P.S. 37, Hague was pelted with rotten eggs and fruit. "Get them little dirty bastards," he screamed into the microphone, pointing at the kids who threw the bombs. Even at Hague's beloved Roosevelt Stadium, Kenny stole the show: Planes trailing his campaign banners buzzed overhead.

Kenny took out full-page ads in *The Jersey Journal*, confidently declaring, "The cynics, the shrug-the-shoulders crowd said it couldn't be done. But it looks as though Kenny will make a killing. A vote for the Freedom Ticket is a vote for Liberty."

In another ad, he warned voters, "It's your last chance to save Jersey City."

The Hague camp knew it was all over the night they and Kenny simultaneously converged on Journal Square for their respective campaign stops. Kenny held a large labor parade on May Day, five days before the election, which wound from Greenville down Bergen Avenue and ended on Journal Square—an impressive place in the 1940s. It hadn't yet become the mini-Calcutta I would come to know. In 1949, it was—like Victory Hall and Kenny—in its prime, a place that songs were written about. The big band hit "Jersey Bounce" proclaimed: "It started on Journal Square. The memory lingers there." The Square even had its own radio station, WAAT, which broadcast as far as the nation's capital. The signal was so strong that a crazy guy from Baltimore who once heard his first name mentioned in a WAAT program got mad and took a bus all the way to Jersey City, where he busted into the studio and tried to stab a singer who was on the air.

Despite the occasional outbreak of violence there, the Journal Square my parents remember is where you took your date on a Saturday night. My mother's first date was on the Square, at age fifteen, at the Spa, a hamburger joint near the Stanley Theatre. She went out with a teenager named Junior Bellino, who got her home past curfew to find my beast of a grandfather waiting angrily on the stoop for them. It was their one and only date.

When my father came along, he took my mother to crowded Journal Square spots like the Art Deco China Clipper restaurant, a curved building on the corner near the Loew's, with a small fleet of airplanes on its sign; the Canton Tea Garden, where red-jacketed Chinese waiters served steaming plates of chow mein to couples snuggled in red booths; Oyster Bay, a place that covered its tables with tablecloths, even for lunch; and Robinson's Steakhouse, which made the best cocktails in town and where my great-uncle Sam—Pauline's brother—always hung out, Scotch in hand. He was the uncle who'd gotten his head stuck in the Morris Canal.

Teachers took kids on field trips to the Square in the 1940s. My mother remembers going there during World War II to visit a Japanese midget suicide submarine, which had been captured at Pearl Harbor and taken on a national tour to encourage the sale of war bonds. The kids were made to crawl inside, where they met a wax Japanese sailor face-to-face. My mother almost had a heart attack.

It was a time when Journal Square was never quiet and never empty, a time when people took first the trolleys and then the Hudson Tubes from downtown to pay their utility bills in person. Before the discount stores and sleazy motels invaded, the Square was known for Russell Lou's beauty parlor, Cara Carson's boutique, the Glove Shop, Five Corners Bakery, and State Gown, a high-class dress shop made famous when a man pumped a bunch of bullets into his girlfriend there.

The burgers at Bickford's cafeteria, where Hague's spies often took notes of overheard enemy conversation, competed with the ice cream sodas at Liss's drugstore and the crispy hot dogs at the new Boulevard Drinks, its pink neon installed that same year, 1949.

The night of the Kenny parade, thousands came out and gathered at the grandstand even though it threatened to rain. Banners were waved. Traffic was stopped. Speeches were made. A bricklayer took the microphone and yelled, "Let it rain! This crowd is going to stay here no matter how hard it rains." The crowd thundered back its approval.

Dozens of cops patrolled on horseback, and the Hudson Boulevard police, dressed, like the Gestapo, with chaps, high boots, and helmets, waved their clubs to keep the mob in check. Nearby, a hook and ladder truck was set up so newspaper photographers could get their shots. Just a few hundred feet away, the Hague/Eggers ticket held its gathering at the Hotel Plaza, a classy place where my godparents spent their honeymoon night, sipping drinks at the Montmartre piano lounge downstairs. But the crowd on Journal Square wasn't there for the Eggers meeting. On their way out into the street, Hague's people knew they would be defeated. Commissioner Arthur Potterton took one look at the Kenny mob and smirked. He knew right then that the Hague machine was about to be traded in for a new model.

Kenny, with a big nose, big ears, and bad teeth, was a man of the people. Unlike Hague, Kenny always blended in with the crowd. While Hague was still riding around in limos with bodyguards, Kenny used the Hudson Tubes and broken-down cars to get where he was going. Some say it had nothing to do with modesty, that Kenny was just a tightwad. Even after he made millions, he would eat at the cafeteria and tip the busboy only a quarter for carrying his tray to his table.

Kenny's "Ragamuffin Army" followed his thrifty cue. The 'Forty-niners, as they came to be known that fateful year, wore knitted ties, mackinaws, and mismatched jackets and pants. They were a colorful bunch—and fit right in with the riffraff of Jersey City. One Kenny sidekick, a guy named Barney Doyle, matched Yogi Berra in his propensity for dumb witticisms. He once criticized a mayoral candidate as being so stupid that he couldn't be a lifeguard in a car wash. He said that his own team could run with five parking meters and win the election, that Judas Iscariot was the patron saint of all politicians, and that his political club's slogan was the same as the word on the back of a vegetable truck: *produce*. The inflection was all wrong, but somehow Barney was always right-on, in a Jersey City sort of way.

On May 10, 1949, Kenny was swept into office, winning eleven of the twelve wards in the city and beating Eggers by 22,200 votes. To celebrate, men stood ten deep at bars like Casey's, a pub around the corner from the Hotel Plaza, where a big floral arrangement declared KENNY IN MAY. Everyone with a car got in it and drove through the city, honking the horn and picking up friends along the way, my relatives included. They moved in a long line, headlights beaming, through Journal Square, past a woman on a sound truck who repeated over and over again, "You're free. You're free. The people of Jersey City are free." A Greyhound from out of town pulled up. People on the bus looked out their windows, very confused. What the hell was going on here?

My mother was downtown, sitting on a stoop with her best friend, Ann, who was nine months pregnant and ready to burst. They got caught up in the rowdy crowds as they marched by on Grove Street, streaming down toward City Hall. One group of guys went by carrying a gray coffin with a sign that read HERE LIES THE REMAINS OF THE HAGUE MACHINE, 36 YEARS OF AGE. In a photo taken that night, my mother is in the left-hand corner of the frame, wearing a white turban on her head, smiling up at the coffin.

My uncle Robby, just thirteen at the time, rode his bicycle down to City Hall, JVK written in chalk on the back of his jacket. To him and the other poor kids in Jersey City, Kenny was a hero, like Joe DiMaggio.

He and his friends arrived at City Hall before all the ballots were counted, hoping to cop some free soda or ice cream. But there wasn't any. The crowd at City Hall was mostly adults, and they were too excited to even think about eating or drinking. Some danced on the roofs of cars or on the grass at City Hall in front of the tired statue, music blaring from the sound trucks. One policeman stood on the City Hall balcony waving a broom. Inside, the coffin drifted overhead upon a sea of bodies.

In another photograph that captured the moment, a somber-looking girl sits alone in the background at City Hall, away from the mob, to the right of the coffin sign. That's my aunt Mary Ann, looking blankly off into the distance. A kid with big ears and a wide smile lights up the foreground of another picture. That's Uncle Robby. When he saw the coffin go by, Robby got scared, thinking Hague's body was in it. Ever since his brother, Sonny, had fallen off the truck and died, Robby had been afraid of coffins. Now, he got down on his knees, crawled out of the crowd, and ran all the way home.

In one more black-and-white snapshot taken that night, the most posed of the bunch, another family member smiles for the camera. Grandpa, all decked out in a freshly blocked fedora and suit and tie, is one of two men holding a sign that reads UNDER NEW MANAGEMENT. A crowd of seven men and boys are gathered around them and the plate-glass door to the mayor's office, flashing the two-fingered V signal.

For victory. For John V.

Grandpa must have been overjoyed, but his face, the only one in the picture that is cast in dark shadow, betrays only a slight grin. Everyone else looks grim or surprised, worried that Hague might walk out any second and punch him in the nose—or, worse yet, see the picture the next day in *The Jersey Journal* and have him hunted down and killed.

Despite their disbelief that Hague was truly out, Jersey Citizens partied until dawn. One 'Forty-niner played taps outside Eggers's home at 3 A.M. There were rallies in the street, from Greenville down to the Horseshoe.

"Let us bid farewell to fear," said Kenny in his victory speech. "Let us say good-bye to corruption. Let us walk forward now as free men and women."

Because of Kenny, an investigation was finally launched into Hague's three-decades-long rule. Needlenose Malone—not Hague—was indicted on charges of corruption, and pleaded guilty after thousands of city workers signed affidavits attesting to Rice Pudding Day. Malone, not a well man, was given a suspended sentence. Eventually, Hague was informally exiled from New Jersey. If he stepped within its borders, he would be served with a subpoena. Traveling back to Jersey City five years later for the wake of his nephew, Hague was handed a subpoena by a deputy sheriff. Hague threw the subpoena to the ground and ignored it, but from then on stayed the hell out of Jersey City, funerals and all.

Some say that in his last days, he had trouble sleeping in his Park Avenue apartment, plagued by thoughts of all the families he'd damaged. Now and then he would call old friends in Jersey City and have them check on the survivors of breadwinners he had crippled or killed. My family never got a call.

Hague died, without apology, in 1956, on New Year's Day; Grandpa died seventeen years later on Christmas Day.

Though he had promised reform, John V. Kenny simply carried on where Hague left off. Patronage flourished. When Barney Doyle was appointed county superintendent of weights and measures, Gene Scanlon, a reporter from *The Jersey Journal,* called him for an interview. At the end of their chat, Scanlon threw him a giant softball.

"How many ounces are in a pound?" he asked Barney.

"How the hell do I know?" snapped Barney. "I just got the job."

Like Hague before him, Kenny also encouraged illegal betting. He loved the horses and spent all his free time at the track. Legend had it that the Turnpike extension in downtown Jersey City was built to accommodate Kenny's frequent trips to Monmouth Park, the racetrack on the Jersey shore.

One of Kenny's best friends was the notorious bookie Newsboy Moriarty, who, with his fortune, bought a new altar for St. Michael's Church—Kenny's parish. Moriarty was a former newspaper hawker who never wrote down a bet: because of his photographic memory, he kept it all in his head. Since there were no records, it was difficult for the police to arrest him, even though he always had large wads of cash—upward of $7,000—in his pockets. Newsboy, who ran a $10 million operation, did some time in jail, but it was a small price to pay for being a millionaire—tax-free. When the cops chased him, he would throw money at them. It was guaranteed to slow down the pursuit.

Newsboy was a rich man, but he never boasted. He drove an old car that had cost him around three hundred dollars, wore tattered clothes, and always ate sandwiches, never fancy sit-down dinners. He lived with his two unmarried sisters in an old brownstone. He dated a girl from Newark for years, and every night, though he had the money to buy a fleet of stretch limos, he put her on a bus back home.

In the early 1960s, the Mafia started to infringe on Newsboy's territory. The inside story goes that New York Mob boss Crazy Joe Gallo was given the okay to run the numbers racket in Jersey City and that Newsboy was ready to make a stink. The two were to meet at the Harmony Bar in downtown Jersey City's Italian Village section, a known hangout for the local mobsters.

Kenny's chief of police had Newsboy picked up from the streets before he could meet Gallo and start trouble. To get even with Kenny, Newsboy started a rumor that some of Kenny's payoff money was hidden in a car trunk in a West Side garage. Since most of it was earmarked for Kenny, it was no loss to Newsboy when two carpenters found the $2.4 million inside an abandoned 1947 Plymouth sedan. Stacks of the money disappeared, and once Newsboy claimed the rest, a big chunk of it went to the IRS. It was Newsboy's revenge for Kenny letting the Mob in on his turf.

Kenny had no choice, though. He was already in too deep, and well known down on the waterfront, where he had controlled the 6-for-5 shylock business before becoming mayor. Longie Zwillman had put up $350,000 in street money for Kenny to pay off voters. In that very first election, Kenny paid fifteen dollars a vote to Hague's five.

In 1952, Kenny double-crossed a gangster named Mo Manna and was hospitalized for pneumonia and phlebitis, according to the papers. Word on the street was that the Mob had given Kenny a bullet in the ass.

To make peace with Kenny, the Mob put Mo's son, young Anthony "Bobby" Manna, at the mayor's disposal. If somebody in the city needed fixing, Bobby would take care of it.

That same year, Kenny was called to testify before the Waterfront Commission, and denied having ties to the Mob. The commissioners knew he was lying, had proof, and threatened him with a perjury charge. A week later, he made a public announcement saying his testimony was a lie. Kenny stepped down as mayor, but he remained the unofficial boss of Hudson County. It wasn't until 1971, the year I started first grade, that Kenny finally lost his power, sentenced with Mayor Whelan in the Hudson Twelve case.

7

LUCKY STRIKE

Great-Aunt Katie was Grandpa's sister, a tough, gray-haired woman who kept a handgun in her dining room sideboard and smoked unfiltered Lucky Strikes. She said it was the filters that gave you cancer. Every day, to go with her cigarettes, Aunt Katie drank a shot of Canadian Club. She said it cleared her lungs and kept her going.

For my mother, Aunt Katie was a replacement for Grandma, even though she wasn't anything like her. Katie was squat and muscular, with short hair that made her look like a little man. Grandma had always worn dresses. Aunt Katie always wore pants.

She was the only woman I knew who really knew how to gamble. When Aunt Katie went to Atlantic City, she didn't play the slot machines like the other old ladies. She shot craps—and had to stand on a box to reach the pit, because she was so short. Many a night, after a big win, the casino sent her home in a limo. Whenever she went to Florida to visit one of her sisters, Aunt Katie was sure to lay some bets at the dog track.

I loved spending time at Aunt Katie's house, especially in her back-yard. It was the same house where she and Grandpa and their ten other siblings had lived. It was my grandparents' first address together, the place where Pauline's water broke when she was pregnant with my mother.

While Aunt Katie and my mother drank coffee, I played with Katie's dog, Buddy, who was so smart that he knew how to open the door from the hallway. Katie treated him like a human, and often sang the old war tune "My Buddy" to him. "Nights are long since you went away. I dream about you all through the day. My buddy. My buddy." His ears would perk up and he would place a soft paw in her lap.

From Katie's backyard, where Buddy's doghouse stood, I could hear the bells of St. Mary's ringing nearby. The St. Mary's neighborhood, back when Grandpa and Aunt Katie were young, was still an Irish neighborhood, a bad place for a bunch of Italian kids to be raised. Because of her name, many people thought Katie was Irish, so she fared a little better than Grandpa had.

St. Mary's was the church where Grandma Pauline converted to Catholicism from the Russian Orthodox religion in which she was raised. Aunt Katie backed her, getting Grandma in touch with the priest and helping her study for each of the sacraments. Aunt Katie was there when Grandma was rebaptized, when she received First Holy Communion and Confirmation, and on the day she remarried Grandpa. Grandma and Grandpa were remarried in St. Mary's so that the marriage would be recognized by the Church and Grandma could receive Holy Communion every week.

It always astonished me that Grandma married Grandpa not once but twice.

During the ceremony, which was held in the parish rectory, Grandpa had a claustrophobic fit. He could never stand tight spaces, and I guess the chapel and the thought of getting remarried made him want to run. Grandma should have let him.

Because Aunt Katie had been so good to Grandma, my mother loved her. So did I. When I cried, Aunt Katie made me laugh by telling me that the water from my tears was making my eyes shrink. I had squinty eyes to begin with, and the thought of them growing even smaller made me stop crying.

Aunt Katie knew I hated being short like she was, so she told me that someday she would buy a racehorse and, since I was so tiny, I would be its jockey. I looked forward to those days at the track and imagined myself in photo finishes, my family raking in big bucks from lucky bets on me and my trusty steed.

The horse never did materialize, but Aunt Katie provided other distractions. She could throw a mean fastball in the backyard, or imitate a crowing rooster—that is until Uncle Al, her longshoreman husband, came home. As soon as Uncle Al came in the door, he would order Aunt Katie around. But she would make funny faces behind his back and "yes him to death," as she called it.

Uncle Al's face looked like one of the faces on the Indian-head coins that Grandpa had stolen from the library. He was Polish, but he looked just like an Indian chief. Though he wasn't as crazy as Grandpa, he could be just as mean. He was stubborn, too, and insisted that Aunt Katie buy Tip Top bread. "Tip Top bread makes Tip Top toast," he said without a hint of humor in his voice, as if he were a staff sergeant. Since Tip Top was expensive, Aunt Katie would buy regular A&P bread and put it in a leftover Tip Top bag. Uncle Al never knew the difference. Aunt Katie was very resourceful.

If Uncle Al lost his temper, he could go into a frenzy and break all the kitchen furniture. Aunt Katie always had a new kitchen set. When he was drunk, Al could be as abusive as Grandpa. But Aunt Katie knew how to handle Al. She was much smarter than he was.

After Uncle Al came in stinking drunk one night and terrorized her, Aunt Katie got an idea. "I'll fix him," she said. While Al snored, she smoked four cigars and a half pack of Lucky Strikes and left the stubs in ashtrays on the table. She sloppily spilled some Canadian Club into glasses, took a few swigs, and left the glasses sitting half empty. She dealt a round of playing cards and tossed some furniture around. Then she went to bed.

When Al got up the next morning, his head pounding with a hangover, he found Katie sitting at the table crying. She was a good actress.

"What's all this?" he asked.

"What do you mean?" Aunt Katie sobbed. "Don't you remember?"

Uncle Al looked at her blankly.

"Last night you and your fucking friends wrecked the joint with your poker game," she said, waving her stubby arm. "Look at this mess. They were cursing and drinking and smoking. One of your buddies even made a play for me." She cried a little harder, to show how traumatized she was by the near-rape experience.

Uncle Al was horrified at his and his friends' behavior, and even more horrified that he couldn't remember a minute of it. That day, he went to St. Mary's and took a pledge never to drink again. He kept his promise for two long years.

Aunt Katie could handle anyone and anything that came her way. She once explained what to do in case a rabid dog tried to attack me. "Take your coat off and wrap it around your arm, like this," she said, winding an imaginary coat around her forearm. "Then stick your arm out so the bastard goes to bite it. When he jumps up, you give him a swift kick in the balls." I never got a chance to use the rabid-dog defense, but it was good information to have in downtown Jersey City, where an occasional pack of wild dogs would roam into my part of the neighborhood.

Katie was full of life lessons. But best of all, she could tell a funny story—like the one about the time she was cutting her toenails and one of them flew into her sister Eva's eye. You had to hear Aunt Katie tell it.

It was Aunt Katie who told us about our Italian ancestors, about my great-great-grandmother Vita, the life-giver of the Italian-American line. Vita—Beansie's grandmother—was married to a man named Francesco, who got involved in a fight during a card game in Bernalde, a town in the district of Matera, a lawless, godforsaken corner of southern Italy. Somehow, maybe in defense, maybe because of the temper that I inherited decades later, Vita killed the man. At least that's what Aunt Katie said.

Perhaps Vita stabbed the cardplayer and twisted the knife a bit before pulling it out, or maybe she hit him over the head with a very heavy saucepan. Maybe the whole story was a fable. But Vita did escape to the United States around 1897, taking with her the last name of her lawyer or lover. The stolen last name was Vena. In Italian, the name means "vein," as in the vein that runs through your arm, or through your family history. Figuratively, *vena* can also mean a talent or gift passed down from generation to generation. In our case, a talent for making trouble. The scandal was a blessing in disguise and a good excuse to leave Matera, which was well known for its violent card games and bandits, its chalky landscape, its cave dwellers, its pagans, witches, poverty, and malaria, its frescoes depicting original sin, and its Via del Riscattoò—"Street of Vengeance." If Jersey City was hell, it was only the first circle. Ancient Matera was the core of hell, from which my ancestors—Vita and her children—barely escaped.

Vita left her husband behind and traveled by ship, in steerage, with her three young sons. One was lost in transit. Maybe while Vita was gaping at the Statue of Liberty in awe, looking away from her boys, her little son slipped away, stolen by a black-market adoption ring or child-labor slave trader. Perhaps he fell overboard, greedily sucked in by the waves.

Between the missing son, the homicide, and the escape from Italy, Vita was a wreck by the time she arrived at the Jersey City railroad terminal. Like my Russian great-grandmother, Irene, who had arrived four years earlier, Vita put down her bags and gave up in Jersey City. The Statue of Liberty pedestal may have read, "Give me your tired, your poor," but if Jersey City had had a statue in the harbor, it would have said, "Give me your completely exhausted, completely broken, completely hopeless and weak, who have no train fare to go any farther." Vita lived to a ripe old age, but in keeping with the family's flair for drama, she didn't die of natural causes, naturally. She was accidentally killed while walking down the street when a mischief-making neighborhood kid hit her in the head with a rock-filled sock on Halloween night.

Vita's two remaining sons were named Leonardo and Valente. My great-grandfather Leonard—Beansie and Katie's father—grew up to be a barber, and opened his shop right across the street from Hague's headquarters at City Hall, only three doors from the Majestic Tavern. Leonard was a small man with a full moon of a face. He was so good and clean that you could smell his fresh barbershop scent when he walked past you. Opening the barbershop so close to City Hall was a brilliant move, since it guaranteed a steady clientele, including Hague and all his cronies. The shop was in a basement, a few steps down from the rotating red-and-white barber pole.

From his perch on a bench in City Hall Park, Grandpa could look straight inside and watch his father cut infamous heads. They sat in a row of old-fashioned chrome-and-leather barber chairs—state-of-the-art at the time—their dishonest faces thrown back at them in the bank of mirrors along the wall.

It was Leonard's difficult job to make them look clean and fresh, to comb over their souls with hair tonic and shaving cream. Combs floated in antiseptic jars. Shaving brushes and straight-edged razors lay out like a surgeon's tools. Each regular had his own shaving mug sitting on the shelf. Business was so good that Leonard even hired a female manicurist, who kept the politicians' hands soft and their nails clean and trimmed.

Though the politicians were his main clientele, Leonard served the working men of Jersey City, too, whose hands were callused and dirty. One afternoon, just as a local man was stepping up to the chair, Hague came strolling into the shop.

"Leo, I'm in a rush," he barked. "I need a fast shave."

"Mayor, I understand," said Leonard, bowing his head and pointing his scissors. "But this man is next. He's been waiting."

Leonard was lucky Hague didn't haul off and punch him in the nose. Instead, the mayor grabbed his shaving mug, left, and never returned.

Though he was the best barber in the neighborhood, with a thriving business, Leonard never taught his sons to cut heads. Maybe they refused. Grandpa preferred to hang around across the street. And his older brother Frankie worked nearby, right outside City Hall.

Frankie would stand in plain view of his righteous father and swindle young lovers. He'd stop those who had come to get married—and who didn't know the system—on the City Hall steps and tell them not to pay the exorbitant City Hall prices for a marriage certificate.

"Come with me," Uncle Frankie would say, then lead them to the dining room of an associate, where they'd meet a "judge"—another criminal, who had stolen a judge's robe and marriage seal. Sometimes, if the couple was more religious, Frankie would take them up to Union City, to one of the cathedral chapels. Charging them a discounted price—twenty-five dollars for a normal affair; a hundred for one with singing and flowers—Uncle Frankie would have the couple "married."

Dozens, if not hundreds or thousands, of marriages in Jersey City are fakes because of my uncle Frankie. Even one of our Vena cousins from Brooklyn fell for Frankie's scam and lived for years, unknowingly, in unholy matrimony.

Frankie was simply no good. Aunt Katie said that he would often take his girlfriends to Holy Name Cemetery to have sex with them on the graves or beside the bones in the mausoleums. Aunt Katie made excuses for Frankie, like she did for Grandpa, saying that when he was a boy, Frankie had suffered a terrible trauma, worse than getting hit by an ice truck. The house caught fire and Frankie, in an effort to save his little brother, dragged the baby carriage out of the burning building, but he stumbled and dropped the carriage down the stoop. The baby died. And Frankie was never the same. He drank for years, and was given the nickname Clearwater.

Urged by his father to get a real job, Frankie became the cashier at the Majestic Theatre. It was just a few doors down from the tavern, the barbershop, and my childhood home and was a nationally known vaudeville theater that attracted such acts as Bing Crosby and Mae West. By the time I came around, the Majestic Theatre was long closed, boarded up, and at the center of a restoration battle. For most residents, the Majestic was a small slice of beauty and proud history still left standing in Jersey City. It seemed a shame to knock it down.

But I knew a little too much of its history. The Majestic's former manager, Charles Suozza, testified at one of the many Hague inquiries that the mayor regularly shook him down for $100 "to keep from being bothered."

Uncle Frankie's Majestic job didn't last long. After a while, word spread and couples would come looking for the marriage broker at the Majestic. But that wasn't the reason Frankie lost his job. He lost it because he plotted with some friends to rob the theater of its large cash box and safe. Frankie stashed the $3,800 in advance. Then his friends stuck a gun in his face to make it look like a real burglary. A few days later, the scam was uncovered and Frankie and his friends were arrested. The story ran on the front page of *The Jersey Journal* on October 30, 1923: SAY MAJESTIC CASHIER STAGED HOLD-UP. It embarrassed poor Leonard.

Frankie was not much better than Beansie. He was just more

crafty. When Hague was rounding up the usual suspects, Frankie high-tailed it home and hid out for a few days. If the cops cornered Frankie, he would bullshit his way out of a beating. "Officer," he would lie. "I went to the doctor yesterday and he told me I have a very bad heart condition."

Grandpa, even if he hadn't committed the crime, spit in the cops' faces. That was the crucial difference between the brothers. That, and Frankie's organized marriage scam. Grandpa was more of a freelance criminal, committing crimes whenever the opportunity arose.

Without his two eldest sons to help him in the barbershop, Leonard turned to his daughter Katie. She had a steady hand and, as a young girl, helped her father shave the customers. She was so skilled with a razor that many of the men requested her when they came in the ring-ing door. Although she was not the prettiest, Aunt Katie was the smartest and spunkiest and the favorite girl in the family. It was in the barbershop that Katie learned the tricks of the trade—not just cutting hair, but working the political machine.

Katie was so charming that New Jersey governor A. Harry Moore asked Leonard if he and his wife could adopt her. "Leo," said the child-less Moore. "You got so many children. Why don't you give us one?" He knew there were eleven other mouths for Leonard to feed, so he would be willing to take this one—this special one—off his hands.

Leonard was flattered by the offer and told the story to everyone who walked into the shop. But he loved Katie too much to give her away. Katie stayed close. Little did Leonard know that when he wasn't looking, Katie would steal change from the barbershop to shoot dice with the guys on the corner.

Each week, Leonard gave Katie two dollars for each child in the family, which she was to put away in the bank. When cleaning the closet one day, her mother came across Katie's coat, which held in its pocket all the bank deposit slips. The money had never been deposited.

There was also the time Katie got up onstage at school and recited a poem she claimed to have written. Everyone clapped and cheered ex-cept one of her sisters, who knew Katie had plagiarized the poem. But she didn't rat her out. She loved Katie too much. Everyone did.

When she wasn't stealing words or money, Katie was watching out for her younger brothers and sisters—a role that prepared her for her job as a neighborhood committeewoman for Hague. When her little brother fell in with the neighborhood gang and started to play hooky, Aunt Katie went to the ice cream shack where the gang leader hung out and beat the living shit out of him. She was only twelve. And the boy, probably around the same age, was forever disgraced for being beaten up by a girl.

With the money from his barbershop, Leonard bought a home for his family in the neighborhood where all his Irish customers lived. My grandfather and his siblings were the only Italians in the St. Mary's neighborhood, and were often ridiculed and beaten for being dirty guineas. Beansie, who had serious problems with authority to begin with, had to fight his way through life. Had he lived in the Italian Village, just a few blocks north, he probably wouldn't have developed such a complex. He probably would have become a full-fledged gangster, not a two-bit criminal.

Katie was smart, and would never be outdone by the "Irish bastards." As a little girl, at Christmastime Katie watched with envy as a neighbor held her new baby doll up to the windowpane. But Aunt Katie thought fast and did the girl one better. She ran inside and grabbed her little sister Tessie, still a baby, and held her up for show. The little girl sulked away, jealous that Katie had a real baby.

In 1931, at the age of twenty-two, Katie became a committeewoman. Jersey City's population was then at its peak, around 316,000, and through her father's barbershop Katie had met all the right people, the players and the dealers.

Katie's territory consisted of two city blocks, from First to Third and from Henderson to Grove, and included eight hundred voters. She was so in tune with her constituents that she could tell on Election Day how many votes the Republicans would get—usually as few as three or four. She eventually became the first-ward women's Democratic leader. Her district usually won six to one.

The committeeman or -woman was the point person you went to see when you had a problem in the neighborhood—any kind of problem: a problem with your landlord, a noisy neighbor, you name it. Katie, big sister to the whole neighborhood, knew all the judges and department heads. If a kid had trouble and it didn't involve a gun or drugs, Katie was his get-out-of-jail-free card.

Like the time my uncle Robby accidentally ran over a traffic cop's toe in a borrowed '37 Chevy the week after he got his license. The cop pulled him out of the car through the driver's side window, roughed him up, then drove the car, with Robby as his captive, down to the Seventh Street precinct house, where he planned to book him. Robby was smart enough not to mention that his father was Beansie. But he did mention that he was Katie's nephew. She was called down to vouch for him, and Robby was set free.

Aunt Katie was always looking out for the family. Had she not been such an insider, Grandpa would have wound up like Michael Rombolo, the Italian guy who got the chair for killing an Irishman. When her mother got sick, Aunt Katie took a hospital bed from the Medical Center. I'm not sure if she rolled it out in one piece or took it bit by bit— headboard, mattress, box spring, and frame. My great-grandmother Concetta died in that luxurious bed, courtesy of the Medical Center, but in the comfort of home. Since the bed was returned after Concetta died, the family likes to say it was a loaner.

If you needed a job, Katie would hook you up with the ward leader, who in turn would put you in touch with the mayor's office. If you were new to the neighborhood, it was Katie's job to help you move in, then get you registered to vote as soon as possible.

Katie and the ward leaders were the foot soldiers of the Hague administration. And Katie was one of the best, serving for over three decades. Though she had spent only two years in high school, she understood the political machinery and the voters better than anyone. Her mentor, a committeeman named Joe Fay, who lived next door, told Katie, "Always do a favor for the people, but never let them know how you did it. Because once they know that, they don't need you anymore."

Katie made everyone feel she was their best friend. She once gave—rather than loaned—her big, new broiler pan to a new neighbor. Around the holidays, she would go door to-door to the Newark Avenue shopkeepers and schmooze them into donating turkeys for the baskets for the city's needy. In one year alone, she sold five thousand books of 50/50 chances for a St. Mary's fund-raiser.

At her city job in the Complaint Department at City Hall, she never condescended, but almost unconsciously, she could change her voice or accent to match yours and make you feel completely at ease. And Aunt Katie loved to sing, particularly a little ditty she wrote about Jersey City: "They called it Paulus Hook in sixteen hundred and four. A little piece of heaven along the Hudson shore." At the St. Mary's CYO dances, painted in blackface, Katie entertained the crowd with "Ol' Black Joe" and "Bye Bye Blackbird."

If she had been a man, she would have someday been mayor. But the idea of equal rights—urinals and all—was decades away. Instead of becoming mayor, Aunt Katie got married to Uncle Al and gave birth to two sons. But as a woman, she pushed the boundaries. During the war, she read a leaflet that encouraged women to "work, not wait, for victory" and took a job as a riveter at the Continental Can Company, building P-47 Thunderbolt fighter planes. Aunt Katie earned seventy-five dollars a week, starting at dawn and working late into the afternoon. When a jealous male worker started throwing rocks at the female riveters, Aunt Katie and her coworkers made sure he got his—a beating and his walking papers.

Between her jobs—at Continental and as a committeewoman—Aunt Katie found time to invent a few gadgets. One in particular, a clothespin dispenser, received a patent but never caught on.

Aunt Katie's greatest invention, though, was Aunt Katie. She was constantly reinventing herself, and never lived in the past, as most Jersey City old-timers did. When Kenny ran for office, Katie followed her intuition and became one of his 'Forty-niners. Then, when an Italian from the neighborhood named Thomas Gangemi decided to run for mayor in the late 1950s, Katie threw her three decades of experience and power behind him.

In her heart, Aunt Katie hated the Irish as much as Grandpa did. She never forgot that her parish, the very Irish St. Mary's, had given her a hard time about joining the Rosary Society because she was Italian, that they had even tried to deny Italians Holy Communion in the old days.

For years, Aunt Katie held it all in, waiting for just the right moment to strike.

8

STRAW KATIE

An Italian mayoral candidate was Katie's best revenge. For the time being, anyway. I imagine that for Jersey City, an Italian running for mayor was equal to the excitement Polish people felt when John Paul II was made pope. About fucking time, they all said. What took you so long?

Thomas Gangemi was known as the Watermelon King because of his fruit-vending business downtown. He was better looking than your average Jersey City Joe, and taller than most downtown Italians. But good looks could only take you so far in such an ugly place. Gangemi's poor grammar and street-tough background scored him points with the voters. They liked his "dese," "dem," and "dose" vocabulary. It didn't matter that he'd been accused of being a no-show on Hague's payroll or that he'd been responsible for the county's unwise purchase of pricey marble-topped (Italian, no doubt) office furniture, said to cost more than President Eisenhower's.

The Italians loved him, including Aunt Katie.

In 1961, with her help, Gangemi was elected mayor. But he only served two years. The thing that got him into office—his Italian roots—also got him thrown out.

As part of a public relations stunt in 1963, Gangemi was to travel to Italy to escort a man named Christopher Columbus—a direct descendant—back to Jersey City to march in the annual Columbus Day parade with him. The parade was a big deal, with the city's entire Italian community gathering on Journal Square at the tall, bronze Christopher Columbus statue and marching up Hudson Boulevard, soon to be renamed Kennedy Boulevard.

With the first Italian mayor ever, accompanied by a man named Christopher Columbus, the Italians were sure to whip themselves into a frenzy. It was their chance to thumb their noses at the Irish politicians who had run the city for decades. But the plan went to hell when Gangemi applied for a passport to go to Italy and the U.S. Immigration and Naturalization Service discovered he was not an American citizen. Which meant that he could not hold office.

Before the story broke, and before his staff even knew what was happening, Gangemi checked himself into Columbia-Presbyterian Hospital in Manhattan, claiming he didn't feel well. To throw *The Jersey Journal* off the trail, the paper's editor was immediately appointed Jersey City's ambassador to Italy and sent to the old country in Gangemi's place. Flying first class on Alitalia, with a seat next to Cardinal Spellman, the editor was to meet Christopher Columbus and escort him to the parade. Gangemi, meanwhile, hid under the hospital covers.

When *The Jersey Journal* city desk found out about Gangemi's passport troubles, they called the Rome airport, just as the editor's plane was landing. He left Columbus in Genoa and took the next flight home. Columbus traveled alone to Jersey City. Though Gangemi was no longer mayor, he was still chairman of the Columbus Day Committee. He donned his morning suit and marched alongside Columbus anyway.

Some people, particularly the city's Italians, think Gangemi was set up, that Kenny knew for years about Gangemi's illegal status, and kept that card in his pocket for a time when he would need to play it. Gangemi's supporters went so far as to say that Bobby Kennedy had had something to do with his downfall—that because of Gangemi's Italian roots, the attorney general assumed he was connected to the Mob and had it in for him.

Whether the passport fiasco happened accidentally or not, the fact was Gangemi could not hold office. The rush for a new mayor was on. Gangemi was promised that his son, Buddy, would get the nod. But at the last minute the city council elected Thomas Whelan, a handsome World War II veteran, six feet tall, two hundred pounds, with blue eyes and a lovely wife. He was another in a long line of Irish mayors whose strong-arm tactics echoed those of Hague's zepps of the 1940s.

During the racial unrest of the 1960s, Whelan gained favor with the predominantly white community by playing on residents' fears. There had already been riots in Rochester, Harlem, and Brooklyn; the violence was creeping closer and closer to home.

Whelan saw his opening. After one small skirmish in August 1964, with just a few black people arguing on the street, the police were sent in. Rumors spread that a young black woman had been hit with a blackjack. A rock was thrown, then a bottle, leading to a series of arrests and an announcement by Whelan: "We will not tolerate anarchy in the city by any person or any group of people." Wink-wink. To make the black politicians happy, Whelan threw in a quote from Abraham Lincoln. "Law without enforcement is only good advice."

Police cars rolled into the black neighborhoods, with cops holding shotguns through their windows, aimed at the crowds in the street. Old-timers liked to say that Whelan "kept the blacks in their place." That's why the people loved him.

While Whelan was striking his tough-guy pose, Gangemi was busy learning about George Washington and memorizing the Pledge of Allegiance. He finally became a citizen and then launched an attack against Whelan in the 1965 election.

Whelan's team circulated a picture of Gangemi talking to a black politician with the catchy kicker *What are these two guys whispering about?* Jersey Citizens, with the "riots" and Gangemi's nickname Watermelon King echoing in their racist brains, fell for it.

Well, most Jersey Citizens. Aunt Katie turned her back on both Gangemi and Whelan. She had her own secret weapon. Despite her long list of accomplishments, Katie was still a woman, and as a woman, her main job was raising her boys, Mike and Chubby. She poured all her political knowledge into her older son, Mike, a naturally smart kid, whom she sent to college and to Harvard Law School. If Katie couldn't be mayor, then maybe Mike could be. Like any parent who isn't able to attain her own dreams, Aunt Katie put her hopes into her child. Having her son run against the machine cost her her job at the Complaint Department at City Hall. But she thought that with Mike in office, everything she had done and worked for would pay off—the years in the barbershop, as a committeewoman, district leader, good neighbor, and entertainer. None of it would go to waste.

I always wondered if Aunt Katie, in her effort to anoint Mike the chosen one, paid too little attention to her younger son, Chubby. From the time he was five years old, his parents told him he would be a longshoreman like his father. And when he grew up, Chubby became one. Even though he was muscular and looked like a boxer, Chubby was a sweet and gentle guy, very soft-spoken. I liked Chubby. He had been in the army, but there was something fragile about him.

When I was a kid, Chubby got beaten up by the Jersey City cops for a traffic violation. The morning after, my mother was on her way to work when she bumped into Aunt Katie, who was headed to court, carrying Chubby's bloody sweatshirt as evidence of police brutality. Maybe Chubby's burly appearance was the reason the cops had hit him so hard. Or maybe it was Aunt Katie's politics. But the cops had been relentless, kicking him in the head and knocking something loose. The family won a large settlement against the police, but it didn't help much. After the beating, Chubby was never the same. He eventually killed himself with a shotgun.

Resourceful to a fault, Aunt Katie sold the gun.

———

Mike made his first bid for mayor during the 1965 election, while Chubby was still alive and well. Chubby helped him campaign. Everyone in the family did, even my mother. She went over to Aunt Katie's and helped stuff envelopes. I was just a baby, sleeping on a bed in the next room.

Mike was the first college graduate I ever knew—never mind Harvard graduate or law-school graduate. In Jersey City, people were actively illiterate and proudly went around saying things like "I never read a book in my life." They boasted that they had managed to get so far without reading a single page. I wanted to say, Well, good for you, you idiot. Look where you are. You're still in Jersey City.

I looked up to Mike, because he was smart and because he admitted that he read books. He spoke to me like my parents did—like I was a person and not a stupid little kid. He showed me his Norman Rockwell prints and talked to me about the novels he'd read and the films he'd seen. It was called interesting conversation. Most people I knew talked about sports scores, the good old days, and the veal parmigiano they just ate and the agita it was giving them. Or they gossiped about yet another neighbor with a tumor. It got old after a while. For me and a lot of other people, Mike was a breath of fresh air in the polluted sky of Jersey City.

Mike was born on the same day as Hank Aaron, the man who had broken Babe Ruth's home run record. He was the first of a new generation, a new wave of politicians in Jersey City who could finally tear down the old order and dismantle the political machine.

Mike had inherited Katie's brains but, unfortunately, not her warmth. He looked as smart as he was, with horn-rimmed glasses and soft hands. Though he did have a Jersey City accent, Mike spoke to everyone in the same direct, lawyerly way. Even me.

I admired him for his large vocabulary and his ability to use mnemonic devices to remember everything. Katie had prepped Mike well—maybe too well—sending him to St. Peter's Prep, the best school in the county. To give him a worldview, she encouraged him to take a Fulbright scholarship to Italy, where he studied the effect of economics on political change. At Harvard Law, he often won debates against fellow student Michael Dukakis. Ruth Bader Ginsburg and Antonin Scalia were also classmates. Roscoe Pound lived in the same hotel in Cambridge as Mike, and though he wasn't a poet like his brother Ezra, he was capable of interesting conversation.

After graduation, Mike considered staying in Cambridge, where people could understand what he was talking about. But Hudson County called out like a sickly uncle. And Mike came to the rescue.

Though he understood the city and state tax system better than anybody, his knowledge was unappreciated by the unsophisticated residents and politicians. In an effort to explain the tax situation to the voters, Mike tried comparing taxes to a poker game, explaining that everyone had to throw in their fair share of money and that Jersey Citizens were being hustled by the dealers.

He tried to explain, to make them understand—in the simplest terms—that Jersey City residents paid one of the highest residential property tax rates in the country ($113 per $1,000), that the once great Medical Center was now operating at a $5 million deficit, that unless an honest mayor was elected, the city would become, "as one Harvard sociologist has already predicted, the first total slum city in the United States."

Mike's biggest fault was a belief in the American system of democracy in such a corrupt place. In a newspaper article that appeared in 1965, Mike naively declared, "I have great faith in the common sense and basic fairness of American people—that's why I have a chance to win." Common sense was abundant in Jersey City. Without an education, common sense was all you had to go on. We called it street smarts. But fairness? In Jersey City? That was something else altogether.

Before the election, Gangemi summoned Mike, telling him he should drop out of the race, that he wanted Mike's help on *his* campaign. Mike tried to explain his theories about high finance but got nowhere. Unable to convince Mike to bow out, Gangemi used the only strategy he could think of: "You should support me because I danced at your mother's wedding." Jersey City logic. Common sense.

But Gangemi got nowhere, and started to get frustrated. "What do you wanna run for? You're gonna waste your money," he told Mike. Gangemi was so confident Mike was wasting his time, he bet him $25,000 he couldn't get two thousand votes. But Mike was more confident. He took the bet and raised it to $30,000. The two made a date the following Monday for Mike to drop off the certified check. When Mike showed up, Gangemi's secretary said he was at a wake. Gangemi never placed the bet.

Whelan wanted Mike out of the way as much as Gangemi did, especially since Mike drew the coveted A1 position on the ballot. One night a Whelan operative came to see Mike. "I heard you're doing well," he said. He congratulated Mike. Then he promptly offered him a $50,000 bribe to get out of the way.

"Joe, that's real nice," said Mike, "but I'm gonna stay in it." Mike, who had been practicing law in Manhattan for the past few years, didn't need the cash. What he needed was the political exposure. He had no illusions that he would win the election. He just wanted to make a name for the next time around. Mike had a long-term strategy.

During that 1965 election, bookies were making bets that Whelan would get more votes than all the other candidates combined. Big bets. Hundred-dollar bets. Mike's father, Uncle Al, was tempted to lay down some cash. "Down the piers, they're betting," Uncle Al told his son. "It sounds like a good bet."

But Mike knew better. To build his political base, Mike was campaigning door-to-door, with the help of only twelve political-science students from local St. Peter's College. "You got nice credentials," the voters told him, "but we're voting for Whelan." Mike knew Whelan would win big-time and told his father not to bet, that the bookies were right.

When the election was over, Whelan got 57,000 votes. Mike got a healthy 10,000 votes. And the rest of the candidates got 45,000. The smart-money bookies won the bet. But it was close.

To prepare himself for the next mayoral election, Mike organized an independent legislative ticket in 1967, including four senatorial candidates, eight assemblymen, and three freeholders who ran against Kenny, still the county boss. Mike financed the ticket himself but decided not to run. He had his eye on the 1969 mayoral race. He knew you could only run so many times and lose before they write you up as a perpetual loser. But Mike's ego got in the way. His friends talked him into joining the ticket as a senatorial candidate. With help from the family, Mike's ticket gained momentum. Our cousin Sonny from Brooklyn knew a printer who made campaign cards. Aunt Katie called in all her favors. Things were rolling.

The Democrats won, but Mike's ticket had a good showing, with 20,000 votes in the county. The Republican party, by contrast, got only 12,000 votes. The editor of *The Jersey Journal* called Mike and told him he should become a Republican.

———

In 1969, Mike ran for mayor a second time, with Whelan and Gangemi his main opponents again. In a *Jersey Journal* article published that

May, Mike, still the political idealist, quoted Alexander Hamilton: " 'Someday the great American city will rise on the west bank of the Hudson,' " he said. "Alexander Hamilton meant Jersey City and he knew what he was talking about."

Unfortunately, most voters didn't know what the hell Mike was talking about. In one campaign ad, he shot way over their heads, using terms like *confiscatory* and *tax ratables*. He called for "the elimination of nonproductive jobs and the ending of the use of the city payroll for rewarding political hacks." A few too many political hacks made up the voter base. The ad simply translated as "Mike will take away your no-show job." It didn't matter that *The New York Times* had called Mike "a refreshing new voice in the morass of Hudson County politics." No one in Jersey City read *The New York Times*. Few knew the definition of *morass*.

Mike opened a political club on Journal Square, choosing ten reform candidates as the nucleus for his movement. One day Grandpa walked into the club, thinking it would be an old-fashioned ward club, with guys in fedoras smoking cigars, offering bribes over the phone, and collecting street money to try and get the vote out. By then, the committeeman system Hague had built was in tatters. Worried that history would repeat itself, a paranoid John V. Kenny started dismantling the system, afraid of getting stabbed in the back by a "loyal soldier."

Full of violent energy, Grandpa was ready to roll up his sleeves and help Mike campaign. But Grandpa was still lost in the era of ward leaders and bat-wielding sluggers. When Grandpa saw all the college kids hard at work, clean and scrubbed, with glasses rather than fedoras, he realized it wasn't his place. He wished Mike good luck, shook his hand, and walked out. It was an oddly graceful and humble moment. I could almost feel sorry for Grandpa, if I didn't know what a bastard he was.

Mike lost again in 1969. But in 1970 he was given another chance when Whelan, Kenny, and the rest of the Hudson Twelve were indicted. By then, Kenny, the man of the people, was spending winters in Florida and summers at the Jersey shore, as Hague had before him.

Two of the Hudson Twelve became government witnesses. The

others either pleaded out or were convicted in federal court. The trials were as colorful as expected. One former county Democratic chairman testified against Whelan, admitting that the mayor, so nervous about being exposed, had given him $50,000 in cash to bribe a witness in the case. The chairman had hidden the money in a trash can in his basement. The prosecutor wheeled the can into the courtroom and revealed the $50,000 hidden inside.

During another trial, the blind treasurer of the Mosquito Commission, wearing dark glasses and tripping on his way into court, testified that city exterminators embezzled money by simply placing illegal checks in front of him to sign—sight unseen, naturally. His testimony gave new meaning to the phrase "rob the city blind."

Over the years, former mayor Kenny stole as much money as he could get his hands on. He had fooled the people into thinking he was one of them. But once again, Jersey Citizens got screwed. When they found out that Kenny had reneged on his promise to make Jersey City a better place, the disappointment was so overwhelming that many residents abandoned the city for good. The population took a sharp nosedive, from around 300,000 at Kenny's election in 1949 to 260,000 in 1970. People left in droves. Except for my family, of course. We stayed behind.

If ever there was a time for a reform candidate, it was the early 1970s. It seemed everyone and his mother was running for office. Mike was one of eighteen candidates.

To save the city, Mike knew that the waterfront had to be developed. He campaigned on the tax issue again, but this time emphasized that a shortage of commercial space in Manhattan would bring companies across the river and build up Jersey City's tax base.

Mike's father and brother were longshoremen, after all, so Mike knew the potential down at the docks. He called the waterfront the eighth wonder of the world, the passageway to the West. He claimed to have private bankers from New York behind him, men who could raise millions to build up the waterfront. But by the time the election rolled around in 1971, Mike's ten handpicked supporters decided not to support him, since he had run twice before. They decided to back the president of his political club instead, another young, nerdy-looking man with horn-rimmed glasses. Paul Jordan, a doctor who had never run for mayor before, won the election. He became known as the man who opened the city's first methadone clinic—a wonderful addition to beautiful downtown Jersey City.

Mike blamed himself for his downfall. He should have hugged more babies. Should have been warmer. But it's hard to be warm and fuzzy when talking about tax reform and development. Maybe he should have played up his mixed ancestry. A young journalist had once told him he was the only Pole with an Irish-sounding name who spoke Italian and looked like a Jew. She told Mike to marry a Puerto Rican girl with a black father "and you'll have all your bases covered."

But Mike's biggest blunder occurred in 1970, when Whelan called Mike's house and said he wanted to meet to talk about taxes, finance, and economics. Mike was excited that Whelan was finally going to listen to his ideas. "Christ," said the still wide-eyed, horn-rimmed Mike. "This is good. This is what I've been trying to get the son of a bitch to do since 1965, to understand this issue."

Whelan came down to the basement at 222 First Street, the same basement where I played with Buddy the dog, the very same basement where Aunt Katie kept her .22. Whelan and Mike talked for about two hours, during which time a reporter from the *Hudson Dispatch* showed up. Before Whelan left, a photographer took a picture of the two of them chatting.

Here he was fighting against corruption, and Mike winds up in a picture next to Whelan, the most recent incarnation of Jersey City political evil. In Mike's own home, no less. Now it looked like Mike was looking for a county job, or at least aligning himself with the forces of darkness. It never occurred to the voters that Mike was just trying to get his point across. No one in Jersey City ever had a point to get across, so how could they understand?

During Paul Jordan's campaign, copies of that newspaper photo were sent to 100,000 people, almost every voter in the city. It ruined Mike's chances of ever being elected.

Though I don't remember the campaign itself, I remember Mike's campaign party, on Mischief Night, October 30, 1971. The car we drove in—my sister's boyfriend's car—was pelted with eggs.

My mother had never let us out on Mischief Night, since bad kids from the neighborhood would hit you with flour-filled socks. Or eggs. Or worse. So it was a thrill to be out, to see firsthand what really went on. The sidewalks were slippery and yellow with egg yolks and the streets were nearly empty, since everyone knew to take cover. We drove past gang after gang of rowdy boys hurling eggs at our car. The windshield wipers couldn't do much. They smeared the egg whites and eggshells and made the view worse, but we somehow arrived safely at the party at the Polish Home on Liberty Avenue.

It was in full swing. Red, white, and blue bunting hung from a stage, upon which a band was playing popular songs that were no longer so popular. People were dressed up, even Aunt Katie. She had on a dress and a faux straw hat made of white Styrofoam, with a red, white, and blue band. The real hats—the straw kind—were called straw katies. I asked Ma if they were named after Aunt Katie. Maybe, she said, laughing. Maybe they were.

Aunt Katie was also wearing her partial dentures, so I knew this was really a special occasion. Whenever she wore the false teeth, which was rarely, Aunt Katie looked a little scary—not like herself, but like somebody else's aunt or like that horse she kept promising me. The teeth looked too big for her mouth.

I had just gotten my first pair of eyeglasses, so it all seemed very clear to me. Things had been pretty blurry before, but until I got my glasses, I had no idea about the details I'd been missing.

That night, coincidentally, was the same night my sister lost a contact lens. It's strange, the facts that cling to your brain at that age, when you can see things clearly and starkly. While we searched around on our knees for Paula's lens in the lobby, Aunt Katie was onstage singing "Bye Bye Blackbird." The election wasn't over yet. But everyone knew it was over for Mike. They had all gotten the picture of him and Whelan in the mail.

I had never seen Aunt Katie cry, but tonight she couldn't make it through the song without her voice cracking. She had bet everything she had, even Chubby's future, on a sure thing—her fortunate son Mike. The years with Hague, Kenny, and Gangemi—they were all just a dress rehearsal for her son's ascension to mayor of Jersey City.

"Pack up all my cares and woe, here I go, singing low, bye bye, blackbird," Aunt Katie sang as we made our way from the lobby to our table. "Where somebody waits for me. Sugar sweet, so is she, bye bye blackbird." Cousin Chubby, big and burly and just a few years away from suicide, stumbled up onstage with a bouquet of two dozen red roses for his mother, as if she were the one running for office. "Where somebody else can understand me," she sang. "Oh, what hard luck stories they all hand me."

By the time Aunt Katie was through, we were all in tears—Chubby, Mike, Uncle Al, Paula, Ma, me. Even Paula's boyfriend was misty. I wasn't sure what I was crying about as I took my new glasses off to wipe my eyes. But I knew that whatever it was, it was very sad, since even Great-Aunt Katie was sobbing.

9

PENNIES FROM HEAVEN

Even though she never got a driver's license, Ma got a job at the Division of Motor Vehicles in 1964, just before she became pregnant with me. She worked right through the pregnancy, her belly protruding under the counter while she typed. I liked it under there, she told me, soothed by the noise of the electric typewriter. It was the first time my mother had worked since having gotten married back in 1952. She loved the DMV because, like Aunt Katie, she liked helping people with their problems. Working also gave Ma a sense of independence.

Though she had to quit when Grandma died, Ma got her job back after I went to school in 1970. The office was just a block from home and from City Hall, and the hours were flexible. A few years later, my sister got a job at the DMV to pay for her night classes in college, and Ma was promoted to head clerk.

My mother had known the DMV agent, Frank, for thirty years, ever since his days as a teenage salesman behind the candy counter at the Capitol Theatre downtown. Frank looked like Van Johnson. I knew Van Johnson from the song-and-dance number he did on *I Love Lucy*, the one where he and Lucy sing, "I like New York in June, how about you?" Sometimes I imagined Frank and my mother dancing and singing that song, trading lines and wisecracks. But then I'd remember Daddy and feel bad for thinking it.

All the DMV offices were state offices, but each was like a franchise, with a private agent, like Frank, running the place. Since it was government-controlled, the DMV was almost like a political appointment. You had to be somebody to be the agent. And Frank was somebody. He had a long political history. His uncle had been Mayor Kenny's closest adviser. Frank had been a city councilman but had a political falling-out in the late 1960s because he didn't get along with Mayor Whelan.

Now that Whelan was going to jail, Frank was planning his own political comeback. Bumper stickers and pens bearing his name circulated throughout the city.

Frank was a favorite to win because, like Aunt Katie and Ma, he was always doing good things for people. Favors, my mother called them. Frank was so kindhearted that he even did Grandpa a favor and gave him a job, back before he tried to shoot us. Ironically, it was Grandpa's job to make sure that people stayed in line. On busy days, he would walk up and down and straighten the DMV line, pushing people around. It was his dream job.

Frank had a way of making you feel special. He once told me he needed to buy a present for his niece, and asked me to accompany him and my mother to the toy store to pick something out. I was honored he would put such trust in my taste. After careful consideration, I chose a Baby Thumbelina doll, which I had secretly wanted. I would never admit it to anyone, being a tomboy. But I knew Frank's niece would love it.

I hadn't realized that my seventh birthday was just a few days away and that Frank had had me pick the doll out for myself. I wasn't yet suspicious of everyone's motives. Only most people's.

Later that week, when Frank handed me the present, everything clicked. I knew what it was before I unwrapped it, but I felt that strange new sensation called surprise: feeling both happy and duped at the same time. I knew Frank's lie had been a good lie. There were good lies and bad lies. It wasn't always so easy to tell the difference.

Frank was a dream boss. He offered big bonuses and understood our working mother's busy schedule. If one of us had a fever, forcing Ma to stay home, Frank never complained. And he never docked her pay. To most people, the DMV was a nightmare of long, messy lines and nasty civil servants. But to me, it was a refuge. The building had twelve gray steps that led down to a wonderful place: a backyard. Frank convinced the "girls" at the DMV to let us kids play back there after school. For the first time in my life, I came close to having a normal childhood, with backyard clubhouses and lemonade stands.

The DMV backyard was better than Aunt Katie's backyard, because there were other kids to play with. Buddy the dog was smart, but he couldn't play army or help me climb a tree. This new yard was my paradise: There was grass—a twenty-foot stretch of it to the back fence, where a large tree bloomed. To the right were a small white shed and a white wall made of cinder blocks, ideal for scaling. To the left was a small chain-link fence, through which you could see clear through to the other backyards.

My playmates included Joe Wendolowski and his older brother, Frankie, whose mother, Angie, worked with Ma. Joe, who was the same age as I was, never took off his baseball cap. He was my first crush. All the girls in our class were in love with him.

Ronnie Pawlak, my mother's coworker who rented an apartment above the DMV, unloaded her young son, Adam, in the yard as well. He became the first man in my life, the first boy I ever kissed during a game of Spin the Bottle.

Other local kids soon joined us. The Puerto Rican kids whose house abutted the DMV heard the laughter and merriment and climbed the fence to join me and my growing harem. A boy named Eggy and, occasionally his little sister, Iliana, the only other girl in the backyard day-care crowd, became regulars.

My mother's good friend Jane Liana, who lived just around the corner and worked as the sales manager at the Rainbow Shop, a women's clothing store on dilapidated Newark Avenue, brought her son, Alfred, to the backyard. Alfred was one of my best friends. We took baths together in our bathing suits at my house.

Alfred was the kindest boy I knew. Once when we were out with my mother on a trip to the Battery, she bought us both helium balloons. I lost mine. Alfred, who felt bad, selflessly let his balloon float away too. We watched both of them trail off together in the direction of the World Trade Center. (Years later, when my boyfriend and I broke up a week before the junior prom, Alfred proved his mettle once again and came as my date.)

Having been raised with an older brother, it didn't faze me that I was surrounded mostly by boys in the backyard. Together, using the tools from the white shed, we built clubhouses made from wood stolen from the next yard over. Eggy was the bravest, and would climb the tree to venture over the high back wooden fence to retrieve old doors, chicken wire, and planks studded with rusty nails. Beneath that tree, with its trunk as a foundation wall, the clubhouse would rise as we sawed and hammered away. Once it was built we'd hold a meeting. Frankie was president, since he was the oldest. I was vice-president, since I was bossiest. Alfred was treasurer, and Adam was sergeant at arms.

Each night, after our club meeting was over and our mothers punched out for the day, Kelsey, the building janitor, would tear our clubhouse down. Kelsey was a stickler for order. Once Grandpa went to jail, it was Kelsey's job to straighten the moblike crowds of DMV customers gathered in the waiting room each morning. He did a better job than Grandpa.

Kelsey never told us he was the one who knocked the clubhouses down, and he never stood in the way of our building a new one. But he scowled and shook his head every time new construction began. So the game continued, week in and week out. We'd construct architectural masterpieces only to have them torn asunder while we were home eating supper.

Between contracting jobs, we played other games, usually war games or hide-and-seek, squatting in the cool shade of the shed, under the stairs, or in the tall tree. On rainy days, Ma brought me inside, where I sat at the counter and typed drivers' permits or poems.

One hot summer day in the yard, during a challenging game of combat, all the boys took off their shirts. Since I was sweating just as much as they were, I followed their lead. They all laughed as I stood there, toy gun in hand, bare-chested and flat as the rest of them. I ran inside, crying to my mother. She stopped what she was doing, rounded up the boys, and yelled at them for making fun of me. She then knelt down and told me, ever so gently, to put my shirt back on. I was not happy about it, but when my mother asked you to do something, you just did it. She always had a good reason.

Most days in the DMV yard passed without incident. Though there was the one time the kids and I greased the gray stairs with soap in the hopes that a particularly scary car dealer would come out and slip down the stairs. His name was Louie and he walked with crutches because he had the gout. We figured that when he fell, the change in his pockets would scatter and we would be rich. Fortunately, we were found out by Kelsey, who mopped up the slippery trap before Louie had a chance to break his neck.

There was also the day Eggy robbed Alfred's catcher's mitt and painted it with black shoe polish to disguise it. But we all knew it was Alfred's. Jane visited the backyard, retrieved her son's glove, and gave Eggy hell. He never stole again, as far as we knew.

One afternoon, bored by the clubhouse, we built a lemonade stand, which was patronized by car dealers, who our mothers guilt-tripped into visiting the backyard. Car dealers came into the office regularly to register new fleets of Cadillacs, Pontiacs, Oldsmobiles, and Lincolns. They were given special treatment by being taken off the long DMV line—the least they could do was buy some lemonade. Each of them came back and peeled off a few bills, then told us to drink the lemonade ourselves. With no output and a steady customer base, we made over a hundred dollars' profit in a day.

Our other form of income came from Frank. Every week, after balancing the books and closing out the machines, Frank would assemble us kids in the front waiting area of the office, take all the accumulated change—mostly pennies and nickels—and toss it into the air. Frank, a redheaded Irish tenor, sang "Pennies from Heaven" while we screamed and scrambled for our take, stuffing our pockets until they overflowed.

Because of Frank, the staff at the Montgomery Street DMV was the happiest around. Drivers from across the county went out of their way to go there because of the unusual, smiling clerks. For Ma and the rest of the girls, boring clerical work became a comedy with Frank in attendance.

The customers provided the punch lines, unintentionally.

My sister once asked a customer if he had a lien on his car. "No," the man answered, "but it tilts a little to the left."

When filling out a permit application, one old lady failed to fill in the box for SEX. When asked why, she blushed and whispered, "My husband's been dead for a long time."

Our mothers often helped illiterate drivers fill out their paperwork, particularly local Gypsies, who claimed to have forgotten their glasses at home. At other DMV offices, the staff would ridicule people who couldn't read and send them away without helping them. But not on Montgomery Street.

"Darling, sweetheart," the Gypsies would say. "Can you read this for me?" My mother always obliged, never condescending, never laughing out loud. While helping a foreigner fill out his paperwork once, my mother asked how many doors his car had. It was part of the usual description—either you had a two-door or a four-door.

"Three," the man answered.

"Three?" my mother asked.

"One fall off," he replied in broken English. Ma somehow kept a straight face.

My mother was often tipped for her kindness and patience, virtues she'd developed while raising three kids. One customer showered her with compliments, telling her she typed so fast she should be the secretary for the president of the United States.

Ma could have made big bucks by filling out phony paperwork for some dealers, who would offer a one-hundred-dollar cash bribe to fix an odometer reading, change the year on a car, or conceal the fact that a car had been in a flood. Ma never accepted out-and-out bribes. She didn't want to embarrass us by being arrested. But she was not above accepting perfectly legal though slightly unethical presents from dealers, who appreciated being taken off the long line. For Christmas, there were dresses, large bottles of perfume, and gallons of Johnny Walker Red. Free lunches and snacks were abundant: Corned-beef sandwiches or hot dogs that would grow cold on busy afternoons.

Amid all this goodwill, it never occurred to us—at least not to the backyard gang—that something was really wrong. But it was only a matter of time before the truth about the DMV came out.

———

It was noon on a cool day in late September 1972 and my mother, as usual, was at school to pick me up for lunch. I was a finicky eater, and the sight of other children in the OLC cafeteria chewing deviled ham with their mouths open made me sick. Ma and I usually went home for lunch, but on special occasions we would venture to the Greek diner across the street, where I'd have a cheeseburger or chicken soup with orzo.

On this particular autumn day, my mother showed up with Angie and my sister, who joined us for lunch at the Greeks'. "What are you doing here?" I asked Paula and Angie, as they slid into a booth with us. "Who's running the DMV?"

My mother explained that in the morning, when she went to work, the state police were waiting at the front door. Frank had been shot in the head during a robbery. He was still alive, in stable condition, she said. But Ma, Paula, and Angie looked nervous and upset, and talked about stuff I couldn't really follow, about detectives and car titles and money. My mind was drifting.

Would Frank be a vegetable like those people in a coma? What if my friends and I had been there when the robbers had come in? What if they had come into the backyard and taken us hostage? This was by far the most exciting thing to happen since Grandpa had tried to kill us.

That night, I read the rest of the story in *The Jersey Journal*. Right there, on the front page, was a picture of Frank. Under his picture and name, it said, "Shot in head." It was weird seeing someone I knew so well on page 1 with something so dramatic written underneath. Even Grandpa had never made the front page.

I wondered if Frank was going to die. Most of the stiffs I'd seen at the funeral parlor had been distant relatives or old friends of Ma's. I considered Frank one of my friends. I didn't want to have to go to his funeral. I really liked him.

I read the story over and over, or at least the words I understood, and learned that right before 9 A.M., Frank had called the police and said simply, "I have a problem." When the cops arrived, Frank answered the door in a "semiconscious state" (I wasn't sure what that meant), his head bleeding from a bullet wound behind his left ear. There was also a bullet hole in the office wall. Two customers had been standing outside when the shooting occurred, waiting for the office to open. They told the police they hadn't seen anyone suspicious entering or leaving. I wondered if the bad guys had escaped through the backyard.

When my mother and the other girls arrived for work that morning, detectives had them step into the office, past the yellow police tape and over the barely dried blood on the carpet. The cash drawer was open, and money and paperwork were scattered everywhere. Thinking that an illegal-car ring had robbed the DMV, the detectives asked my mother and the other girls to count the titles and permits, which were numbered. But the papers were all there. In the meantime, Frank was admitted to the Medical Center, where doctors removed two .32-caliber bullets from his head after four hours of surgery.

The next day, with Frank's blood cleaned from the rug, the DMV opened for business as usual. My mother had to go in early to open the door, since Frank was still in the hospital. While the police searched for clues to the crime, Ma and the other girls worked the counter. We played in the backyard, lost in games of Red Rover and One-Two-Three Red Light, forgetting, for the time being, all about Frank's terrible head wound.

There were people who were being paid to think about it, though. Detective Michael Borseso, the same detective who had arrested Grandpa when he came to shoot us, noticed that Frank was a southpaw and that the wound was on the left side of Frank's head. Two days after the shooting, Borseso got Frank to confess from his hospital bed that there had been no robbery, that he had shot himself—that he even shot one round into the office wall to make it look like a robbery. Frank told Borseso exactly where to find the gun.

The detective came up behind my mother while she was typing a license renewal that afternoon. "Don't move," he said, bending down and reaching between her feet into the space under the counter.

There, under my mother, beneath the floorboards in a secret hiding place, was a .32-caliber revolver.

Frank's gun.

———

Frank was "despondent over domestic and financial difficulties," the front-page story the next day said. Now that they mentioned it, my sister did notice that Frank had been a bit off lately. He had come to work recently wearing four wristwatches. His hair was a mess. Paula figured he was having a nervous breakdown, but since he was the boss, she couldn't really ask him about it. We, in the backyard, had seen none of Frank's unusual behavior. The closest we came to noticing any financial problems was a slowdown on the "Pennies from Heaven" routine.

Frank survived, since the gun he had used was an antique. Even the bullets were old—they failed to penetrate his skull, lodging just below his skin line. When the bleeding wouldn't stop, Frank stumbled over to the counter, hid the gun, then called the police. It was one thing to die instantly from a gunshot wound. It was another to bleed to death slowly in the waiting area while customers stood outside, banging on the door to be let in for license plates.

I guess dying slowly like that gave Frank some time to think about things, like the fact that he didn't really want to die after all.

Charges weren't filed against Frank for four years, until the feds could rack up a list of sixty-one counts of conspiracy, misapplication of bank funds, and submitting false credit statements on loan applications. Frank had been borrowing money from the DMV drawer and replacing it with money from loans he acquired illegally. Along with a banker friend, he was accused of scamming more than $100,000.

This, I realized, was the bad kind of lying, the kind you went to jail for. It was the kind of lying the mayor had gone away for. Frank faced a maximum of 227 years in prison. I imagined him with long white hair, a long white beard, and long fingernails, like Methuselah in the Bible, standing there all hunched over as the jail guard finally creaked open his cell door.

Frank paid back the money somehow, pleaded guilty to one count, and received just five years probation. I was glad he didn't have to spend 227 years in jail.

His real punishment was that he lost the agency. My mother broke the bad news to me over lunch at the Greeks', telling me the office would have to move to a new location. They would have a new boss.

What would happen to the backyard? I asked. To the tree and to the grass? And to our clubhouse? What would become of Kelsey? Would he move with us? My mother shrugged and smiled and said not to worry, that things would work out. But I had my doubts.

The DMV office was moved up to Journal Square, and a man named Saul Farber became the new agent. He owned a parking lot, a gas station, and a car wash. The DMV was to be the jewel in the crown of his automotive empire. Saul was the kind of outsider the state was looking for after the Frank fiasco: a Jew from outside Hudson County, with no Democratic-machine connections and no Jersey City accent.

I knew Saul was certainly no Frank. The nuns had made me unduly suspicious of Jewish people. There was that story Sister Isabelle had told of God striking down a man named Saul as he rode through Damascus on his horse. "Saul, Saul, why have you forsaken me?" God asked him. I felt like asking Saul the same question.

The DMV girls—like God in the biblical version—grew to love Saul. I refused to speak to him for two years—not because he was Jewish, but because I was sure he'd disappoint me, too.

In a way, he already had. Saul had no backyard, no tree, no space for a clubhouse or for my friends. All Saul could offer was some blacktop and the car wash, where it only rained cold water. Never pennies. Not even once.

10

BAD BOY

Along with the other DMV mothers, Ma was one of the troublemakers at OLC. At PTA meetings she, Angie, Jane, and my aunt Julie, on
my father's side, were the only mothers who got up and protested the
piddling injustices that were done to us at the hands of the Felician
Sisters.

My mother and her friends were tough. Ma would have liked to
have wrestled with an idiotic nun or administrator on the floor of the
church hall during those PTA meetings. But she kept her cool. There
were arguments over favoritism at the school, when some kids were
left to stand outside in the cold on winter mornings before the bell
rang (i.e., me and most of the students) while other kids got to sit inside the warm school (i.e., the fat Polish kids whose mothers worked in
the administration). My mother argued that we should all be allowed
inside.

Ma never let anyone push her or her kids around. She even yelled
at the checkout girl at ShopRite when she bounced our cantaloupe
into the bag. It embarrassed me, but I learned from my mother to stand
up for myself, and to dislike careless and unfair people. There were
quite a few of them living in Jersey City.

Because I was preoccupied with being like Aunt Mary Ann, I didn't realize that my mother was a rebel. There was a lot of Beansie in her. She refused to work Bingo, even though it would have reduced the price of my school tuition. All the mothers were expected to wait tables once a month at Bingo. But my mother and her friends couldn't stand the game or the women with their beehives and long cigarettes, flicking their ashes into lipstick-stained cardboard coffee cups and calling out for new cards in the dingy school basement.

I felt that Ma didn't belong at OLC. Unlike most of the other mothers, she and her crew didn't wear housedresses and curlers when they came to pick us up after school. Some mothers didn't bother to pick their kids up at all even though Jersey City was not a place where you wanted your ten-year-old to walk home alone. My mother, always there at dismissal, made me proud with her pretty clothes and her freshly combed hair, which was never done up in a bouffant. She had normal hair, like me. She hated the beauty parlor and never had a hairdo, even in the hairdo-crazed 1960s.

Every day we'd eat lunch together at home or at the Greek diner. Most mothers at OLC didn't care what their kids ate for lunch. Their lunch boxes were dirty and rusty, with sour milk and old, discarded breadcrusts. One kid came to class with a sandwich of Marshmallow Fluff and liverwurst. Together. Just the thought of it made me want to vomit.

I ate leftover spaghetti or chicken soup, side by side with Daddy, who also came home for lunch, dressed in his blue work uniform. We would watch *The Don Ho Show* together. They were happy afternoons; Daddy got to thaw out for an hour away from the walk-in freezer at work, and I had a full hour away from the clutches of the evil nuns, who seemed to grow meaner as time went by.

In a desperate bid for respect, the nuns trained us to rise when one of their fellow stormtroopers entered the room. As soon as the door cracked open, we shot up from our desks and recited, "Good morning, [insert name of evil nun here]." The first time our new principal, Sister Mary Grace, entered our classroom, we only got as far as "Good mor—."

She cut us off, yelling, "Sit down before I knock ya down." We didn't doubt for a minute that she would punch each and every one of our scared little faces.

Sister Grace was much worse than Sister Isabelle. She bore a strong resemblance to the actor Robert Shaw, particularly in his role as Quint in the movie *Jaws*. One of her front teeth was filled with silver. Or gold. I never got close enough to find out. Behind her back, we called her Orca—a reference to another killer-fish film. The whale's black-and-white body resembled Sister Grace's black-and-white habit. And she was just as fat.

One spring, during graduation practice at OLC Church, one of the boys mouthed off while Sister Grace's back was turned. When the instigator failed to present himself, she resorted to the usual Nazi tactics, punishing the group to rout out the evildoer. The class would stay after school until she got a confession. Of course, it didn't work. I started to think that maybe the nuns didn't expect results, that maybe they simply liked punishing us. I hadn't yet heard the word *sadist,* but the day I learned its definition—a person who takes an abnormal delight in cruelty—a picture of Sister Grace popped into my head.

When the evildoer failed to step forward, Sister Grace threatened to cancel graduation. The girls were in tears. They had all bought their white graduation dresses. The corsages were already ordered. My cousin Stephen, my aunt Julie's son, stepped up and took the blame. He wasn't the guilty party, but he bravely offered himself up so the rest of the class wouldn't suffer. It was an incredibly noble moment for a fourteen-year-old boy. But soon Sister Grace figured out that Stephen wasn't the true instigator. She called him stupid and slapped him across the face. He stood there, unflinching. He didn't even blink. Stephen was the most stoic kid I knew.

The next day, when Aunt Julie got wind of the story, she took off from work at the Beehive Bank and came marching to school, ready to rip Sister Grace's head off. When Julie walked through the big wooden front doors, the principal was at the top of the stairs, waving her big, beefy hand. "Come on, come on," Sister Grace taunted. "I know you want to fight." I can just see her metal tooth glinting in the hallway lights.

Julie stormed up the stairs and gave it to her good. "How would you like to get hit across the mouth?" she asked Sister Grace. Sophie, the gym teacher, stood behind Sister Grace with her fist clenched, mocking the nun and encouraging Julie to peel one off. But Julie kept her composure. She walked away, and never spoke to Sister Grace again. I wished Julie had knocked her sparkly tooth out. But Julie knew, as Ma did, that she was better than all that.

Aunt Julie was too good for OLC and for Jersey City. She had almost escaped once. As a testament that you couldn't run away, the story of my aunt Julie was often invoked in OLC circles. Julie was the pioneer on my father's side of the family, like Aunt Mary Ann was on my mother's side. In the 1970s, she had gone to Arizona with her husband, John, and her son, Stephen.

John looked different from most of my uncles. While most wore white shirts and dress slacks, he was always decked out in jeans, western shirts, and cowboy boots. All he needed was a horse. But as I already knew, you couldn't keep a horse in Jersey City. Uncle John yearned for the wide open spaces. And Julie was madly in love with him. We all were. Even my father, a very quiet guy, liked talking to John. He was different, in a place that didn't encourage individuality. He played drums in a jazz band. Julie was different, too. Unlike everyone she knew, she didn't have her first child until she was thirty-seven. In Hudson County, she and John were practically freaks. But in a good way.

When Stephen was three years old, Julie and John loaded him and their belongings into a camper and drove out west. John found work as a carpenter and, later, as a manager of a sign shop in Chandler, Arizona, while Aunt Julie helped out in a small hotel. She loved Arizona—the beauty of it, the independence that comes with being anonymous in a new town, the freedom of not knowing every person who walks down the street.

Not that you personally knew every man, woman, and child who walked down the street in Jersey City. But you knew them well enough, could immediately see down into their dusty souls. You knew they had eaten hot dogs at Boulevard Drinks, had gone to the matinees at the Loew's, had relatives who worked for either the Parks Department or Public Works and had paid that 85-cent toll on the New Jersey Turnpike a few too many times. You knew what their wardrobe looked like, what their dates looked like, and the kinds of teachers they had—what they had learned or, more important, what they had failed to learn at a place like OLC.

Julie's feeling of freedom was fueled by the knowledge that there was a better, bigger world out there, past the gray skies and dirty gutters of downtown, around the weed-infested corners of Hudson County, and beyond the entire joke of a state. That feeling came from not being afraid to go away. And stay there. And live there.

It didn't last long for Julie.

Uncle Henry called our house one night. It was later than his usual numbers call. When I answered the phone, I was surprised to hear his voice on the other end asking for Daddy. He rarely made social calls.

We knew something was wrong when, after a few minutes, Daddy pulled up a kitchen chair and sat down. They were not gabbers, he and Uncle Henry. And this call was lasting quite a while. We gathered around Daddy and watched his frown grow deeper than usual. He nodded his head slowly, his forehead wrinkling like a strip of bacon, and he murmured, "uh-huh, uh-huh," signaling Uncle Henry to continue whatever the hell he was saying on the other end. The suspense was too much.

Between nods, Daddy said, "It's John. There was an accident."

That afternoon, John had gone pistol shooting in the desert with his boss and the boss's brother. Julie went to a flea market with a friend. After shooting practice, the guys locked their guns in the boss's jeep and went to hear a musician friend play at a local bar. As they drank their final beer, some words were exchanged with an army sergeant seated at the bar. Or something John and his friends said was overheard. It's unclear. But the sergeant angrily walked out of the bar.

John left a little later, and while walking to the jeep, he was almost run over by the sergeant's car. John knocked on the guy's window to yell at him. The sergeant rolled the window down, put a 9mm German Luger to John's chest, and pulled the trigger. As John fell into his boss's arms, the guys thought he was fooling around, that he couldn't possibly be shot.

The shooter sped off toward the Mexican border, but he got nervous and returned when the cops started searching for him. He told the police he'd merely tried to scare John, that he hadn't meant any harm.

That night, Julie called Uncle Henry, since he was the oldest in the family. And Uncle Henry had called Daddy.

As he hung up the phone, Daddy put his head down and gripped the kitchen chair for support. "John is dead," he said without looking up. I think he was crying and didn't want us to see. The bullet had hit John's main artery.

At an inquest a few days later, the killer said he had been listening to John and his friends' conversation and thought their insults were directed toward him, that he was being harassed. He was never charged with the shooting. Julie blames his eighteen-year record in the service and says that the government whitewashed the whole affair.

The other mothers at OLC glommed on to Julie's tragedy as a lesson in hubris. "She thinks who she is," was an all-too-familiar refrain. According to them, it didn't pay to leave, to think you were better than everybody else. Sooner or later you'd find yourself right back in Jersey City, sorry you ever left. John went all that way, they said, just to get shot. He could have done that right here on Jackson Avenue.

Julie didn't want to come back but, like Ma, she didn't drive. And in Arizona you had to have a car. A driver's license was one of the basic requirements for escape.

She had bragged about the fresh, dry air of Arizona and its wide open spaces, but Julie found herself back in smelly old Jersey City, getting a bouffant like my other aunts. The problem with leaving was that if you ever did have to come back, the place looked even uglier than it had before you left.

———

I was glad Julie came back to Jersey City, because Stephen was my favorite cousin on the Polish side. We goofed around a lot. Once, we put toothpicks in Aunt Julie's hair. They stood up like antennae. Aunt Julie didn't even know they were there, since her hair was so high off her scalp.

Stephen and I saw *Star Wars* together. For us, seeing that movie was like the day JFK got shot. Everyone we knew remembered exactly where it had happened and who they were with at the time. Daddy came with us to see it, but he stood in the back of the theater through most of the movie and smoked. He preferred movies about real things and real people. Science fiction was not for him. "Garbage," he said, scowling.

But Stephen and I loved *Star Wars*. We even had fake light sabers, which we used to clobber each other over the head. I liked boys better than girls, because they didn't cry when you hit them over the head. They were more fun. Hitting each other, climbing poles and trees—when you could find one in Jersey City—was much more entertaining than playing with dolls.

I calculated that I had no fewer than ten cousins at OLC at one time, all from Daddy's side of the family, most of them boys: Stephen, George, Mark, Andrew, Victor, Phillip, Scott, Melissa, and two Michaels.

Our cousin George once told Stephen that if he ever needed any-one beaten up, he would do it for him, since Stephen no longer had a father. Not having a father could be a problem in a tough place like Jersey City. And George knew about it firsthand.

George always seemed much older than the rest of us, as if he thought that shooting bottle caps or playing TV tag were pointless, silly exercises. He participated, but reluctantly.

He was a distant—fourth—cousin and we weren't particularly close. If you saw him on the street, George would look just like any other kid. He was polite, always said thank-you, and always put his toys away at the end of the day if he came to play at your house. He was short, and blended into the background with dark hair and thick glasses. People called them Barney Google glasses, after a cartoon that used to run in the Sunday funnies.

To me, Stephen, and the other kids, there was something unusual about George. Behind those glasses, he had a light in his brown eyes that was missing from most of the other kids' eyes. George seemed smarter, or wiser. You would think that it was just his glasses that made him look wiser. But there were other kids at OLC with glasses—like me—and we didn't have that same George quality. There was a vibe hovering around him, as if the air around his body were charged. More than anyone I knew, George had that crooked, reluctant Jersey City smile.

I knew why. And it wasn't just that he had no father.

We all knew George's story, though we never talked to him about it. It was just another of the many hard-luck Stapinski tales. On a foggy night after Valentine's Day 1971, when George was just four years old, he woke his mother up in the middle of the night because he had to pee. Mary Ann, a cousin on my father's side, groggily took him out into their hallway, to the building's communal bathroom. On the way, they saw George's father standing in the doorway. He looked like he was standing on his tippy toes. In the dark, it seemed as if he were staring at them.

"What's the matter?" Mary Ann asked him. When he didn't answer, she asked again. But then she realized that he was hanging from the doorway by a belt around his neck. She nervously let George pee, then hurried him out of the hallway.

George's father had been a heroin addict, so it was just a matter of time before something bad happened to him. His death was listed as a suicide. Some people, like George's mother, thought he had been murdered. Either way, George no longer had a father.

Having Grandpa try and shoot us was pretty dramatic, but seeing your father dead like that was something else. Even Stephen had been spared the details of his father's death. I tried to imagine what it would be like to see Daddy hanging in a doorway by his black leather belt, the one with the cracks and the metal buckle. The thought was so terrible that I pushed it from my mind and tried never to think it again.

George supposedly didn't remember the incident. But I knew that first memories were the ones that stuck, that they were the memories that struck hardest, even if we didn't want them to. I wanted to talk to George about his father, and to tell him about Grandpa, but George wasn't very approachable.

The kids treated him differently because of what he had seen. We were in awe of him, or afraid of him, or maybe afraid for him. George's story was the only lesson we needed that you shouldn't do heroin. Forget the OLC film strips and the lectures from Officer Friendly. We had cold, hard facts.

Though he said he didn't remember the tragedy, you could tell that George carried it around with him, like heavy luggage. It weighed him down and made him mad. Sometimes it made him do bad things. Like the time he and his friends picked a fight with me and my friends after school. I remember George cursing us out. He was the first boy ever to do such a thing, and the shock of it set me off. I told him off right on the spot that he should leave us alone and that he was a disgusting pig. George just smiled that crooked smile. He gave me a knowing look filled with sexual innuendo—too mature for a twelve-year-old kid.

George scared me, because the thought flitted across my young mind that he was a distant cousin, the most dangerous of my Polish cousins, and that it would probably be legal for me to kiss him. There was something exciting about the danger that lurked beneath George's skin—something mysterious, sad, and smart. He was the class bad boy. And as the bad boy, he possessed that special quality that made you want to run with him but then save his soul at the end of the day.

For the first time, I realized that bad boys were much more interesting than good boys. For the first time, in my first flash of wisdom, I understood finally why Grandma had fallen for Grandpa.

11

GONE AWAY

All my knowledge of Grandpa came from family stories, repeated over and over again until I knew them by heart. Though wakes and funerals provided an unending chorus, the best place to hear a Grandpa story was at my cousin Gerri's house in North Bergen. The township was never anything to write home about, but its ugliness paled in comparison to Jersey City's. As did its reputation.

North Bergen was shaped like a semiautomatic handgun. But people felt it wasn't half as tough as Jersey City, Hudson's largest city and the county seat. When we visited North Bergen, kids would step back an inch when they heard where I came from, as if I were carrying a .44 in my back pocket. I didn't mind, really. Being from Jersey City made me feel taller.

There were no brownstones in North Bergen, mostly wood-frame or brick houses built on incredibly steep hills. Some houses were on such an incline that North Bergenites couldn't get reception from their antennae, since they faced the meadowlands and not New York City, where the signals were sent out from the Empire State Building.

I always considered North Bergen the suburbs, because it had hills and trees. But the towns of Secaucus and Kearny and Harrison—connected to Jersey City by a street called Fish House Road—were even more suburb-like. Its residents were often embarrassed to be associated with the rest of Hudson County.

On my trips to New York and to Hudson County's other towns, I started to piece together a map of my world in my head. If I surgically removed Kearny, Secaucus, and Harrison, which protruded from the western edge of Hudson County like polyps on a cancerous host, I was left with a strip of land floating between the polluted Hackensack River, Newark Bay, and the Hudson River. This strip of land, which consisted of Jersey City, Bayonne, Hoboken, Union City, West New York, Weehawken, Guttenberg, and North Bergen, lay directly across from Manhattan.

The strip resembled a wrench or some other blunt object aimed at the back of New Jersey's head. To me, the state looked like the bust of a hunched-over little man wearing a fez. He was in profile, and had an overbite and a big nose, which pointed toward the rest of America. He was giving New York the cold shoulder because New York thought it was so great. Which it was. I wanted to live there someday. Eventually, all my Hudson County reference points would have to do with Manhattan.

If I waded into the Hudson from downtown Jersey City, swam less than a mile, and didn't die from the undertow or PCBs, I would be in New York City's financial district. If I looked at the city from Hamilton Park in Weehawken, I had a perfect sight line down Forty-sixth Street, straight to the horizon. Or if I took a dive from Frank Sinatra Drive in Hoboken, I could doggie-paddle over to the Empire State Building. New York was so close that I worried its skyscrapers would fall and hit my house if there was ever an earthquake. I should be so lucky.

People thought places like North Bergen and Bayonne were a step up from Jersey City. To visit my cousins who lived in those towns, we had to take a bus or get a ride down Kennedy Boulevard, originally called Hudson Boulevard. The boulevard was the county's main artery, filled with plastic flag–fringed car dealerships and low-lying bowling alleys.

Most of the other towns along the boulevard were populated by former Jersey Citizens who had moved on to two-family, aluminum-sided homes with driveways and bathroom mat–size backyards. In some ways, those other towns were worse off than Jersey City. People there were lulled into a false sense of security. They had toxic waste, just like us. Sometimes even more.

Their mayors were no better, either. In 1970, Mayor John Armellino of West New York was found guilty of taking bribes to protect illegal gambling; U.S. representative Neil Gallagher of Bayonne, once a potential candidate for vice-president of the United States, pleaded guilty to income tax evasion. Then in 1976, Guttenberg mayor Herman Klein resigned when prosecutors threatened a case concerning his no-show county job. Klein was reelected a few years later, demonstrating the forgiving nature of no-show city workers.

That same year, North Bergen mayor Angelo Sarubbi was convicted of taking bribes from a contractor. But North Bergen's most notorious character was town clerk Joey Mocco. Prosecutors were constantly accusing Mocco of all sorts of things. He was indicted and arrested on charges of embezzlement and fixing votes in favor of his brother, mayor Peter Mocco, but was never convicted. Eventually, Joey got twenty years for bribery, official misconduct, and illegal dumping. When he was sentenced, the judge told him, "You plundered and pillaged your town and treated it as a fiefdom as if you were a medieval lord."

Parts of North Bergen looked better than Jersey City, but the danger was there, lurking just below the surface. Kids in those satellite towns were lost in some kind of netherworld—not urban and not suburban, but the worst of both worlds. North Bergen kids wore concert T-shirts, faded Lee jeans with patches of the Rolling Stones tongue on their butts, and lots of suede and brown corduroy. They wore their hair long in the back and short in the front, as if they lived in white-trash Middle America. They hardly ever visited New York. For some reason, Manhattan seemed farther away from places like North Bergen and Bayonne than it did from Jersey City. But the rest of America seemed closer, with its pickup trucks and country music.

In Jersey City, kids listened to R&B and disco and dressed up when they went out. They were better groomed, in general, with shorter, cleaner haircuts. In the other towns, kids were more racist, since they were exposed to very few blacks or Puerto Ricans. Even in Union City, which had the biggest population of Cubans north of Miami, people were racist. The Cubans, many of them formerly doctors and businessmen in their own country, looked down on other Latinos.

Jersey City wasn't exactly enlightened, but at least we had black and Puerto Rican friends and neighbors. We knew they were the same as we were. My brother's best friend was a black kid named Jay, who taught him how to dance the robot, which he did, very well, at the high school Ebony Club dances. Stanley was the only white guy in attendance, and was voted best dancer in the class of '75. His nickname was Brother Kielbas, as in kielbasa.

The African Americans lived mostly in the Bergen-Lafayette ward, made up of beautiful Victorian mansions next to burned-out and abandoned buildings and drug dens. The neighborhood had once been an elite shopping district, but white flight had left the area with a few liquor stores and check-cashing joints, a white-owned cheap-furniture store, and little else.

Kids in Bayonne and North Bergen were afraid of black people, so they called them names, something my mother forbade. I remember one of my cousins choosing sides for a game of freeze tag once and singing, "Eenie meenie miny mo, catch a nigger by the toe." I couldn't believe she said the *n* word. We always said "catch a *tiger* by the toe." She must have picked it up from the kids in her neighborhood.

One other crucial difference was that kids in towns like North Bergen attended public school. Jersey City's public schools were so bad that only the poorest of the poor went to them. Any parent who could scrape together the money sent her kid to Catholic school. Even Protestants and Muslims. It was a flawed system that we had inherited from the days of Hague.

Catholic schools like OLC were lame, but public schools were much worse—even in Hudson County's other towns. In public high schools, there were fistfights and drugs for sale in the hallways, as well as apathetic, tenured teachers who couldn't care less if you showed up for class. The nuns were bad, but at least they instilled discipline. That was my mother's rationalization for subjecting us to Sister Grace. The only good thing about public school was that you could wear your own clothes every day.

Though we had junkies and dealers on our corner, it seemed there were more drug-addicted hippie teens in North Bergen High School. It was the only place in Hudson County where I had heard of kids doing LSD. There was the urban legend about the girl who tripped out at White Castle in North Bergen after eating a mini-burger laced with the drug. She danced on the tables and scared everyone out of the restaurant. There was something wild and scary about North Bergen. I loved going there, and whenever I could, I'd convince my mother to let me sleep over at my Italian cousins' house.

Whenever I visited Gerri and her siblings, we didn't have to get up early on Sunday to go to church. My cousins only went to mass on special occasions, which seemed like a great idea to me.

In North Bergen, I was allowed to play in the street, especially the many dead-end streets. I liked dead ends, because there was less traffic zipping past. It was on one of those streets that Gerri taught me to ride a bike without training wheels. There were fewer cars, not to mention an abundance of hills and rocks, on which we'd climb in the summer and slide down on cardboard boxes in the snow of winter.

Whenever I was there, I felt a certain freedom that I didn't get at home. I felt more grown-up. When I slept over, we made Aunt Millie breakfast in bed. My cousins and I would get up before she did, perc a pot of coffee, poach two eggs, and make triangles of white toast. It was a special treat for me, since my mother never let me near the stove for fear I would set my hair on fire.

Aunt Millie worked nights, as a career waitress, so during the day she usually slept. My uncle Jerry liked to tease her about snoring so hard that when she inhaled, the curtains would blow off the windows and the ships would come in from the harbor. Uncle Jerry was the family comedian. To make a living, though, he drove a bus. I thought he might get on his bus one day and keep driving and never come back to North Bergen. He longed to leave Hudson County, and did so whenever he could. He visited Aunt Mary Ann more than anyone else in the family. When he didn't have time to go to Florida, he'd drive to the airport and watch the planes take off for foreign destinations, places he wanted to fly to. He could do almost any accent—Russian, Greek, whatever. And he could imitate all of the Muppets. So could my uncle Robby, the family storyteller. When he and Uncle Jerry got together, we were entertained for hours.

At Gerri's house, over Aunt Millie's famous meatballs, Uncle Jerry told the story about Grandpa forcing Mom and Aunt Mary Ann to go get a block of ice from the iceman when they were little. The ice weighed more than they did, but they managed to carry it up the stairs. Or most of the stairs. Just as they got it up to the top of the long flight, the ice slipped out of the pan and bounced down, step after step. Whenever Uncle Jerry told that story, I watched that block of ice slip and bounce, step by step by step in my mind's eye, eternally falling as Grandpa came running out like a maniac, cursing them, then grabbed the ice under his arm and took it upstairs himself. Every time Uncle Jerry told the story, we laughed and laughed, imagining Ma and Aunt Mary Ann as skinny little kids.

There was also the story about Grandpa's ridiculous visit to Uncle Robby's army base in Indiana when he went to borrow some cash. And the story of Grandpa taking the settlement money after a flying bowling pin hit Uncle Jerry in the nose while he was working as a pin boy to help support the family. Uncle Jerry's nose was still crooked after twenty years.

When Uncle Jerry and Uncle Robby told the stories, they seemed funny, not tragic. Living in poverty and having rats run under your bed seemed comical when they talked about it. Their sense of humor had helped them survive it. That and the fact that the family was so close. Getting together to talk and joke about the bad times helped a lot. It was their therapy. My family didn't believe in psychiatrists, and never had the money for them, even if they wanted to believe in them.

While they were telling stories about the bad old days, the one about Grandpa trying to shoot us would sometimes come up. My cousin Gerri said she couldn't remember that night. I thought it was strange, since Gerri was a few years older than I was. How could she not remember? Maybe she was like George, with the awful memory clinging somewhere back there in her brain like a big tumor, pushing, pushing. But Gerri didn't seem to be haunted like George. She was an optimist, and remembered the good things about visiting our house: the hot roast beef sandwiches my father made, the lobster tails, french fries, and Sara Lee cupcakes.

Gerri was everybody's favorite cousin. My sister, Paula, was Gerri's sponsor for her Holy Confirmation, so they had their own special bond. Even Daddy loved Gerri, since she had such a good appetite. He and my mother were Gerri's stand-in godparents. Her real godmother was a friend of Aunt Millie's who'd forgotten about Gerri and never sent her cards on her birthday. Ma adopted Gerri and always sent her a birthday card with money inside.

I felt close to Gerri, because our birthdays were just three days apart. I tried not to remember that Grandpa's birthday was only a day before mine. I didn't want any special bonds with him. Not after hearing all about him. But I never tired of the stories, Christmas after Christmas, family wedding after family funeral, until the family soul was recycled and we got together again for a baptism.

My brother would grin his crooked grin. My cousins Susan and David, the same age as I was, and the youngest in their families, too, would sit with me and giggle. Gerri smiled her big, toothy smile, her eyes sparkly blue like Grandma's. Unlike me, she had an open face, without shadows or doubt, and a great laugh, which flowed clear and clean like the spring water we had to buy whenever a water main broke.

When we got a little older, the family get-togethers and storytelling sessions were often held at my sister's house. Paula was the oldest girl cousin in both the Italian and Polish families, so she became the natural hostess when she moved out and got her own place. Paula married a banker from Hoboken named Basil, and traded in her difficult-to-pronounce three-syllable Polish name for an even more difficult to pronounce four-syllable Italian name. She had a baby, whom she named Paul, after herself and Grandma and her favorite Beatle, Paul McCartney.

Paula and Basil would have the whole clan to their modern high-rise apartment three blocks from the Majestic. They lived in the newly built Gregory Apartments, named after the first mayor, Dudley S. Gregory. Cousin Mike helped the city secure the financing for the three buildings' construction.

My best friend, Liz, lived in the Gregory building across the street from Paula, and when I slept over at my sister's house, Liz and I would wave to each other while talking on the phone. It was from Paula's seventh-floor apartment, high above the crowded buildings, that I watched the sun set for the first time, the sky smeared with the vibrant reds and purples that only serious air pollution could provide. It was at Paula's apartment that I tasted, for the first time, Kraft Macaroni & Cheese and Chef Boyardee ravioli in a can—two things Daddy didn't have at the Cold Storage. In her own way, my sister rebelled.

When Gerri, the next girl in line, came of age, she got her own apartment, too, in North Bergen. Gerri had a family get-together every Christmas, putting out a big spread of cold cuts and beer and wine. I looked forward to it every year. I looked up to Paula and Gerri and hoped someday I could have family parties at my apartment. I imagined what my bachelorette pad in New York would be like—with beanbag chairs and plastic beads hanging from the doorways and a view of the tall buildings surrounding me. I couldn't wait. Everyone would come to my luxurious apartment to tell their funny stories. Even Aunt Mary Ann.

She came from Florida to my sister's house a few times. I remember one time, everyone was gathered together, each with a big plate of antipasto on their lap: roasted red peppers, provolone cheese, salami rolled like little fleshy cigars. Cousin Susan always liked the black olives, and would place one on each finger and then eat them one at a time.

As the stories were told, I watched Aunt Mary Ann's face. I figured that she, my favorite aunt, would outdo my uncles with her hilarious memories. But the ice story and the Indiana story didn't make her laugh at all. Aunt Mary Ann didn't say a word. She looked like that picture of her the night Kenny won—there but not there, her mind floating somewhere off in the distance, somewhere you didn't want to go.

After that night, I found that the stories about Grandpa didn't seem as funny anymore. All of sudden I saw them through Aunt Mary Ann's eyes. The older I got, the more I blamed Grandma for staying with Grandpa and subjecting her children to a life of torture. I could understand how Grandma wound up meeting Grandpa and why she thought he was attractive, being the bad boy and all. But why had she married him? If you looked at Grandpa's arrest record and listened to the stories, without the laugh track, you could see what a terrible person he was.

Aunt Mary Ann was right. It wasn't funny at all.

In the early days of their marriage Grandpa didn't need to work, because of Grandma. With her three siblings, she'd inherited the row of brownstones on Grand Street when her father died. Her siblings did well for themselves with their inheritance and with their lives.

Her brother John had some problems early on, when his wife and baby both died while she was in labor, because of a tubular pregnancy. But Uncle John persevered. He became a Wall Street stockbroker, married a member of the Daughters of the American Revolution, and settled in Brooklyn, first on Dean Street, where Grandma had lived with him for a little while as a teenager, and then in Flatbush. We visited him there about once a year, usually around Easter. It was always an adventure. My cousins and I would pile into Uncle Jerry's car and ride, squished, through the Brooklyn-Battery Tunnel. Susan got in the car with dog-doo on her shoe one time, and we threatened to throw her out the window. We were just kidding, but she cried all the way to Brooklyn.

Uncle John's wife, Aunt Frances, looked like George Washington and had an impressive collection of Revolution-era antiques. Uncle John collected rocks, which was much more impressive to a kid. Every time we went there, Aunt Frances cooked lamb, another food that Daddy never brought home from the Cold Storage. I liked it, but it made Paula gag. So I ate her portion. I was always sad to leave Uncle John's house when night fell. Though he had had a traumatic childhood, he managed to make himself a happy home.

Uncle Sam, the one who got his head stuck in the Morris Canal, had a wobbly start in life as well. His daughter, Rose, died of pneumonia when she was two years old. Then his wife left him for a cop whose beat was Journal Square. But Sam, like John, bounced back. He remarried and became a professional bowler, then managed a bowling alley over the Canton Tea Garden. He retired, like most of the city's elders, to Miami. We saw him whenever we went to visit Aunt Mary Ann. Sam's swimming days were over, but he taught me how to fish in a canal near his house.

Even troubled Aunt Helen, the one who discovered her Russian mother dead in bed, made a better life. After getting out of the youth house, she became a flapper, got a job at Lord & Taylor, and met a Puerto Rican strawberry-shortcake baker from Lindy's in New York. Aunt Helen and Uncle Jesús retired to Puerto Rico. On a visit to our house once, Jesús was fed lobster and french fries by my father and was sent home with a Butterball turkey so large that it was still frozen when their plane landed in San Juan.

Grandma didn't manage her inheritance, or her life, quite as well as her siblings did. She let Grandpa handle the finances. He pissed it all away, gambling, drinking, and taking a vacation to Canada, of all places. By himself. He could have at least gone to Italy or somewhere romantic. But Canada? Within a year, Grandma's money was gone. Grandpa even hocked the wedding ring he had given Grandma, forcing her to go to Woolworth's and buy a cheap replacement.

Using pop psychology, I figured Grandma married him because he was a brute like her father, the Russian wife-basher. Grandma was continuing the cycle. Grandpa beat his children regularly—when he wasn't in prison, anyway.

Even Grandpa's sisters couldn't understand why Grandma stuck around, and they repeatedly tried to get her to leave him. After one of his violent binges, one of his sisters went to Grandma and begged her to pack her bags. "Get dressed, get lost," my aunt whispered. "Get the boat to China. Anything. Just get going." Instead of leaving, Grandma had a fight with Grandpa and wound up telling him what his sister had said. When Grandpa saw his sister, he attacked her, wrapping his hands around her throat, yelling, "Why the fuck are you telling my wife to leave me?"

Grandpa could not—or simply would not—hold down a job to support his wife and five children. He tried working as a union deliverer for the *New York Sun,* a good gig during the Depression. But a life of crime appealed to him most. When Grandma needed milk, Grandpa would go out and come back immediately with three or four bottles, having robbed them from the doorsteps of the neighbors. The only time he ever put food on the table was the night he came home, drunk, with fruit that he'd stolen from a local vendor. It wasn't a lovely fruit basket. It was a big, stinking freight box full of rotten oranges, which were probably headed for the garbage anyway.

Grandpa would steal whatever he could lay his hands on. His conscience knew no bounds. One afternoon, the local Jewish door-to-door salesman came to collect on a statue of the Blessed Mother that my grandmother had purchased. Grandma was paying for the statue on time, a quarter a week. The statue of the Virgin, dressed in blue, with her arms outstretched, was about two feet tall and encased in a bubble of glass, like a bell jar.

Not only did he refuse to pay, but Grandpa threw the salesman down a long flight of stairs, the same one where my mother and Aunt Mary Ann dropped the block of ice. The salesman never returned. But Grandma got to keep the holy statue, free of charge. My mother inherited it when Grandma died, and whenever I helped Ma clean the house, it was my job to dust its rounded globe. I never opened the glass bubble, but I peered at the saint safe inside. Though it would be a poetic story, it was not the same statue my aunt Mary Ann tried to beat Grandpa with years later.

Thanks to Uncle Al, Grandpa landed a job as a stevedore down at the Linden Avenue docks, stenciling names of places he would never visit onto wooden boxes destined for the high seas. He stole the long, chrome stencil guns and brought them home, thinking he was doing the family a favor. He quit the job because, he said, it was too easy. But there may have been more to it than that. Grandpa got into a fight with a fellow member of the International Longshoremen's Association while eating with his brother Bicky at Nedick's diner in the Grove Street PATH station. While Grandpa was eating a hot dog, a dock worker named Joseph Wykoff hit him in the forehead with a portable coffee urn. But Grandpa retaliated.

The next day, my mother was waiting for a train at the PATH station when she overheard some guy say to a cop, "Hey, what happened to the pay phone?"

"Oh, fucking Beansie pulled it off the wall and beat some guy in the head with it." Everybody knew Beansie. And it was just another one of his tantrums. My mother slinked away, but later that day she read all about the fight in *The Jersey Journal*.

This time, Grandpa was the victim for a change. All the detectives in the city were on the lookout for Wykoff, whom the papers described as a "dock character" and "an ally of Frank 'Biffo' DeLorenzo." Ma wasn't sure who Biffo was, but with a friend named Biffo, Wykoff had to be bad. When he hit Grandpa with the urn, Wykoff was already under indictment for breaking-and-entering and possession of burglar tools and was out on $15,000 bail for possession of a dangerous weapon.

After getting stitches at the Medical Center, Grandpa talked to the cops about Wykoff, and was released. But early the next morning, Grandpa was picked up for his own disorderly-person's charge. When questioned about Wykoff, he changed his story from the day before and said he got hurt when he fell and hit his head on the curb. Who knows why he changed his story. Maybe Grandpa was afraid Biffo and Wykoff would strangle him for ratting. Or maybe the bad guys felt they had to stick together, like all those criminals on *Batman*.

In 1935 Grandpa was arrested at least four times. His first victim, Gabriel Gurman, worked at a butcher shop and was cleaning up the blood and bones one March evening when Grandpa and a friend came through the door. At first they asked Gurman for five cents, which he gladly handed over, in the hopes they'd leave him alone. But then, always the overachiever, Grandpa asked for ten cents more. Gurman, starting to get nervous now, gave Grandpa the ten cents.

Sensing the butcher's weakness and unwillingness to fight, Grandpa snatched a large butcher knife from the countertop while his friend stood lookout in the doorway. Grandpa held the knife over Gurman's head while he riffled through the poor guy's pockets with his free hand. He came up with $32, and ran. Maybe some cop on the beat noticed the robbers burst out from the butcher-shop door, or maybe Gurman screamed for help. After a short foot chase through the downtown streets, the cops cornered Grandpa.

While out on bail two months later, Grandpa was arrested again for assault and battery. His crimes often overlapped, one on top of the other, like a deck of cards when you fan it out during a magic trick: Pick a crime, any crime.

When he wasn't out stealing, Grandpa was out drinking and fighting. Most nights, after a bout, his kids could hear him coming, weaving down the street and growling like a mad dog. He would often come home smelling of booze and covered in blood, and would then pass out on the kitchen floor, leaving his kids to drag him into the living room, where he'd sleep it off night after night.

From the next room, the family could hear Grandpa sing himself to sleep. There was no radio, since he had hocked it to play the horses. A cappella, Grandpa would sing an old Bing Crosby tune: "When day is done and shadows fall and twilight's due, my lonely heart keeps sinking with the sun. Although I miss your tender kiss the whole night through, I miss you most of all when day is done." Grandpa liked "When Day Is Done" so much that he once recorded it at a booth in Coney Island, dedicating it to Grandma. "Hey, Boobie, this is for you," the record began. (Years later, after Grandpa died, my mother and her brothers found the haunting recording and burned it.)

Grandpa's worst binges were always around Easter. Maybe because the moon was guaranteed to be full—since Easter Sunday is based on the Paschal full moon—Grandpa always lost his mind during Holy Week. One Good Friday, Judge Zampella refused to lock Grandpa up after he broke every piece of furniture in the house. Grandpa was a Catholic, the judge reasoned, and it was Holy Week. My aunt Mary Ann cursed the judge over his Jersey City logic and was almost locked up herself. The rest of the kids kept their mouths shut.

The morning after a particularly harsh fight, Grandpa would send one of them to the Palace drugstore for three or four sticks of eye makeup to cover his black eyes. He would sit in front of the mirror and blend the different shades until they were perfect.

Grandpa was incredibly vain, and blamed baldness for ruining his life. His hair started coming out at age twenty-six, and by the time he was twenty-eight, he was pretty bald. Not completely bald, but close. Whenever his son Robby combed his own thick black hair in front of the mirror, Grandpa flew into a jealous rage and threatened to kill him.

To give his skin a healthy glow, Grandpa liked to sunbathe on the roof, reading a detective magazine or smoking marijuana to pass the time. When he wanted, Grandpa could be handsome and even charming. But those times were rare. He was usually covered in scabs and bruises, cursing out everyone around him.

One of his favorite objects was his gun—a .45, which he kept in a strongbox without a lock, stowed away on the top shelf of the kitchen closet. We're not sure if he ever used it to kill anyone. Or if he simply preferred his bare hands.

In August 1935, Grandpa was arrested for atrocious assault and battery, the crime that would seal his reputation as a murderer. Though it was by far his most serious crime, it was the one we knew the least about. The complainant's last name was Craig, from Brooklyn. I often wondered if he was related to Joseph Craig, the boxer Hague had managed years before. But there were no stories written about it in *The Jersey Journal,* and the records were sketchy. My mother tried to find out more about the crime after Grandpa died, but the county worker in charge of such documents said that the only records kept were those filed under homicide. And this wasn't quite a homicide. Back in the 1930s, without a dead body, atrocious assault was the highest charge the cops could bring.

Ma suspected that the records were on file somewhere but that the clerk was just too lazy to look them up. The ancient files were kept inside Murdoch Hall, the old Medical Center building where Grandma had worked back in the 1940s. Because of a broken window, a family of pigeons flew inside one of the file rooms and took up residence. Many of the criminal records were covered in bird droppings and were ruined. Others simply sat there, yellowing and decaying. If they still existed, Grandpa's files lay buried beneath a ton of long-forgotten murders and homicides, file upon file, box upon box, row after row, and room after room of other families' crimes, tragedies, and sorrows.

All we had to go on were our own family stories. Aunt Katie said that during a campaign rally for Hague, a riot broke out. Craig was clubbed in the mayhem, and Grandpa was framed for the attack. Craig eventually died, but too late for the cops to charge Grandpa with murder. Knowing Hague, it's not a stretch to think that Grandpa was framed. Especially if Craig was related to the boxer Hague had managed.

But then again, Grandpa was a man who, a few decades later, would plot to murder his own children and grandchildren. It seems as if Grandpa could have willingly beaten Craig to death. He would probably even have enjoyed it.

While out on bail a month later, Grandpa was arrested again, for breaking-and-entering and larceny. He pleaded not guilty to all his charges but was sentenced to seven years for the assault on Craig. In 1935, Grandpa went away—not to the country or overseas, but away. In Jersey City, when someone mentions that a relative has "gone away," it means they've gone to jail or to the crazy house in Secaucus. Jersey Citizens, though they'd have you believe they've seen it all, were never enthusiastic travelers.

Grandpa went not to Atlantic City or Miami, two popular destinations for the most adventurous Jersey Citizens, but to Trenton State Prison. With time off for good behavior, he spent five years in the "Big House," the state penitentiary, where the electric chair was kept.

They were wonderful years for my mother and her brothers and sister—Beansie-free years. But the times he had hit them, knocked them down the stairs, stuck a live Christmas tree into the coal-burning stove, balls and all, and almost burned the kitchen down, were still fresh in their young minds.

And it wasn't long before Grandpa was back from Trenton State, re-creating all those precious family moments. My mother was sitting outside her house the day he was sprung, and she saw him come down the street. She was only nine years old, but she recognized him right away. Grandpa bent down and kissed her, then walked inside, where Grandma was curling her hair, getting ready for his big entrance. When she saw him, she dropped the curling iron on the floor and was swept up in his embrace. They hugged and kissed like in a movie. It was the worst day of my mother's life.

Soon Grandpa was assaulting them again. He beat my uncle Sonny up so bad that he threatened to kill Grandpa someday. When my uncle Robby asked to go play in the pumps on a hot summer day, Grandpa filled the tub up with ice-cold water and viciously threw him in it. Then, when my mother had her hair up in a towel and was drinking a glass of milk, Grandpa unleashed this particularly obscene string of compliments: "What are you drinking milk for, you Hindu dying-looking fucking pimple-faced cocksucker? You'll get more pimples on your fucking face."

Ironically, my mother always had beautiful skin, just like her father.

With a monster like that for a husband, Grandma should have packed up the kids and left. But she couldn't leave Grandpa. She was afraid. Not for herself, but for her children. Grandpa told her that if she left, he would track her down and kill the kids. That was why Grandma stayed.

Though he scared them, hurt them, and threatened to murder them, Grandpa embarrassed his children more than anything. The other kids in the neighborhood called Uncle Jerry, Uncle Sonny, and Uncle Robby jailbirds, beat them up, and wouldn't let them play ball with them in the lot. All because of Grandpa.

My mother didn't have to worry about stickball, but she had her own problems. She once woke up for school and found a half-dozen restaurant sugar shakers on the kitchen table.

"Where'd they come from, Mama?" she asked.

"Your father brought them home in his coat last night," Grandma answered, shaking her head and wringing her small, white hands. "He was drunk."

The next day, my mother and her girlfriends walked uptown to go swimming at Dickinson High School, the neoclassical Parthenon-like structure that's visible from the New Jersey Turnpike approach to the Holland Tunnel. Like the Art Deco Medical Center, Dickinson's elaborate architecture seemed somehow misplaced in Jersey City. The high school looked lost up there on its hill, like a crisp, new dollar bill you found lying in the gutter.

After swimming at Dickinson, my mother and her friends walked down the long hill, their hair drying in the warm sun. Along the way, they stopped for hamburgers and coffee at the local Greek diner. The owner, Poly, brought them their order, but when they asked for sugar, he threw up his hands.

"Some sonofabitchin' drunk came in last night and stole all our sugar," he yelled. My mother cringed and almost slid under the Formica counter.

She was actually relieved when Grandpa wound up behind bars again, out of their lives once more. It didn't take long. While the rest of the country was at war, Grandpa was arrested and went away again in October 1943 for robbing a guy named Stanley Miniski, of Northport, Long Island, of three hundred dollars and a watch and chain after the two had been out drinking together in a saloon.

This time the crime made the paper, with the headline FATHER OF FIVE SENT TO PRISON. According to the story, Grandma passed out in the courtroom, but not before shouting, "Whatever is to become of my five children?" As if Beansie were a positive role model and great provider. The kids could surely steal their own bottles of milk, smelly oranges, stencil guns, and shakers of sugar.

If only the government had had the foresight to ship Grandpa off to Germany, he could have terrorized the enemy rather than his family. But he was too old for the service and had too many children. Instead, he was sentenced to three-to-seven. He was in prison barely a month when he was let out again, bound in handcuffs and shackles and accompanied by prison guards, taken from his cell just long enough to attend the funeral of his son.

12

FALLING STAR

———————

Sonny was my eternally adolescent uncle. There were times, as I approached my own adolescence, when I tried to imagine him as a grown man who had made something of his life, left something behind, or at least spawned his own children. I imagined birthday cards coming in the mail from Uncle Sonny with twenty bucks inside, just like the ones my other aunts and uncles sent each year.

I knew Uncle Sonny's story well, so well that I felt I knew him. Sometimes it was like he was still alive, since the older I got, the more I learned about him. Every year, on April 10, his birthday, Ma went to church, even the years it didn't fall on Easter Sunday or during Holy Week. It was like she was going to visit him. Like he was waiting for her in one of the church pews.

My mother and Sonny were a year and six days apart and looked exactly alike, so much so that some people thought they were twins. Uncle Sonny didn't like to eat, not that there was ever much to eat in their house. My mother was always hungry, always felt an emptiness in her stomach, so when Uncle Sonny hid his vegetables under his plate, my mother would eat them for him. They had a good thing going.

Grandma was the provider in the family, with help from Sonny, the oldest of the five. Because he was the oldest, Uncle Sonny was very serious. He worked for the local butcher delivering meat to downtown brownstones and tenements and gave all the money he earned to Grandma so she could provide an unsteady diet of lentils and stale Italian bread. While Grandma worked at a local luncheonette, my mother cleaned the house and took care of the younger children—Mary Ann, Robby, and Jerry, whom they used to call Junior, since he was named after Grandpa.

Uncle Sonny's story starts on a Tuesday night in 1944, when he was fourteen. It had been a hot week in August, with temperatures bubbling over a hundred degrees. It was too hot to sit in the house at night, so the whole family, and everyone in the neighborhood, was out on their stoops. While they were sitting there, Grandma argued with Sonny about what he was doing the next day, his day off. He had plans to work on his clubhouse, in an empty lot on First Street, with his friends. But Grandma wanted him to go to the movies instead. As they argued, a shooting star streaked across the sky. The kids were excited. But Grandma said that whenever you saw a falling star, it meant that someone was going to die.

The next morning, Sonny stubbornly left the house to meet his friends. Before he slammed the door, he turned and looked at his brothers and sisters seated at the wooden kitchen table. My mother got a good look at him before he stormed out, like a slow-motion part in the movies she saw at the Stanley Theatre: his jet-black hair, straight like hers, covered in a sailor hat that he'd borrowed from his brother Junior, striped polo shirt over a skinny seventy-five-pound body, black sneakers, and baggy jeans bulging with swimming trunks underneath. Sonny wore the trunks in case he and his buddies decided to go swimming down by the docks later that day. It was that kind of day, so hot it makes you want to do something stupid, like swim in the dirty Hudson.

Grandma went to work at the luncheonette and told my mother to meet her there when she was done cleaning the house. If her boss wasn't looking, Grandma could serve my seventy-pound mother a bowl of soup or a ham sandwich, and maybe even give her some food to take home to the others, who were now out playing in the vacant, garbage-strewn lot next door.

That afternoon, while finishing her chores, my mother happened to look out the window and notice a green-and-white police car, the old kind, with running boards and rounded hood popular in gangster movies from the 1930s. Because of the Depression, the war, and Hague's stolen tax money, new police cars hadn't been bought in years.

A cop in a dark blue uniform, the badge above his heart glinting in the high summer sun, walked over to the neighbors' stoop across the street. A group of kids soon gathered around and began looking up at my mother in the window. Her first thought was that Grandpa had broken out of jail. The cop looked up at the window and yelled to her, "Is your mother home?"

"No," she answered. "She's at work."

"Well, tell her to come to the police station after work," he said, walking back to his car.

After he pulled away, Annie, Grandma's best friend, called to my mother to come downstairs. When she got to the bottom of the rickety staircase, Annie was standing in the vestibule, closing the door gently behind her. She placed her hand on my mother's bony shoulder and said, "Junior's been killed by a truck."

"My little brother," my mother thought as a small bomb exploded in her brain. She couldn't speak. She remembered the shooting star from the night before.

As my mother stood there in the vestibule, dumbstruck, Annie went to find Bill Barrett, a boarder in her house who was one of the few people on Second Street who owned a car. She called Aunt Katie, who lived around the corner. With my despondent mother, they all gathered in Annie's kitchen and tried to work out a strategy for telling Grandma the bad news. Suddenly, the door opened and Junior walked in. Since he was supposed to be dead, they all flinched when they saw him. For a second, my mother thought it was Junior's ghost.

"Junior," my aunt Katie yelled. "What the fuck are you doing here? You're supposed to be dead." The hopeful thought that maybe this was another family's burden flashed in their heads. But my mother knew what was happening. She remembered the sailor hat. She knew it was Sonny who was dead. The cops simply had the wrong name, she told Aunt Katie.

Knowing Sonny was the firstborn, the police had thought he was named after his father, and therefore a Junior, the name stitched inside the cap. The cap Sonny had borrowed from Junior.

With the *new* news, the knowledge that Sonny was dead, Annie, Katie, Bill, and my mother climbed into Bill's car and headed for Montgomery Street, to the luncheonette.

"Sonny's been hurt," Annie hedged when she saw my grandmother behind the counter. "You better come home." On the short ride, less than a mile, Grandma wrung her hands, and my mother placed her skinny arm around her shoulders.

When they got home, Aunt Katie knelt before Grandma, who sat in a kitchen chair. Katie laid her hands on Grandma's hands and said slowly, "There's nothing you can do. Sonny is dead."

Grandma heard a sound like leaves falling inside her head. Then she fainted and fell off the kitchen chair.

At the morgue, they wouldn't let Grandma see Sonny, because his chest had been crushed in the accident. But she knew it was her son. She was told he was wearing swimming trunks beneath his pants.

Sonny's best friend, Vinnie Antoniack, later told my mother what had happened. Sonny and his friends were on their way to the Gypsum Company at the edge of town to try and scam some shingles from the dumping ground for the roof of their clubhouse. Sonny was pulling a wagon, so the trip was slow. Diadato DiTorio, a local truck driver, saw the boys and offered them a ride on the running board. I imagine them as the cast of *East Side Kids*—dirty, dressed in baggy clothes, always in black and white, jumping onto the running board of the truck. When they jumped off a few minutes later, Vinnie noticed that Sonny wasn't with them.

"Where's Sonny?" Vinnie asked the other boys. He looked down the street and saw the frail body of his friend lying in the gutter. Vinnie ran over and knelt down, shouting, "What happened?" to his friend. When he lifted Sonny's head for an answer, blood gushed out instead.

Diadato was taken into custody while the cops investigated. They determined that Sonny accidentally fell from the truck and was dragged underneath it when his wagon got caught in the wheels. Grandma didn't press charges. Friends encouraged her to sue, but Diadato had five small children of his own. His knowing he had killed her oldest son was punishment enough, Grandma said.

Grandma's hair began to turn white that night, and would be completely white by winter. Her four remaining children climbed into bed with her like kittens, and stayed up throughout the night crying.

It was standing room only at the Introcaso Funeral Home the next night. Sonny was small for his age, but he was a smart kid, the smartest on the block, and everyone liked him. The front-page story in *The Jersey Journal* that day told about the clubhouse and the kids' new plan to name it after Sonny—the Sonny Vena Victory Club. They would place a photo of Sonny inside as a tribute.

Sonny's popularity and the front-page news brought people who didn't even know Sonny to the funeral parlor. Italian relatives wailed in the heat of the room, the smell of the embalming chemicals smothered by so many bouquets of flowers. Instead of giving Grandma gardenias, Aunt Katie had gotten Uncle Al to collect money from the other longshoremen down at the docks. Though it was a beautiful gesture, Uncle Al gave Grandma only half of the collection. He and Katie kept the other half.

As soon as he died, stories of the supernatural started to attach themselves to Uncle Sonny. At the wake, people said he had once seen Jesus' face in the sky and pointed it out to everyone else, and that the *Hudson Dispatch* had snapped a picture of it and printed it in the paper the next day.

Aunt Katie said that when Sonny was little, he had carved his initials into the hot, black tar on Second Street. While he was bending over, a bee flew over his head and buzzed around three times. Years later, after Sonny died, cousin Chubby went back to the very same spot, took his knife, and cleaned out Sonny's carved initials. A bee flew over his head and buzzed around three times. It was Sonny's way of marking Chubby, of letting him know he was waiting for him in heaven and that it wasn't so bad up there.

At Sonny's wake, my mother stayed far away from the coffin, because the body inside didn't resemble her brother. The way she could tell it was really Sonny was by looking at his hands. Those were the hands she knew, their fingernails chewed and bloody, like Grandpa's. Ma didn't understand why the women were saying things like "He looks so good. So peaceful." To her, Sonny looked dead.

In the next room lay a man who had died of a heart attack. His widow was screaming loudly and singing sad songs that seeped through the thin walls. My mother was afraid to stay in the room with Sonny, but because of the sounds outside, she was even more afraid to leave. She wouldn't even go to the bathroom.

When the wake was almost through, one more guest arrived. It was Grandpa, chained in handcuffs, escorted by prison guards. He cried, tears sliding down his reddened face as he hobbled over to the coffin that held his son's crushed body. The guards let one hand free from the cuffs so Grandpa could stroke Sonny's cheek. My mother had no love for her father, but she felt sorry for him, like she would feel sorry for any stranger who sees his dead son for the first time. Some friends of Grandma's were angry to see him there. Who was he to cry? Never around to feed those kids. How could he even show his face?

At Holy Name Cemetery, where most of my relatives were buried and where Uncle Frankie met his lovers, Sonny's grave lay under an old apple tree, littered with decaying apples. There was no tombstone, since Grandma didn't have the money. A house brick marked the grave. My mother and the other children tossed small handfuls of apple-scented soil into Sonny's grave as his coffin was lowered.

After the funeral, Grandma and her four remaining children went to Annie's house for ham, rye bread, and potato salad. Grandma never returned to her job at the luncheonette, because it reminded her too much of Sonny. When he was old enough, Uncle Jerry got two jobs to help feed the family—setting up pins at a local bowling alley by night and delivering newspapers by day.

Grandma was never the same after 1944. Sonny had been her favorite, though his birth was the source of most of her life's pain. It was because of Sonny that Grandma had had to marry Grandpa. Until I was an adolescent, I hadn't realized that Grandma married Grandpa because she was pregnant. People had said that Grandma "got into trouble." I thought that simply meant she had met Grandpa.

For me, Grandma was no longer so pure. She was finally human. More important, Grandma had a good excuse for marrying Grandpa.

My mother, to retain Grandma's saintly image, insisted that she had been the victim of a splash pregnancy. That would make Sonny the blessed child of an immaculate conception, which would make his untimely death more meaningful than it actually was. He was the sacrificial lamb of Second Street, the savior who died too soon.

To make themselves feel better, the family concocted a reason for why Sonny died so young: Had he lived to be an adult, he would have eventually killed Grandpa, and the sin of patricide would have been an even greater tragedy than Sonny's birth or death. God took him while he was still innocent. But I always thought it would have been a good thing if Sonny had killed Grandpa. Years of pain and suffering could have been avoided.

A sadness, like Sonny's ghost, stayed with my mother and her siblings in that Second Street apartment for years, until Grandpa came home from Trenton and replaced the sadness with terror. Aunt Mary Ann got enough money together to eventually buy Sonny a tombstone. It infuriated Grandpa, because he wanted the money for himself.

But Grandpa could never lay another hand on Sonny. With a front-page story above the fold all about him, a victory club in his name, and local sainthood granted forever, Sonny was probably better off dead.

Had Sonny lived, he very well may have killed Grandpa. Or maybe Grandpa would have killed him. Or maybe—worse—Uncle Sonny would have lived a mediocre life, working himself to death in a factory or getting beaten up by the cops like Chubby. Instead, Sonny was as prized and as safe as that Virgin Mary behind the glass bubble, canonized and finally above it all.

———

Almost a half century later, I decided to check out Uncle Sonny's story for myself, to relive his posthumous, adolescent moment of glory. I walked over to the library on Jersey Avenue, in a huge limestone building, the same library where Sonny and my mother had done their homework together, the same library where I had researched school papers, the same place Grandpa had worked as a security guard in the 1960s, before he tried to shoot us.

Remembering all the objects Grandpa had stolen from there, I nervously took the worn marble stairs to the second-floor reference room two at a time, worried that someone might notice a resemblance and demand I return the encyclopedias and Indian arrowheads. I could have taken the elevator, but it had been one of Grandpa's jobs to run the elevator when he worked there. It gave off bad vibes. I thought that in a final fit of rage Grandpa might send me hurtling down to the basement to an early death.

The 1944 reel of microfilm was thick, dark, and shiny and felt good in my hand, so heavy with all the stories from that year, with the story of Uncle Sonny. The machine was not easy to operate. I wound the film through the take-up reel and figured out which buttons to push. I sped through winter, January stories passing in a blur, stories of grieving families whose sons were killed in the war, picture after picture of young heroes in uniform. That blurred into spring ads for Easter clothes and hats. And then there was summer. In search of August 10, the day after Sonny died, I sped past the steamy months of June and July, with their baseball stories and weather reports. When I hit August, I slowed down, using my fingers to turn the thick reel. I didn't want to miss it.

August 7 . . . August 8 . . . my head and eyes hurting from the blurred microfilm, the focus off enough to be annoying. I felt a little nauseated, both from the moving images and the anxiety of getting closer. I found August 9, and then the last page, the editorial page. . . . And then, there, on August 10 . . .

A big black hole where the lead story should have been.

There was a left-hand column story on FDR, a tear, and then nothing. Where was Sonny? Before I even finished asking myself, I knew the answer. I knew what had happened. I knew that Grandpa had torn the story out while working in the library years ago. It felt as if his hand had reached from the grave, through the soil at Holy Name Cemetery, and ripped the clipping right from under my eyes.

I felt a pain, a dull ache in my chest, the pain my mother must have felt whenever her father did something horrible. The pain Aunt Mary Ann still felt, even years later. I'd heard those bad stories about Grandpa so many times, I thought I'd become numb to them. But this was a new one. I felt like Grandpa had whacked me in the gut. My hands shook as I fingered the reel and tried to figure out what to do next. But what could I do? Like Grandma, Ma, and her siblings years ago, I was helpless. I wanted to point to the screen and scream, yell out, tell the people sitting on either side of me what was missing. That Grandpa had stolen it. But no one would understand.

I couldn't even complain to the librarian. I knew who had stolen this story, this evidence, and I was too embarrassed to even mention it. The story was Sonny's only glory, his fifteen inches of fame in the local paper, and the family's only printed news story without an arrest attached to it. Grandpa had wiped it out, in one swift tear. It was Grandpa's final, posthumous act of stupidity and violence. His sucker punch in the face of family history.

I did the only thing I could do. I pressed the rewind button and watched the microfilm go whizzing back in time. Summer turned to spring turned to winter and the new year, 1944.

13

THE HEIGHTS

When my sister was pregnant with her second baby in 1980, she decided to move out of the Gregory and out of downtown altogether. Paula had been the first in our family to drive a car and the first girl to go to college. Now she was the first to buy a house. We moved with her—Ma, Daddy, and I into the first floor, Paula and her family upstairs. Stanley took the basement apartment. Cousin Mike, the lawyer, did the closing on the house, as a favor to Paula. It helped having a lawyer in the family.

The house was a mother/daughter two-family yellow brick on a street called Summit Avenue—as if we'd reached a mountaintop or some other high point in our lives. We had, in a way, thanks to Paula. Summit Avenue was part of the Heights, the northernmost ward of Jersey City. Since it was mostly populated by German Americans and other fair-skinned residents, it was known as Little Johannesburg. The area was also populated by lots of mosquitoes because of the nearby meadows and reservoir. One of the biggest parks in the Heights was called Mosquito Park.

Paula's house was a fixer-upper, but it was beautiful. Out front was a big porch, surrounded by a pretty, black wrought-iron gate with loops and swirls. There was a huge hallway and a wide staircase with a sloping wooden banister that ended on a landing lit by an oval stained-glass window. The floors were polished parquet, with swastika-like patterns around the borders of each room. The bottom half of the walls were covered in embossed antique leather.

Paula even got a dog to go with the house. His name was Marty, and he was a golden retriever. He was the only dog in Jersey City who was fed steak on a regular basis. I had always wanted a dog, but our apartment above the Majestic had been too small. When I was really little, I wanted a dog so badly that I pretended to be one for a few weeks, crawling around on all fours and drinking water from a wooden salad bowl. My favorite TV show had been the exercise program with Jack La Lanne, because at the end of the show, Jack brought out his German shepherd, who looked just like Buddy. By the time we got Marty, I was fifteen, too old to enjoy him. I had better things to do than play with a dog. I had new friends to make in my new neighborhood.

The move to the Heights was a major change for all of us, but it was most traumatic for Daddy. Since he didn't drive, he had no way of getting downtown to the Majestic. He couldn't place his bets with Uncle Henry, who also didn't drive, so I had to buy Daddy a Pick-It lottery ticket every day. I think he was too ashamed to do it himself. The Pick-It was for old ladies. The number was what guys played.

But the legal lottery was becoming more and more popular. Hardly anybody played the number anymore. As overzealous prosecutors tried to make names for themselves, illegal gambling became more and more taboo. In 1984, Uncle Henry was fined $5,000 and sentenced to five years in jail. Not St. Lucy's, but jail. Fortunately, he was allowed to serve his time in the Hudson County Jail Annex, a much less dangerous prison in Secaucus. That way he could visit Uncle Tommy on weekends at nearby Meadowview.

Each day, I would buy Daddy a lottery ticket and leave it on his clock radio at night when I came home from gallivanting, as my mother liked to call it. Without the Majestic downstairs, Daddy stopped drinking, except for special occasions. I knew what a loss moving away from the tavern was for him. At the turn of the century, when Dziadzia arrived in Jersey City, he and practically every one of his brothers had opened his own tavern. The Stapinskis were tavern owners by trade. And tavern lovers by nature. During Prohibition, Dziadzia made home brew to keep his downtown business afloat. One night in 1927, while Dziadzia was out, Babci had to tend bar. She was pregnant with Uncle Tommy at the time. That night, an Elliot Ness wanna-be wandered in and noticed the bottles without labels on the shelves. The tavern was raided, and Babci was so upset that she fainted and fell to the floor. Dziadzia was taken to the Seventh Street precinct and arrested for bootlegging.

That autumn, when Uncle Tommy was born, he began having spells. He had epilepsy, the doctors said, and Babci blamed herself. She thought that if she hadn't fallen down on the night of the raid, maybe her baby would have been born healthy.

Because of the home brew, Dziadzia's tavern was closed down, and he paid a fine. Because of the Tommy tragedy, he never opened another bar, but he continued to patronize the family's other Gammontown establishments. The night Dziadzia was attacked and hit on the head, he was on his way home from one of those neighborhood bars, Wozniak's on Morris Street.

In a way, I was glad Daddy didn't find a bar in our new neighborhood. Tripping up the stairs on the way home from the Majestic was one thing. But I didn't want him wandering around outside getting hit on the head like Dziadzia. For the first time in my life, I worried about Daddy. I didn't like the feeling. I was happier when it was the other way around, and Daddy was worrying about me. But I couldn't help it. Daddy needed looking after.

While walking out on the porch one day, he stepped on a nail. By the time he showed it to us weeks later, red streaks were running up his leg. He went to the hospital, and our incompetent family doctor almost killed him by giving him a glucose-water drip. Daddy, it turned out, was a diabetic, which was why he didn't feel the nail in his foot and why the sore on his foot hadn't healed. It was a no-brainer.

Daddy almost lost his leg but got away easy, with only four toes amputated. He had to wear special orthopedic shoes. Standing on the platform at the Cold Storage wasn't so easy for him anymore. But he had no choice. My mother had lost her job when the DMV office closed, its latest agent involved in yet another scandal, this one involving stolen sales-tax money.

Ma blamed Daddy's diabetes on all the Sara Lee cake he had brought home over the years. But there was more to it than that. Drinking for forty years hadn't helped. Neither had smoking. So Daddy stopped smoking, cold turkey. He left his last pack of Marlboros on the mantelpiece in the new house, a trophy of his accomplishment. With all his free, sober time, he liked to sit out on the porch and watch the unfamiliar faces go by. Now and then he'd throw a tennis ball down the stoop for Marty to run after.

I knew virtually nothing about the Heights. But I soon discovered that the local kids were like the kids in nearby North Bergen: into suede, corduroy, long hair, hard drugs, and kegs of beer. By my sixteenth birthday, I was wearing peasant blouses and Lee jeans, complete with a patch of the Rolling Stones tongue. I was also smoking pot and drinking under the gazebo at Mosquito Park. I didn't consider smoking pot a crime, since I rationalized that drugs should be legalized. And drinking? I was just picking up where Daddy had left off.

Compared to my friends and boyfriends, I was a goody two-shoes. The kids in the Heights had more money than the kids I'd grown up with downtown, so they had more disposable income to spend on mescaline and LSD. My downtown friends had been happy with a pint of malt liquor and a loose joint.

Crimes in the Heights were committed out of boredom, not need. A guy I went out with for four weeks in 1982 turned out to be an ex-con who had stolen money from the safe at the Foodtown supermarket. Another boyfriend was regularly beaten up by the local cops for being a druggie and all-around troublemaker. My serious high school boyfriend, whom I took to the senior prom, was a cousin of Bobby Manna, the mobster who had befriended Mayor Kenny. I didn't know it until my mother interrogated my boyfriend one day to find out who exactly her baby was dating.

For the first time, Ma really started to get on my nerves. I had to carry mouthwash with me so that she wouldn't smell the smoke or beer on my breath when I walked in the door. She forced me to lie to her constantly about where I was going and who I was going with. It was for her own peace of mind that I failed to tell her about the ride my friends and I got to the Cars concert in the back of a shag-carpeted van with five stoned guys we didn't even know. Or the time I went camping with my friends—but had to sleep alone in a tent with my boyfriend. Or the many Saturday afternoons I spent smoking pot and hanging out at Washington Square Park in Greenwich Village.

My friends' parents weren't as strict as Ma. Why couldn't she be more like them? Whenever I hung out "down the tracks"—near the old railroad cut on the West Side—I had to sleep over at my friend Gretchen's house. There was always a bonfire at the tracks. One stoned girl set her long, blond hair on fire while dancing around it. I never got that close. But the smoke left me smelling like I'd just gone out to fight a blaze with Engine Company Number 9. Gretchen's mother didn't notice the smell. Either her nose was stuffed or, more likely, she was a complete idiot. My mother would have been all over me if I'd come home smelling like that. After a night down the tracks, I'd sleep at Gretchen's, then wash my clothes before going home.

My friend Tammy did mescaline right in her own bedroom. She even convinced her parents to get her a Mustang, which we'd drag-race down at Caven Point, near where the Black Tom explosion had happened years ago. We'd drive over a hundred miles an hour on the concrete pier, Jimi Hendrix blasting from Tammy's state-of-the-art speakers, Budweiser nips clamped and sloshing between our knees. The only reason we didn't crash and burn was that Ma was home saying her rosary.

The greatest thing about becoming a teenager was learning to drive. A whole canon of fifties songs was written about it, but I thought I was the first teenager ever to feel liberated by a steering wheel and a motor. I realized that greener pastures actually existed within driving distance. Going on vacation was one thing, but getting in a car and just going somewhere, anywhere, wherever I wanted, was truly exhilarating. With my friends, I drove to Garrett Mountain out near Paterson or went camping on weekends at the Delaware Water Gap. I drove past farms in western Jersey and beach towns in south Jersey.

To get out of town, you had to be subjected to the worst possible strip of pavement. It was as if the city planners had saved the absolute worst street for last. Tonnelle Avenue (pronounced *TON-lee*) was filled with chemical plants built next to toxic-waste sites, jug handles, auto-paint shops, sex-video stores, a place called Hubcap World, and the occasional hooker motel. If you drove fast enough, it all sped past your window in an unrecognizable blur. There was no sidewalk on Tonnelle Avenue. It was built for cars and tractor trailers, as if humans were not driving them. It was the outer fringe of a place that was already edgy, the puss-filled nodule on a rotted limb. But once you got past Tonnelle, you were out, headed to somewhere green, away from the decaying buildings, burnt piers, and dirty streets.

While out gallivanting, I realized that the Heights wasn't all that different from downtown. Most of my new friends' families lived on swag, just like we did. Donna, a girl who lived around the corner, sobbed one Christmas night after showing us the three dozen sweaters—mostly velour—that her father had given her. We couldn't understand what the problem was. A few of the sweaters were ugly, with orange and green velvety stripes, but for the most part it was a nice haul. Donna would never have to wear the same sweater twice.

Between sobs, Donna explained what the problem was. "He didn't buy any of this," she sniffled, waving her arm over her bed, desk, and carpet, where the offensive sweaters lay. "What kind of gift is that?" It had never occurred to me to complain about the merchandise that fell off the truck. Maybe it wasn't always what you would have picked out had you been able to do some proper shopping. And maybe it didn't always provide for the perfect gift. But swag was part of everyday life.

And then it hit me. Christmas was not every day. Swag and Christmas did not mix. Wrapping it up and giving swag as a present was unacceptable. It was tacky, and much more morally wrong than swag itself. A girl would rather get Fruit of the Loom underwear and socks—a typical Hudson County Christmas present—than swag. It just wasn't done.

Then again, Donna's father was connected. He wasn't in the Mob, but it seemed he could have been pretty close to it. She was lucky he was even alive to give her presents. Besides, Donna wasn't exactly a saint herself. Many an afternoon we would wind up at the local drugstore, Donna shoving cosmetics into her faded Lee jeans. I was always terrified of shoplifting. Swiping ashtrays was one thing—restaurants expected you to steal them. I figured it was free advertising for them. But shoplifting was illegal, something you could go to jail for, the Hudson County Jail, the house of horrors where Grandpa had spent several years of his life.

My friend Nina had shoplifted a few times from the downtown Woolworth's. Eventually, an old clerk in the store saw her and told her mother, an apathetic woman who was known for taking other people's chicken bones home from parish affairs. "For the dog," she claimed. But who ever heard of giving your dog chicken bones? My mother felt sorry for her and said she probably made soup from them. My mother—who kept her eye on everyone and everything—let me know that she knew that the Woolworth's clerk knew about Nina. It was an indirect warning. But I would never shoplift, mostly because I never could let my mother down like that.

What made me even more uncomfortable than going "shopping" with Donna and Nina was going to church with my friend Molly. Her father would give her the family envelope to place in the collection basket each week. Every Sunday, Molly would steal the money and deposit the empty envelope in the basket. It made my stomach turn, but not out of fear of God or guilt about the Catholic Church. By then, I was developing into a smart-ass teenage agnostic who believed the Church was a corrupt, sexist, homophobic multimillion-dollar tax-free business. My fear stemmed from knowing that someday Molly would be found out.

At the end of the season, when the church bulletin listed how much each family had donated that year, there was a big fat zero next to Molly's family's name. Her father, unlike Nina's mother, was not so apathetic. He was apoplectic. Molly was grounded for much of sophomore year.

I stole. But in a socially acceptable way. When I was old enough, I carried on my father's tradition of coming home after work with a brown paper package under my arm. My first job was as an ice cream scooper at Carvel on Journal Square. The place was at a very bad intersection, across the street from a White Castle hamburger joint, which back then was a hangout for the neighborhood bums. I kept waiting for somebody to trip out on acid there, like at the North Bergen franchise. It never happened, though lots of other shit went down at the White Castle—which we nicknamed White Casket. When you got hungry enough, you might take your life into your hands and venture over to the Casket, where you were guaranteed to see at least one person sprawled out on the tile floor.

By comparison, Carvel was clean and wholesome, filled mostly with young kids and ice cream-a-holics, who were weird but usually not dangerous. The Vanilla Fudge Man, who came in every night and purchased one pint of hand-scooped vanilla fudge, was in his sixties, wore a stocking cap and a shy smile, and probably lived nearby with his elderly mother. Except for his trips to Carvel, he was likely a shut-in. But he was harmless. The Cherry Vanilla Man was another story. He was younger, and liked to flirt with me and my teenage coworkers. One night, when my friend Michelle wouldn't respond to his advances, he got a little crazy and hurled his cup of cherry vanilla ice cream at her.

I had my own run-in with a local Sikh, who bought a sheet cake one Saturday afternoon. As a service, we would squeeze a birthday greeting or some other celebratory message onto your cake with sugared gel, free of charge. The man in the turban handed me a long note in his native language and insisted that I copy the entire paragraph onto the ice cream cake, verbatim. I tried, but screwed up, which sent the man into a rage. Maybe I wound up cursing his mother on her ninety-fifth birthday. But what did I know? He left, without the cake, screaming a slew of foreign curses at me. I was left to scrape the squiggles off the sheet cake for recycling. Nothing at Carvel got wasted. Almost nothing.

One time, I got stoned before going to work. I tripped out—not as badly as the girl at the North Bergen White Castle did, but it felt just as bad inside my head. I remember washing aluminum cake molds in the industrial-size sink in the back of the store and thinking that I had become a robot. I could see myself washing and washing, removed from the action. I washed mold after mold after mold after mold. (There were only five shapes, from which all Carvel cakes were fashioned: round, rectangular, log, Cookie Puss/leprechaun/Abe Lincoln/pilgrim, and Fudgie the Whale/Santa/Elf/guitar/tennis racket/ghost.)

Minutes dragged on like hours, and after a while I started to worry that maybe I was dead and this was purgatory, washing mold after mold in the back room of Carvel. I freaked myself out so badly that I wanted to go yelling and screaming from the store, hurling Fudgie the Whale molds onto Kennedy Boulevard. But I somehow managed to stay calm. Once I came down, I swore I'd never smoke pot again. At least not at work. It was too dangerous.

There was a robbery at Carvel once, on my day off. A scooper named Chloe was working with the owner, a little Paul Simon looka-like. When the robber came in, the owner was in the bathroom, reading the paper on the bowl. Chloe was forced to sit on a tub of ice cream inside the walk-in freezer while the guy emptied the cash register. She was shaken up, and almost quit. Especially when the owner emerged from the john too late and scolded her for giving up the cash.

He was my first lesson in hating the boss. The owner was not from Hudson County. He owned a Mercedes and commuted from the suburbs each day. He was so stingy when mixing his tubs of ice cream that customers dubbed the rum raisin "rum raisinless." His chocolate chip mint was so light on chips and mint flavoring that people thought it was lime sherbet. We were taught to make parfaits the tight-ass way: brush a little syrup around the inside of the cup, then fill it with ice cream. From the outside, it looked like the syrup was swirled throughout.

He taught us the "S" method of scooping ice cream, something he was probably taught at Carvel College. The S motion was designed to place as little ice cream in the scooper as possible, filling the center of the scoop with air. The ball of ice cream—light as Styrofoam—often fell off its cone perch with one lick. The licker, usually a small child, would scream until his parents bought him a new ice cream cone. Customers got one for the price of two.

On a regular basis, our boss ignored Carvel College rules, using unsanctioned Disney characters and drawing copyrighted Smurfs onto sheet cakes. But his worst offense was making obscene ice cream cakes for bachelor and bachelorette parties. On at least one occasion, he made a cake shaped like a penis. He used the log-cake mold but had to improvise the rest. While sculpting the cake, he ran back and forth to the bathroom every few minutes to check on his still life. And never once did he wash his hands. When he was done with his masterpiece— covered in flesh-tone peach ice cream, with colored coconut for pubic hair—he told us he was leaving early. He left us with the cake—and the dirty work. We were barely sixteen years old, the age when you're most easily embarrassed, left to face the man who came to pick up the penis.

We were horrified to find that he was black. Peach ice cream was out of the question. My friends and I poured chocolate shell over the shaft, which hardened on impact. It was a brilliant Carvel move, some- thing they didn't teach at Carvel College.

When the owner wasn't there, my friends and I took our revenge. We dug deep into the tubs and gave kids their fair share of ice cream. Then every night, before mopping and closing up the store, I would call home and take my family's order.

Paul, my little nephew, always asked for a cup of chocolate ice cream with chocolate syrup, chocolate crunch, and chocolate sprin- kles on top. My mother and sister loved the ice cream sandwiches, called Flying Saucers, and my brother, a hot fudge sundae. Basil, my brother-in-law, liked vanilla fudge in a cup. And for Lauren, the baby, I brought home a small cup of soft vanilla. On special occasions, I'd swipe a Cookie Puss cake. I always brought my father a plastic con- tainer of Thinny-Thin, the sugar-free ice cream, because of his dia- betes. But I would have loved to have brought him a big banana split every night, dripping with wet walnuts, fudge, and whipped cream, with a cherry on top. The Great Provider deserved more than a Thinny- Thin and a Pick-It ticket at the end of the day.

With a large paper bag in my arms, just like the kind Daddy used to carry, I'd walk in the door each night. Until one night the owner staked us out from the White Casket. The next day, my friends and I were fired for stealing merchandise.

I was outraged. How dare he fire us? He was lucky we didn't report him to phlegm-throated founder Tom Carvel for all his franchise and copyright infractions. But it was probably for the best that we were let go. With all that free ice cream, my nephew was entering what would later become known as his chubby phase. My brother was sprouting love handles. And I was starting to grow hips.

14

THROUGH THE TUNNEL

I made a break for it after high school, escaping to New York University, commuting every day on the PATH train. Greenwich Village was only a few miles away, but it may as well have been in another solar system.

At first I was intimidated by the other students. I sat at the back of the classroom most of that first semester, trying to hide. Every time I opened my mouth, I was embarrassed by my accent. I was convinced everyone was smarter than I was, that I didn't belong there, and that one day the dean of the School of Arts and Sciences would discover my existence, find out about all the criminals in my family, and have me escorted from campus.

NYU was the first school I'd attended where the students and teachers were not like me: Catholic, working-class, heterosexual, and jaded from years of living in Hudson County. There was a woman at my work-study job who was a lesbian and a girl in my Italian class who, ironically, wore a flowered housedress and had dyed blue hair. It was bright blue, not the old-lady bouffant-blue that I was used to. It was a whole new world.

Everyone at NYU thought I was Jewish, not because of my last name, but because of the cases of "free" Manischewitz matzo and macaroons that one of my uncles would send from his job at the Jersey City plant for me and my college friends.

Catholic, Jewish. It didn't matter. I wasn't even sure I still believed in God. Heaven and hell were definitely out—concepts that society had created to keep all the workers in line. I had come to NYU believing in heaven and hell. But it was all called into question during freshman year on the afternoon I overheard a conversation the girl with the blue hair was having in my Italian class. She was ridiculing a TV show she had seen the night before in which real people gave their accounts of "going to the light" and "traveling through the tunnel." Everyone was laughing with Blue Hair about it. And I suddenly felt stupid and naive. I had always assumed that there was life after death. No one I knew had ever questioned it. The afterlife was a given, like toxic waste, political corruption, and bodies washing up in spring.

But by sophomore year I nearly forgot all that existed. I found a boyfriend who played acoustic guitar. I was busy going to art films or to classic black-and-white movies that stood the test of time. I realized Hudson County was often used as a backdrop for corruption. Directors making movies about beautiful places never chose it as a setting, but both Elia Kazan and Woody Allen had used Hudson as a grim set—in *On the Waterfront* and *Broadway Danny Rose*. Sid and Nancy, in the movie version, lived out their seedy punk existence on Hudson's grungy streets.

I spent less and less time on those streets. I went to fewer family functions, and stopped going to mass on Sunday. I crashed most nights at a Ukrainian friend's $90-a-month rent-controlled railroad flat in the East Village. It was next door to a row of Indian restaurants, and at night the smell of curry would waft up into Lana's bedroom. It was a new smell for me.

In the East Village, there were still mumblers and rejects, two-bit criminals and crazy people. I just wasn't related to any of them.

To channel the temper I had inherited from Grandpa, I took up playing the drums and writing articles for the school paper. I found a new newspaper, the *Village Voice,* which I bought religiously every week on Tuesday nights. I didn't read *The Jersey Journal* anymore. The stories in the *Voice* were long and complicated and got me riled up—but in a different way. When the drums and the writing weren't enough of a release, I went to Washington, D.C., to march against the evil Republicans. There were marches for abortion rights, housing rights, and arms reduction.

I was starting to develop a social conscience and was especially pleased with myself. I read Plato and Aristotle and suddenly despised people who voted for someone because of what they could do for them personally. I even got mad at a Hudson County friend when he voted for a candidate because the guy got his mother a job. I found it despicable. Nobody in Hudson County cared about the common good, just what they could scam for themselves.

Plato talked about the cave and how the unenlightened, shortsighted people inside the cave were so busy watching shadows of themselves on the cave wall that they couldn't see the light outside. It all made perfect sense to me. Hudson County was the cave. Every time I commuted back home through the Tubes, I felt like I had to duck my head back under.

But I had no right to feel so self-righteous. What convinced me was another family story. Normally, it would have been thrown on top of the growing heap of family tragedies and dramas I heard retold every few weeks. But this one was different. No one in the Stapinski family had mentioned it before. When I heard it repeated a few times, it was not by my relatives. The story sounded like something out of the pages of the *Village Voice*. It had been written about in Jersey City history books and social critiques of the Hague years. The town historian had used it to describe the city's corrupt ways, but I hadn't known that it involved a relative. That it involved my last name.

I remember the afternoon the city's history and my family's history dovetailed. It was like finding two matching cards in a game of Go Fish. I should have recognized it sooner, but until sophomore year, I hadn't bothered to turn the right cards over. Daddy never talked about his family. But one day Ma mentioned the story in passing. And that's when I put the two tales together. Suddenly. Finally.

In 1934, Andrew Stapienski, a cousin of Dziadzia's, had a run-in with the police. Though most of the family had settled downtown, Uncle Andrew and his wife, Kunegunda, ran a tavern on Pacific Avenue in the city's Lafayette section, a more upscale neighborhood. Their main customers were recent Polish immigrants whose wives had stayed behind in the old country. They would come to Kunegunda for a home-cooked meal or to rent a room upstairs.

Kunegunda was a shrewd woman, not your typical steerage slob. Even her name was special. In Poland, to have that name was an honor. It was considered high-class. Her namesake, Cunegund, a Bavarian empress around the turn of the first century, was elevated to sainthood around 1200. Her feast day, March 3, was, coincidentally, the same day as Grandpa's birthday.

Kunegunda had a head for business and didn't simply rent rooms and feed her hungry Polish brethren out of the goodness of her heart. When food and drink tabs grew too large to settle, Kunegunda accepted parcels of land outside the city as payment. By 1934, a year after Prohibition was repealed, the Stapienskis had a pretty good thing going. The beer was flowing, and so was the cash.

When Andrew and Kunegunda's son announced he was going to be married, the Stapienskis took it upon themselves to throw the party. Young John was engaged to a Jersey City girl named Anna Lukachyk, who was, rumor has it, already with child. No matter. This was to be a weekend of dancing and drinking, shotgun or no shotgun. The day before the wedding, on a busy Friday afternoon in June, the sky threatening thundershowers, the family was busy with last-minute preparations.

Having been to many a Stapinski wedding, I'm sure the polka band was on tap, as was the beer. The clarinet and accordion were no doubt in tune, ready to dance across pages and pages of sheet music. I can imagine Kunegunda running around in an apron, grinding the meat for the kielbasa, stirring pots of sauerkraut, and folding piles of pierogi. And, of course, bottling the hooch for the Saturday celebration.

Around 11 A.M. on Friday, detectives from the city's Bureau of Liquor Control raided the tavern on an anonymous tip that the Stapienskis were distilling their own whiskey. Detectives Leon Wilzewski and Michael Noonan and a lieutenant demanded that Uncle Andrew show them the booze in the basement. When Uncle Andrew refused, he was beaten.

He was arrested for liquor-law violations and hauled into the station house, along with the evidence—a five-gallon jug of brown liquid, a two-gallon jug of alcohol, a copper funnel, a capping machine, and a quart bottle of spirits.

Twelve hours later, while out on bail and trying to finish his chores in time for the impending wedding, Uncle Andrew was rushed to the hospital. When he was brought into the Medical Center, still very much alive and in pain, Uncle Andrew was placed under anesthesia. He soon stopped breathing and was given oxygen and adrenaline. Doctors tried massaging his heart. But Uncle Andrew was gone, dead from abdominal injuries.

The death made the front page of *The Jersey Journal*: POLICE BEATING BLAMED AS MAN DIES. FAMILY SAYS FATHER WAS BLACKJACKED. POLICE ATTEMPT TO SUPPRESS NEWS.

Somehow, amid the murder and scandal that weekend, the family went ahead with the wedding on Sunday. The rationale was that all the food was already made. What could they do? They drowned their sorrows in kielbasa and what was left of the liquor. The Stapinskis—myself included—have always had a good appetite. Funerals were never an excuse for not eating and drinking; they were just another reason to indulge.

As Uncle Andrew's long funeral procession made its way down Sussex Street toward OLC the following Tuesday, police headquarters became the scene of the investigation. The papers said he was killed over just two gallons of liquor, that bruises under his arms were six by three inches, and that his lips had been cut. It looked like a clear case of police brutality.

The police denied any involvement in Uncle Andrew's death, of course. The chief claimed to have seen him in the station house after the arrest and said, "He made no complaint." I wondered if Uncle Andrew was even conscious at the time. It was hard to complain when you were passed out on the station-house floor.

The medical examiner was right on board with the cops. "The case is closed as far as we're concerned," he said. The official cause of death was "incipient peritonitis following rupture of the intestine and precipitated by syncope due to cardiac dilation and myocardic degeneration."

They claimed that Uncle Andrew fainted because of heart problems. While lifting a heavy beer barrel, they said, he passed out and hit the sharp corner of a metal tub, busting his own gut. But as much as police hoped, the story wouldn't die quite as easily as Uncle Andrew had. The papers milked it for days. Finally, on July 3, an inquest was held. A former judge, Robert Carey, represented the family. He started the proceedings with a dramatic flair.

"A serious crime has or has not been committed," he said, rising to his feet. "If it has, we are here to see justice is done."

Carey was cut off by the assistant prosecutor, who said speeches were not in order. But Carey continued in typical Jersey City fashion, misquoting Shakespeare.

"There is something wrong in Denmark," Carey told the jurors, who probably had no idea what he was talking about. Carey then, thankfully, stalked out of the courtroom and let the real drama unfold.

The first witness was Kunegunda, who testified in broken but defiant English that it was impossible for her healthy forty-six-year-old husband to just up and die. "He never was sick," she testified. "He was a healthy man, God help me.

"He get beat. First detectives come up my house," she said, glancing over at Noonan. "Lieutenant and other guy grabbed him behind arms . . . hit him with fist on chin. Another used first fist, then club." That all happened before they dragged Andrew downstairs.

Andrew's daughter Nellie said that she heard him yell from the cellar, "You have no right to use that blackjack on me."

"Show me where the stuff is," Detective Noonan yelled, punching Andrew twice in the gut.

Noonan and his boys testified that Uncle Andrew had resisted arrest and that they got into a scuffle. They denied using the blackjacks.

"Stop lying!" John, the newlywed, yelled from the back of the courtroom.

Despite four hours of evidence from eyewitnesses at the bar and from among the family, the jury ruled in fifteen minutes, just before 1 A.M., that the cops weren't lying, that they were innocent.

In the follow-up story the next day, the police were quoted as saying that Uncle Andrew must have hurt himself after being arrested, that it was impossible for him to receive an intestinal rupture in the morning, then carry ice, lift a two-hundred-pound keg of beer, and drive an automobile before complaining of pain at 6 P.M. The police didn't know my Polish relatives. They were workhorses. "Strong like bull," we always joked. And when a party was at stake, well, they were known to go to superhuman lengths for a good time.

The Stapinskis never relied on hired help or caterers. Affairs were always run the old-fashioned way, everybody selflessly pitching in and lifting, decorating, and cooking until they nearly collapsed. For my mother's wedding, sixty-one-year-old Babci cooked for a week, rolling stuffed cabbage, cooking huge vats of sauerkraut, and mixing frighteningly large bowls of potato salad.

Despite the jury and police findings, everyone was convinced the cops had killed Uncle Andrew, particularly Kunegunda and the Polish-American community. On July 5, fueled by the patriotic fervor of Independence Day and *The Jersey Journal*'s sensational headlines, three thousand Poles held a protest rally, with Kunegunda, their sad widow, among them. They demanded that a civil-rights committee be appointed to investigate the death and to suspend the police officers involved. Uncle Andrew wasn't the first Pole to be beaten by Hague's zepps. And the Polish community—with no representation in Hague's cabinet—wasn't going to take it anymore.

The rally was held at the Polish American Community Center and made the front page of the paper: POLISH-AMERICANS DEMAND STAPINSKI DEATH PROBE. Another rally was scheduled for Monday, July 9, at Victory Hall.

It was time for Kunegunda—the queen of the family—to shine. It was her moment in the spotlight, to demand justice for her martyred husband. But if you look at the next week's papers, the story disappears, its space filled by other controversies and untimely deaths. There's a story headlined RADICALS DEFY JERSEY CITY POLICE. But these are different radicals, not the Poles at Victory Hall. The news involves striking furniture workers picketing Hague's antipicketing rule. In another front-page story that week, a priest is reported to have died in the chapel at Meadowview while kneeling on the altar.

The follow-up Stapienski story is nowhere to be found—not that week or the next. There's no story about a Victory Hall rally. There are no Polish crowds demanding justice. The furor ends with no explanation. None in print, anyway.

The story that wasn't reported—one that became part of Jersey City legend—was that Kunegunda cut a deal with Hague: She was allowed to keep the tavern at a time when women weren't even allowed to drink in taverns. Kunegunda shut her trap and bellied up to the other side of the bar, continuing the Jersey City tradition of keeping your sights as low as they could possibly go. She didn't reserve the cowardice just for herself. Kunegunda spread it around, like a nasty rumor that no one particularly wanted to hear. She forbade anyone in the family to attend the rallies. Kunegunda quashed the uprising.

The Polish Americans had their martyr. What they needed was a hero. But Kunegunda wasn't up to the challenge. Or she was just too pragmatic, tricked by those shadows on the cave wall.

"You can't bring him back," she was overhead saying of dead Uncle Andrew. "I got a living to make."

As my relatives like to say, Kunegunda "had a finger in it." She made a pretty penny from her husband's well-publicized death, having been told by the cops or Hague—or both—to keep quiet.

———

Realizing I was related to the city's infamous female barkeep did more than embarrass me. I was ashamed. No one at NYU knew about her, but I did and that was enough. Her story was worse than all the crime stories in my family, because of Kunegunda's squandered potential. It seemed that Grandpa never really had a chance. And my Russian great-grandpa was always a bastard. But Kunegunda could have been a hero. She really blew it. Now she was a pathetic, selfish footnote in the sad history of Jersey City.

At NYU, I continued to write scathing articles for the campus paper and to march on Washington, but my heart was no longer in it. I was humbled. I had no right to feel self-righteous, not with relatives like Kunegunda. I felt like I had to get away from Jersey City, and from my history.

I figured that education was my key to escape. I soaked up as much information as I could, majoring in journalism and taking extra credits each semester. I took a music class called "The Art of Listening," then smoked pot and for the first time heard—really heard—Bob Dylan's lyrics and the Beatles' harmonies. I became a walking college-student cliché.

I took a summer class reading the great modern philosophers, and came to the obvious conclusion that life was meaningless. The following semester, I took an extra two-credit class on Kafka, which sent me on a two-month binge of muttering that life was not meaningless but that its meaning was ambiguous. For a fleeting moment, I even understood what the giant cockroach was all about.

When I got over that phase, I took "Observational Astronomy" and climbed to the top of the highest building at NYU every week to observe the few stars one could see through the lights and haze of the city. I loved it so much that I minored in astronomy. Through a telescope, I glimpsed the craters of the moon, the rings of Saturn, and seasonal meteor showers. Falling stars were a regular annual occurrence, scientifically mapped and charted. They were not harbingers of death, like Grandma had said the night before Sonny died.

Using my astronomy text as a guide, I drove up a dark stretch of the Palisades Parkway and pulled over to the side of the road. Lying on the warm car hood, the engine clicking underneath my back, I waited and watched the Perseid meteors shoot past. Right on schedule.

I knew that the farther I got from Jersey City, the less angry I became. In senior year, just when I thought I should sign up for a trip on the space shuttle, it exploded.

I settled on a trip to Europe.

For my college graduation, my family got together and threw me a typical Stapinski bash in the OLC Church hall, lugging giant trays of pierogi and kielbasa and sauerkraut. I made enough money at the party to get to Italy. And back, if I wanted.

That summer, I got as far as Siena as part of the study-abroad program. I visited Venice and walked in courtyards right out of the Stanley Theatre. I visited the real Rialto bridge. I visited St. Peter's in Rome and understood why people liked being Catholic: It was all so sturdy, old, and official.

More important, I did my own laundry for the first time and hung it from the roof of the fifteenth-century building where I was living. I loved the smell of the wet clothes and the way the warm sun made them look so white and clean. One afternoon, while walking in the town of Assisi, I got that feeling of freedom and unbridled joy that Aunt Julie had told me about. It was as if a heavy appliance, like an air conditioner, had suddenly been removed from my back, as if my eyes were wider now that cool air had been pumped into my lungs and brain. I felt as if I'd awoken from a deep sleep that I didn't know I had fallen into. Or was it a sleep I had always been in, one that came with being born in the Margaret Hague maternity wing? In Siena, I lived in a monastery for a few days and thought, amid the cypress trees and medieval frescoes, that in a world so big and so beautiful, there was absolutely no reason to live in a place as ugly as Jersey City.

When I got back home, I could suddenly see how ugly it really was. I felt like I had the day I got my first pair of glasses: Everything was suddenly clear. I hated Jersey City so much I could taste it—bitter and rotten, like the flavor left in my mouth after a particularly bad frat party hangover.

Ironically, as a journalism major, I met all kinds of enthusiastic students whose dream it was to cover crime and corruption, students who wound up getting jobs in places like Jersey City. There was even a campus band at NYU called Urban Blight, a name I never found the least bit amusing. If you'd actually grown up in it, urban blight wasn't hip, and wasn't funny. These people thought the Pulaski Skyway was cool. They'd grown up in bland suburbia and yearned for the grittiness of places like Hudson County.

I longed to escape. Permanently.

I set out to find a job in a whole other city, a whole other state. Maybe even a whole other country. On the bulletin board in the Journalism Department there was a sign advertising openings at *The Sacramento Bee,* and though I'd never been to California, I was sure I'd love it: sunshine instead of industrial-gray skies; sparkling beaches instead of contaminated riverfronts.

If not California, then I'd head to the thoroughly scrubbed Midwest. Or maybe the fresh, pine-scented Northwest. Or maybe I'd fly off to London and rent a flat. The world seemed limitless. And I was only twenty-two.

But that autumn, on the night of the Orionid meteor shower, another Stapinski tragedy occurred, the worst one yet.

Daddy died.

15

TEN PLAGUES

We had been to the hospital with Daddy several times in the recent past—what with his near-gangrene experience and the complications from his diabetes. So on October 22, 1987, when Daddy woke up early in the morning and had trouble breathing, it meant just another trip to the hospital.

I got into the ambulance with Ma and sat next to Daddy on the stretcher. He was wearing an oxygen mask and his face was very pale. But his eyes were open and he was breathing all right. Though he was suffering congestive heart failure, the paramedics didn't seem too worried. He was only fifty-nine, after all. They stopped at red lights and drove slowly through Jersey City's streets. No siren necessary. I should have made them run all the lights and head straight for the Holland Tunnel, to a hospital on the New York side.

When we got to St. Francis Hospital in downtown Jersey City, there was no doctor in the emergency room. While Ma and I waited in the long, dim hallway, the code-red light began flashing and nurses started to run back and forth. Still, no doctor arrived. Before I knew it, my mother was fainting onto the waiting room floor while I tried to pull her up by her armpits and tell her that Daddy would be okay. But she saw the nurse's face before I did. And understood. My father had been right here minutes earlier and now the nurse was telling us that he was gone.

I thought she meant they had transferred him somewhere, to another floor or to another room. But in a terrible moment of recognition I figured that my mother was on the floor for a reason.

The nurse meant Daddy was dead. That was what she meant by "gone." He was gone for good. "No longer with us," she added for clarity.

I couldn't cry, since I had to finish picking Ma up off the floor, make sure she didn't collapse again, get her seated in a safe place, and then call Stanley and Paula from the pay phone. I dialed without thinking and delivered the bad news as if it weren't happening to us. I felt like I had that day I got stoned at Carvel, watching my body perform various tasks from afar, listening to words leave my mouth without even knowing that I was speaking.

When I hung up the phone, the nurse asked me if I wanted to see my father. I didn't really want to, but I had read somewhere that seeing a loved one's dead body helped with closure. I had never had closure, had never been wide open enough to need closure, and wasn't sure if I needed it now. But I nodded and drifted into the curtained emergency room alone.

When I saw Daddy there on the gurney, I still couldn't cry. I was too confused. I had seen dozens, if not hundreds, of dead people at all those wakes but had never really thought much about them. I realized now they had been all made up, in fancy clothes and pancake makeup, with cotton in their mouths to keep their cheeks from sinking. They looked more like big dolls than dead people.

From movies, we're taught to think that when people first die— before the cotton and makeup—they look like they're just sleeping or, at worst, unconscious. But that wasn't true at all. Daddy didn't look like he was sleeping or knocked cold. He looked dead. Gone. No longer with us, just like the nurse said. The blood was drained from his face, and his mouth was wide open—something Daddy never allowed to happen, even when he was asleep.

I was confused, because I knew this dead man. I loved him. But this was not him. Daddy had been right here minutes earlier, and now, now that he was dead, he was inexplicably gone. In a flash. Just like that. This body was here, but Daddy was missing. Where had he run off to?

I looked nervously around the emergency room, then up above me, thinking I might see Daddy hovering there, smiling down with that toothless grin of his. But all I could see was the harsh fluorescent light buzzing overhead. I thought about Blue Hair from my Italian class laughing and saying so confidently that there was no such thing as life after death. I wished she were here right now so that I could punch her in the mouth. Fuck you, I thought, shaking my head. Fuck you.

———

Though I wasn't sure exactly where Daddy had run off to, his body was taken to the Bromirski Funeral Home on Warren Street, the street where you could get a good glimpse of the Statue of Liberty. My mother, the lover of wakes and funerals, had Daddy laid out for three whole days. She didn't want to part with him, and since she was closer to a nervous breakdown than I was, I didn't argue with her.

But it was torture. For three days and three nights I had to sit in the front row of the funeral parlor and stare at Daddy's body while people came and went. They said things like "Oh, he looks so good. So peaceful." No, I wanted to say, he looks dead. Can't you see? He's dead. It's not even him, really.

I know there was a burial at Holy Cross Cemetery in North Arlington, out near where Daddy's sister Terri lived, and a Hi Hat funeral dinner afterward. I don't remember it. But I do remember thinking about Daddy being put into the ground. And I remember wondering whether he would be cold down there all alone now that winter was coming, even though I knew, really knew, and tried to convince myself that I knew, that the body wasn't really him anyway. That he was gone.

I remember being comforted by the cemetery's green grass and trees, which were in the peak of autumn, their leaves dying in vibrant orange and yellow. When I was a kid, skipping around the graves and past the lines of tombstones, I thought that all that nature was wasted on dead people. But now I knew better. The pretty grass and trees and flowers were not for the dead but for the survivors. I wanted to lie down in a pile of crunchy leaves and stay there for a few days.

When we got home, after everything was over, Marty, the dog, looked really depressed, as if he knew Daddy wasn't coming home again. I was depressed, too, though I still hadn't cried. I was exhausted from three days of smiling at my father's friends and relatives. I couldn't wait to go to sleep. I gave Marty a pat and looked over at the clock radio to see what time it was. And there, on top of the radio, was the lottery ticket that I had brought home for my father the night he died. He hadn't seen it, and now he never would.

That's when I started crying, and couldn't stop. I cried in giant heaves, like when I was little, like the times Aunt Katie told me my eyes would shrink. I tried to catch my breath, but the tears kept coming, in waves. I cried for hours, the autumn afternoon turning to night, the stars coming out over our Summit Avenue porch. Between sobs, I took the Pick-It ticket off the clock radio, smashed it into a ball, then threw it away in the kitchen garbage. I didn't even bother to check it against the winning lottery numbers.

Now that Daddy was gone, I couldn't really move out. My plans for westward expansion were over. Stanley had gotten married a year earlier and soon had his first child, Nicole. My sister was busy with her own family. That left me to worry full-time about my mother.

Ma not only fell into a depression; she had to have major gallbladder surgery. She was sure she was going to go next to meet Daddy in the great beyond. It was my job to make sure she didn't. For years, she had scraped together tuition money, raised the cash to send me to Italy, and protected me from a life of crime. I loved my mother. She never asked me to stay. But I felt that sticking around was the least I could do.

Most of all, I was afraid to leave her. I wasn't just afraid that she would die. I was afraid of my own life for the first time. Just when I thought I had it all figured out, life came up from behind and kicked me right in the ass. I had seen death and tragedy and sorrow—our family had so much of it—but it always seemed to be whirling around me, never really touching me. Daddy dying left me stunned for the first time in my life.

Some fortunate nights, I even forgot he was gone. Waking up in the early morning, I thought I could still hear him shuffling in the kitchen, sneaking a coconut cupcake or some Sara Lee cheesecake. But then the reality would hit me that I would never see him again, and Daddy would die all over again for me, my soul curling back up into a ball and weighing me down in bed like a heavy stone.

I was stuck in Hudson County for the rest of my life, too crippled to limp away. The farthest I could crawl was Weehawken, where a friend and I rented a crummy, steamy attic apartment. Though I moved in on Independence Day, I felt no spine tingles of freedom. My street corner was almost as bad as the Majestic corner I'd grown up on. There was even a group of guys who played conga drums across the street in summer. I didn't feel a bit nostalgic.

Since I wasn't going anywhere, I completely surrendered and took a job at *The Jersey Journal*. People in Jersey City always made fun of the paper. They called it a rag and joked that the proofreaders were blind.

The office was housed in an old five-story building on Journal Square, one that I had passed thousands of times in my life. I had never once dreamed of working there. On top of the building stood the unlucky thirteen battered red letters that spelled out the paper's name. The bottom two floors were reserved for the press, which made the building shudder at night. To get to the newsroom, I had to take the elevator to the third floor. I could see that it had once been state-of-the-art, with its big silver buttons and turquoise walls. But that was sometime back in the 1960s.

After the short elevator ride back in time, I stepped out into an even deeper time warp. I had to walk down an eerily quiet, shaftlike hallway devoid of color. Everything was dingy off-white and brown, with a few old gray filing cabinets thrown in for variety. Though it wasn't dirty, *The Jersey Journal*'s office seemed dusty, as if the newsprint from the press seeped through the floorboards into the rest of the building. It was hard to breathe.

In the long hallway, there were wooden doors with windows of frosted glass, with company names stenciled on them, like something out of a movie from the 1940s. I expected to see the name Sam Spade stenciled on one. Instead, at the very end of the absurdly long hallway, I found a door that said KNEWSROOM. Some joker had drawn a K in front of NEWSROOM.

As soon as I walked through that door and into the windowless knewsroom, I knew I wasn't like the other young reporters who were sitting at their computers, busy writing the day's stories. They were all just passing through on their way to somewhere else, like the Jersey City coal cars and freight trains whose contents were destined for fancy homes in New York. The other reporters were Columbia Journalism School graduates or people from Ohio or Colorado who thought that Hudson County was an exciting place to work. I had arrived by default.

My desk was right near the front door, so I could run out if I ever got up the gumption to leave. But I had a feeling I never would. I had walked the long shaft of the hallway, and now I was trapped.

The knewsroom was divided into two camps: the newcomers and the old-timers. I wasn't sure which camp I fit into. Sometimes both; usually neither. I looked like a newcomer, but I felt like one of the old-timers. The new reporters called them B&Rs, for *born and raised*. When the young reporters used phrases like that in front of me, it was as if I were an undercover agent. *I* was born and raised, I wanted to shout at them. But was I bragging or complaining?

One B&R had lumps all over his body. There was the mumbling copy editor, who barked like a dog, and the narcoleptic, who would fall asleep at his desk while typing; the guy with the perpetual neck brace; the reporter with a truss who hadn't had a byline since 1968, on a byline strike for a cause long forgotten; the guy who resembled a cadaver—he'd just forgotten to lie down; the reporter who chewed on his tongue when he talked to you; and the sixty-year-old night editor with the mohawk, who wore leather and chains.

They all scared me until I got to know them better. Eccentrics like them were slowly being edged out by smart-asses like me who had studied journalism in school. But we had a lot to learn.

I was hired as the new police reporter, replacing a guy who went on to work for the mayor's office. In days of yore, he would have simply

taken on both jobs, with the editor's blessing. But things were changing. The year before I arrived, the new editor, Steve Newhouse, fired a
reporter for being on the city payroll. *The Jersey Journal* wasn't *The New
York Times,* but it had its standards.

Each day, it was my job to cover crime, fires, and all the other
breaking bad news in Hudson County. I was a very busy person, since
there was always an abundance of bad news. As the police reporter, it
was my job to interview people on the worst day of their lives. The police beat was like an extended hell week—the job the editors gave new
recruits to see if they could take it. If you survived the Jersey City police, you could survive anything.

Every morning, I called the precincts to see how many horrible
things had happened overnight. One morning, a cop picked a fight
with me over the phone about a story someone else had written. I
fought right back and called him an asshole before hanging up on him.
George Latanzio, my city editor, had to field the cop's complaint minutes later. When he finished calming the desk sergeant, George hung
up politely and walked over to my desk. He was not smiling.

"Next time you have a fight with a cop," he instructed, "hang up
first, then call him an asshole." George smiled.

To check up on my phone leads, every afternoon I drove around to
all the precincts and read the police blotters. At the downtown
precinct, there was a desk sergeant who liked to give me a hard time. I
tried to pretend he didn't bother me.

"Anything happen today?" I would ask, day after day, in as chipper
a mood as I could dredge up from my shrinking, defeated soul.

"There was a rape," he said one day as some of the other officers
looked on. "Why don't you come in the back and I'll tell you about it?"

I took a deep breath. I had had it with this guy.

"You dirty old man," I said, loud enough so the others would hear.
"What makes you think anybody would even look at you twice, never
mind touch you, you pervert?" The other cops applauded and laughed.
I bowed and walked out.

I put on a tough show. But day after day, whether I was on the street
chasing down a story or at my desk in the claustrophobic knewsroom,
I felt like I was drowning. When I was out reporting, I bumped into

guys from grammar school who were now cops, whose faces I never wanted to see again, but whose hairlines I watched slowly recede week after week. I knew some streets so intimately, I could tell you where the cracks were and how many gum marks pocked the sidewalk.

Every time I referred to the paper, I had to catch myself and edit my words before they left my crooked lips. The other young reporters called the paper the *Journal,* a pretentious name that was usually reserved for *The Wall Street Journal.* When I was around them, I did the same thing. But like everyone born and raised in Jersey City, I wanted to call the paper the *Jersey.* I pronounced it with an accent, dropping the *r* just enough to betray that I was from this awful place. Some old-timers actually called it the *Joisey.* They were the same people who called the toilet the *terlit* and the refrigerator the *frigidaire* or the *icebox.*

What you called the paper was an easy test to see who was from here and who, luckily, was not. *Jersey* or *Journal?* I was very conflicted. The paper was, in spirit, the *Jersey.* It contained all that was wrong with Jersey City, wrapped up in a nice little ink-stained package that could be read well within an hour. Most readers thumbed right past the stories we wrote and headed straight to the obituaries, to see which of their friends and enemies had died.

Writing obituaries was the only job more depressing than mine. Each day, the poor guy with that job had to write one feature to lead the page, to try to make one dead person's sad life sound interesting. The obit writer, Wendell, didn't come in until 4 P.M., and for the first couple of hours he would use a desk in the back of the knewsroom, in the Lifestyles section of the paper. We called that section Life and Death. When I left after deadline, at around 7 P.M., Wendell would come and work at my desk at the front of the knewsroom. On my way out, I could hear him making the phone rounds, calling all the funeral parlors in the county, including Bromirski's.

We often covered the same dead people in our stories, but since we worked different shifts, we barely waved at each other. The first conversation we ever had was about a story that came to be known as the Knife-Toss Murder. While writing the victim's obituary, Wendell realized that the guy was only twenty-nine years old. He asked the funeral director what had happened.

"You better talk to the cops," the funeral director told him.

Since I was the police reporter, Wendell asked me about it. I had just written the news story, so I gladly filled him in. A couple of guys in a Bayonne tavern were sitting on their stools, taking turns tossing a knife at a balloon floating above the bar to see if they could pop it, when the knife bounced off a glass hanging over the bar and landed in one guy's neck, puncturing his jugular vein. He died within seconds as his buddies helplessly watched. The prosecutor indicted the friend who had tossed the knife, as if seeing his buddy bleed to death wasn't punishment enough.

It was a terrible story, but it was fascinating in a gruesome sort of way. I spoke animatedly about it, waving my arms and talking with my hands, like I always did, trying to describe how it all happened, the angle at which the knife came flying down, and how stupid and senseless the whole thing was. And how stupid and senseless the prosecutor was.

That's how Wendell and I met. After the Knife-Toss Murder, whenever Wendell came to sit at my desk at the end of my shift, we would chat about that day's horror stories. One afternoon, Wendell came in a little early and we went on our first date, to Boulevard Drinks. The hot dogs and Journal Square were all new to him.

The Square was just as nasty as it had been when I was growing up. Maybe even worse. The bums were replaced by what everyone now referred to as the homeless. I wondered what had happened to Mary, the woman with the dirty raincoat. Had she gotten to wherever it was she was hurrying off to? The midgets selling the newspaper had disappeared. But they were replaced by a woman who looked like the Fat Lady at the circus, and a parade of misfits like characters out of a Fellini film. The crippled pencil seller was still there, as were the vast army of freaks with growths and tumors and the mumblers who walked around arguing with themselves. I was sure I was destined to become one of them.

To try and avoid my sad fate, I got out of town as much as I possibly could, taking my first paid vacation to Miami. It was the first time

I'd gone alone to Aunt Mary Ann's. I thought the visit might give us a chance to bond and compare our many similarities—how I was skepti-cal about marriage and cynical about everything else, how I wanted to escape from Jersey City like she had so long ago. But before I got the chance to tell her, Aunt Mary Ann told me that I was just like my mother when she was in her early twenties. She couldn't believe how much I looked like her, sounded like her, and acted like her. Ma had even wanted to be a reporter at one time.

I'd had no idea. Like most kids, I selfishly assumed that my mother had no ambition before she had me. I figured she liked Jersey City. But maybe she was stuck here because of us. It wasn't easy to pack up and run with three kids.

I came back to *The Jersey Journal* a bit wiser and with a deep tan. But it soon faded. On my next vacation, I took a road trip along the West Coast with Wendell, my new boyfriend. The following fall we took a trip to Paris. Those vacations didn't last nearly as long as I would have liked. The following Monday, we'd end up back in the dusty knewsroom.

Wendell, who loved newspapers, didn't mind *The Jersey Journal* half as much as I did, and he almost convinced me I was lucky to work there. He got me to watch the press run, its clanging, inky parts mirac-ulously belching out our words and bylines in a continuous blur. For about fifteen minutes, I was happy to be at the paper. But I hated Jer-sey City too much.

Around this time, strangely enough, Hudson County started to look a little better, around the edges anyway. While I had been at NYU, the brownstones on Mercer Street were restored as gentrification replaced urban blight. In the late 1980s, Jersey City had become a bedroom community, after years of being a toilet (pronounced *ter-lit*). I wasn't sure which made me more angry, yuppies or drug dealers.

The waterfront's burnt-out piers were being magically transformed into prime real estate for back-office space. New glass office towers were erected in Jersey City and Weehawken. Sidewalk cafés bloomed in Hoboken. Parks were built along the Hudson River. A mall was even constructed near the Holland Tunnel, in a development called New-port. In an effort to separate themselves from Jersey City, though, the developers asked for their own Zip code and tried to leave Jersey City out of their address altogether. They tried to say the mall was in Newport City, a fictional place. I was outraged, and suddenly felt protective of Jersey City.

But Jersey City's planning board, bribes or no bribes, wouldn't let that one slip past. Newport would take advantage of the city's tax abatements, so it sure as hell would keep the name Jersey City in its address. And be proud of it.

Working as a reporter, I knew a little too much of what was going on behind the scenes. I wished I could just sit back and enjoy the new waterfront walkways, cafés, marinas, and boutiques along with most of the other Jersey Citizens. But some people were suffering because of the development, and I felt more comfortable suffering along with them. It was my nature.

In 1989, the Colgate factory was closed to make room for a new development project, devastating a large part of the downtown worker population—Stanley included. He had worked there for nine years and was forced to leave his job as a warehouseman. I was assigned to cover a worker résumé-writing meeting. I wanted to interview the president of Colgate so I could punch him out. How could I be objective when my brother was getting canned?

The counselors on hand were encouraging the workers to relocate to Kansas City, to the Colgate plant there, where several of Stanley's friends got replacement jobs. But Stanley stayed and got a job in a machine shop in Rutherford. Good thing. A year after they relocated, his friends were laid off and left jobless in Kansas City, a strange new land, where they had just taken out mortgages on new houses.

It was another lesson in why you should never move away. You'd just wind up back in Jersey City, defeated.

Aside from the factory closings, I tried to convince myself it was generally a good thing that the waterfront was finally being developed after years of languishing under the control of corrupt politicians and rich railroad companies. But I knew that in typical Hudson County fashion, shortcuts were being taken, not to mention bribes and kickbacks.

When Newport Mall was built, construction crews forgot to bait for rats, so an army of rodents invaded downtown—just like in Gam-montown's heyday. A pack of rats ran past the candy counter in one of the mall department stores one afternoon. Then a small boy was bitten while sitting on the toilet in his own home, in the mall neighborhood. The rat had come up through the pipes and into his bowl. Firefighters visited nearby St. Anthony's High School, where Paula worked as a teacher, to make sure the nuns had all their toilet seats covered.

The Newport rats were only the first round of development woes. While Hudson's politicians turned their heads, buildings were con-structed on top of and next to contaminated land left over from Jersey City's industrial glory days. But people were so used to hearing about toxic waste that they simply shrugged. If they weren't dead by now, they were probably immune, they thought. Everytime I looked at Hud-son County's rising skyline, its blue and green gleaming buildings growing taller each day, all I could think of were the dirty deals the politicians were making.

I wound up uncovering stories about the toxic waste that lay be-neath lots I had played in as a kid. I had memories of playing bartender in one of those lots, pouring dirt—now known to be contaminated—into a Coke bottle while my brother played baseball a few yards away.

Cancer-causing chromium was buried all over Hudson County, left behind by three companies that produced chemicals for paint, ceram-ics, and ink. Sodium dichromate, their main product, was used for the ink on money. Gammontown was one of the few neighborhoods in the city that contained no chromium, simply because the adjoining brown-stones there, crowded together with no empty lots in between, were built long before the city starting burying tons of the industrial slag.

But the downtown school where Hague had been hit by an egg back in 1949 was built next to a chromium dump. The Liberty Science Center, a showcase for the entire East Coast, visited by 850,000 kids, teachers, and parents each year, was built on top of a contaminated parcel of land owned by the state. Before construction, the site was covered over with clean soil and deemed safe by the state Department of Environmental Protection.

I wrote stories about chromium found under the drive-in where Stanley had taken his dates, under the Gregory Apartments, where my best friend, Liz, had lived. Chromium stalactites dripped from the ceiling of the newly renovated Newport PATH station, where I had waited for trains to NYU. A friend and fellow reporter, Dan Rosenfeld, collected some of the crud in a jar and had it tested. He found that the chromium levels were dangerously high. The DEP did its own test and pronounced the station safe.

I covered the chromium stories as if I were on a mission. Which I was.

Objectivity was never an issue.

I remember having an argument with the flack for a Society Hill development project planned for the old Roosevelt Stadium site, next door to the biggest chromium site in the city, where a million tons of waste lay buried and covered over. The flack accused me of having a chip on my shoulder. I wanted to dig up the contaminated dirt and shove it down his throat. That Beansie temper was rising. And the more I learned, the angrier I became.

Some friends and I, frustrated that the DEP would never get anything done, banded together and formed a guerrilla group called Chromium Underground. We stenciled the name at unmarked tainted sites using spray paint the color of chromium slag—fluorescent green. We made flyers designed like PATH newsletters and handed them to commuters outside the cruddy train station.

One night, during one of our spray-paint runs, an off-duty cop on his way home from the precinct stopped his car, pulled out his badge, and asked us what the hell we thought we were doing. We weren't your typical graffiti artists but three smug white women in our twenties.

When I saw his badge, all I could think was how much a conflict of interest this was for me, how *The Jersey Journal* would fire me when they found out I was spray-painting messages at night about subjects I was writing about during the day.

"Officer," I said, trying to sound respectful. "There's chromium buried on this lot and we just wanted people to know that it's here, so . . ."

"I know all about chromium," the cop said, waving at me to shorten the speech. "I'm an environmentalist too." He looked around at the empty streets. "Just hurry up, before somebody else sees you."

He pulled his Pontiac Firebird out onto Grand Street, and left us standing there, spray paint in hand, in disbelief. "Nice cop," I said, ashamed at myself for thinking that was an oxymoron.

Since I had such a problem with authority, objectivity, and keeping my opinions to myself, the wise editors at *The Jersey Journal* gave me my own weekly column. I could pick my subject matter from a wide variety of everyday scandals and then complain about it as much as I liked. As long as it all fit inside nineteen inches.

It was a lucky break, since continuing to cover crime would have been a major conflict of interest. To get back on her feet, my mother had applied for a job as a file clerk in the prosecutor's office. When she went for the interview, she was asked about her relationship to the criminals in the family. A background check was part of the usual procedure for the prosecutor's staff. They asked Ma if she was related to Beansie. Was Henry Stapinski her husband? Satisfied with her answers, the investigators hired my mother. It was her first non-DMV job in more than twenty years. .

After a few months, the prosecutor's biggest fear wasn't whether Ma would tip off any criminals during an investigation but whether she was tipping off her daughter at *The Jersey Journal*. I kept my distance, though, with my new beat. Ma had been through enough. I didn't want her to lose her job because of me.

I chose my subjects—and my causes—carefully. The Loew's Theatre, my childhood refuge, was in danger of being torn down. The thought of a wrecking ball bashing through its coffered ceilings and golden-tiled alcoves made me feel woozy. So I covered that story. Hartz Mountain Industries—makers of dog collars and the corporate parks that had replaced Secaucus's pig farms—wanted to replace the theater with an office building. The theater had closed in 1983 after showing its final unlucky movie, the last installment of *Friday the 13th*.

I attended more than a dozen planning-board meetings, where the fate of the theater was being decided. Jersey City's few political activists—Joe Duffy, Ted Conrad, and Colin Egan—organized a preservation committee to save the Loew's. It was because of people like them, who were still fighting the good fight, that Jersey City had any bright spots left.

While at the paper, I got to know Ted well. He was an architect and lived in a plantation-style house in the Heights, overlooking the Hudson River. His home was filled with architectural models he had built over the years and refurbished antique car seats from the 1950s and 1960s that he had mounted and which he used as love seats. He was tall and lumbering and often wore a cap over his white hair and suspenders to hold up his drooping pants. Ted drove a banana yellow Cadillac and loved to take me out to lunch, where he would fill me in on the latest worthy cause. He lectured me in his gravelly voice and begged me never to leave Jersey City.

Joe Duffy was the physical opposite of Ted. He was a small, nervous ball of energy, with glasses and a combed-over strand of hair that fell in his face when he became agitated. He walked very quickly and carried around a huge stack of documents and newspaper clippings. Joe always seemed flustered, but he was on the ball and got right to the point.

Joe and Ted made sure that every planning-board meeting was packed with people like me, with fond memories of the Loew's.

The Stanley Theatre had been saved by Jehovah's Witnesses, who had turned it into a Kingdom Hall. It was one of life's ironies that the Stanley, the theater that had showcased a naughty Bill Holden and the rabble-rousing music of Bill Haley and the Comets, wound up in the hands of evangelical Christians. Working their way into heaven with each brush stroke and swipe of a rag, the Jehovah's Witnesses shined the copper outside, refurbished the cloud-covered ceiling inside, and painted clothes on naked cherubs and classical figures. But at least they had managed to save the theater from the wrecking ball, something Ted, Colin, and Joe were trying desperately to do with the Loew's.

Ted had successfully saved the old domed Hudson County courthouse, a palatial marble masterpiece, with a rotunda painted in the high classical style, with angels and signs of the zodiac floating in delicate colors above.

Two other activists, Morris Pesin and Audrey Zapp, had saved the historic railroad terminal, through which Vita and Irene had passed a century ago. While everyone was focused on preserving Ellis Island, Audrey and Morris knew that the railroad terminal was sacred ground, too. If not for them, the terminal would be a pile of rubble at the water's edge.

Some buildings were beyond saving, like the old Margaret Hague maternity hospital. It sat abandoned on Clifton Place, sad and haunted looking, its windows broken and doors boarded up, not a newborn baby in sight. The rest of the Medical Center was in rough shape as well. In 1982, the public hospital went bankrupt. Since then, the new, private owners had been trying desperately to find a location for a new state-of-the-art facility. Meanwhile, asbestos was found. Concrete was eroding. Then, in 1991, a brick fell from one of the buildings, totaling a car below. Roofs leaked, floors sagged, and walls cracked. The building's boilers were so antiquated that hospital workers had to make their own replacement parts. Since there were only a few elevators, patients on their way to surgery would often ride up with hospital visitors. Hague's grand Art Deco masterpiece was obsolete. But there were other structures in Jersey City that were worse.

In 1990, *The Jersey Journal* staff covered the closing of the sixty-four-year-old Hudson County jailhouse, one of the most overcrowded and decrepit in the nation, where inmates were beaten to death and a fire had killed seven prisoners. Inmates were always trying to escape. You really couldn't blame them. Three of them succeeded one night, tying bedsheets together and dropping down from the fourth floor onto heavily trafficked Pavonia Avenue, right next door to the courthouse, where my mother and all the judges worked.

Some days I felt like one of those prisoners, waiting for the warden to turn his head so that I could leap out the window on my bedsheets. I was the only reporter, I realized, whose relatives had spent considerable time inside the jail. My mother had waved up to Grandpa from Pavonia Avenue when she was a child. He had waved back from behind bars.

No one complained when the jail was finally destroyed—least of all me and my family, who were happy to see a bit of our criminal history crumble.

The building that brought me—and the city—the most grief, though, was the Union Terminal Cold Storage, where Daddy had worked, the big red building at the mouth of the Holland Tunnel that I saw every time I drove to New York. The building was still standing, but it had closed soon after my father died, its big refrigerator switch flipped to OFF. The abandoned building reminded me of more innocent times: eating stolen lobster tails that Daddy cooked and slathered in butter and lemon; cases of shrimp and steaks; the dry ice for our Halloween parties.

The city's board of health closed the warehouse down after ammonia leaked from a faulty cooling system and sickened some of the toll collectors. They vomited and had to be evacuated. But when the building was closed, someone forgot to remove the 10 million pounds of frozen food inside. Oozing calamari and decaying frog's legs were finally hauled out in the sweltering month of August. Special chemicals were spread to cover up the odor.

The smell lived on. For nearly two years, the wretched stench of rotten fish was the first thing that hit you when you got anywhere near the Holland Tunnel. The approach ramp was unbearable. It was worse than the Newark bone-rendering smell on a bad day—much worse—and forced drivers to close their windows when the wind blew the wrong way. I thought the odor wafted over from the river, from a large pile of dead fish murdered by the PCBs in the water.

Even worse than the smell were the flies and rats that invaded the tunnel toll booths like the ten plagues that had invaded biblical Egypt. It wasn't long before some unlucky son of a bitch discovered the origin of the smell and the flies: One last freezer full of thawed fish had been left inside the building and thousands of bloated, foot-long rats had eaten themselves to death. Food poisoning, experts said.

It turned out the one locker had not been emptied because a three-foot ice floe had frozen outside its door. The ice was no challenge for the rats. An army of them gnawed through that, and then the six-inch layer of insulation around the locker, to get to the rotting treasure inside. Men in moon suits were called in to clean up the mess. They made the front page of *The Jersey Journal*. I tried to imagine what their job was like.

I wasn't sure there was such a thing as heaven. But now I knew there was a hell.

The story ran for several days, with follow-ups about the president of the cold-storage company, who was arrested, spent the night in jail, and was released on a half-million dollars' bail. To get sprung, he had to put up his house—in suburban New Milford, not smelly old Jersey City. The charges against him were dropped after he agreed to pay for the cleanup and the $10,000 extermination bill to get rid of the last of the living rats.

It was one of the worst stories I'd ever heard. But it aptly described Jersey City—the incompetence, the neglect, the extreme ugliness—so close yet so far from wondrous New York City, threatening to wipe out even the tiniest fond memories I had of home.

I was glad Daddy wasn't alive to read about it.

16

ON TRIAL

For most of *The Jersey Journal*'s reporters, covering City Hall was like going to the circus for the first time: The death-defying acts and walks on the high wire were too amazing to be believed. There were clowns and midgets and even a ring master.

I felt too old and jaded for the circus. I had been to the menagerie, after all, with Daddy. I had smelled the lions and tigers up close and had fed peanuts to the elephants. By the time I started working at the paper, I had witnessed quite a bit from that Majestic apartment seat, high above the ring.

Still, I knew that the current mayor, a good man and a dapper dresser named Anthony Cucci, made sensational headlines only once while in office—after visiting Jersey City's sister city, Cuzco, Peru. (Jersey City had sister cities in places like Korea, Italy, the Philippines, China, and India, to reflect its cultural diversity. Because of a growing Peruvian population, Cuzco was chosen as the latest sibling.) While Cucci was there, visiting with Cuzco's mayor, their train derailed. Both the mayors' wives were killed. Though the deaths were first blamed on the Shining Path guerrilla group, it was later learned that the train's driver was simply drunk.

Cucci's tragedy was cited as yet another example of why you should never leave the confines of Hudson County.

To get into office, Cucci had beaten Gerald McCann, who had been mayor from 1981 to 1985. The two had been allies and were so close that people called them McCucci. But they were now sworn enemies.

McCann was a throwback to the old days of Democratic machine rule. He was the 1980s version, with a designer suit and an interest in a Florida savings-and-loan. When he ran against Cucci in 1985, off-duty cops, illegally carrying guns, were positioned at the polls, set to challenge black and Latino voters who came to cast their ballots. More than 1,400 would-be voters sued McCann, claiming that he had cheated them of their right to vote. McCann settled his case, paying out half a million dollars in damages.

After he beat McCann, Cucci scheduled his swearing-in ceremony for midnight, in a rush to get into office as quickly as possible. McCann was on a rampage, forcing people to resign at the last minute and filling city board seats with political appointments. Right after Cucci took his midnight oath at City Hall, a bomb scare sent him and his aides running from the building and out onto Grove Street. When Cucci returned early the next morning, the mayor's complex was a stinking mess: desks and chairs were overturned; rugs were soaked with urine and human feces; glue had been squirted into the locks of most of the office doors. A locksmith was called in.

A file cabinet was missing; Cucci could tell by the imprint left in the piss-stained carpet. There was talk that documents had been shredded, but no one could prove it. The mess was cleaned up, but for months Cucci was reminded of the McCann regime by a big urine stain that remained. Cucci finally got new rugs.

McCann denied relieving himself in the mayor's office. But everyone blamed him and his cronies. He was a class act.

I had never met Hague or Kenny, but I imagined that McCann was cut from the same dirty cloth. He never really looked at you when he spoke to you. His eyes had a busy, nervous jump to them, almost like a rabbit's. They always seemed to be scoping out the rest of the room, darting over your head, past your shoulder—even when he was the one doing the talking. Before he became a politician, McCann had been an accountant. His fingers, and the rest of his mind and body, seemed to be twitching with nervous energy, adding up imaginary figures from big scores he hadn't yet made.

McCann's voice was in the whine family. He rarely conversed. He told you what he had to say in a condescending drone, as if you were an idiot. You always felt as if you were wasting his time, like he had somewhere he had to be and something really important he had to do. He made me, and everyone I knew, feel very uneasy.

What made us most uneasy was that McCann ran again in the 1989 election. Nine other candidates ran against him, including my cousin Mike, who was giving it one more go-around, running on his tax platform. The city's home owners were facing a revaluation of their property, evening out the chips in the poker game that Mike had tried to explain decades ago. People in the Heights and downtown, whose taxes had been unfairly low for years, were now getting hit with huge bills to make up for lower taxes in other neighborhoods. They had to ante up.

As much as Mike tried to lead the reval bandwagon, it was too late for him. Waterfront development, his baby, had already grown up in Jersey City. Telling people "I told you so" when their tax bills came in the mail wasn't enough to get him elected. Mike had other solutions, but as usual, his complicated economics included state tax reform and shot way over everybody's head.

I covered the 1989 election but kept my distance from Mike's ticket. I figured it was a conflict of interest to write about him. Besides, I couldn't even understand what he was talking about half the time. I was assigned to follow one of the front-runners, a black guy who made it into a runoff election with McCann. Glenn Cunningham was a former cop, a decent, honest man who had been a city councilman for years.

He didn't stand a chance.

At one political debate, Cunningham questioned McCann about his lavish lifestyle. McCann lived in Jersey City's most exclusive waterfront development, Port Liberte, which was so close to Lady Liberty that McCann could stick his head out his window and practically kiss her ass. It was a gated community built along canals that separated one cluster of pastel-colored homes from another, which gave it the nickname Venice on the Hudson. It even had its own private ferry to Manhattan. Since he had enough money to live in a place like that, everyone at *The Jersey Journal* suspected that McCann was somehow on the take.

When Cunningham suggested that McCann was up to no good, the audience at the mayoral debate applauded McCann, not Cunningham, and shouted "good for him." Why shouldn't McCann steal money and live in Port Liberte if he could? It was only natural. He should take what he could get while the gettin' was good. It was because of people like them that McCann was elected to a second term.

At first I thought the only explanation for McCann's victory was that voters, overwhelmed by the number of choices, went with the most familiar Irish face, that there was no way a black man was going to get into office. I blamed racism. But now I think their decision was even more stupid than that: Jersey City's voters missed being abused. It didn't feel like home without a criminal in office.

Midway through his second term, Mayor McCann was charged with defrauding money through a scheme that involved a failed Florida savings-and-loan. He was indicted for mail fraud, bank fraud, tax evasion, making false statements to the IRS, and failure to file his taxes. The day he was indicted, McCann called a press conference and hurled excuses, his face growing red and his forehead dripping with sweat. He blamed the Republican party, which, he said, was out to get Democrats like himself so they could cover up the crimes of the Bush family. He blamed Attorney General Dick Thornburgh for using the indictment to boost his Senate run in Pennsylvania.

McCann, playing by the dirty Jersey City rules, didn't simply proclaim his innocence. He lobbed insults at the prosecutor, Michael Chertoff. "It will become obvious that they were insane to bring this case in the first place," he declared. "And we are going to send Mr. Chertoff back to preparing wills. Maybe I can find him a job driving a sanitation truck in Jersey City."

I covered the trial in Trenton every day, usually poking fun at McCann in print. Each morning I had to face his parents, who sat in the front row of the courtroom looking worried and sad. I would have felt better had they yelled at me. But they looked like such kind, God-fearing people. How had they raised such a shyster? Whenever I felt a pang of guilt about the scathing stories I wrote about their son, I would convince myself that McCann had gotten himself into this mess. It wasn't my fault he was a criminal.

Once he got on the witness stand, I felt a little less guilty. His testimony contradicted the testimony of his own accountant, and he often talked right over the arguments of his own attorney. He admitted that when he doctored his tax returns, he scratched a message to the IRS in the margin: "Come and visit me."

Chertoff used McCann's arrogance to paint a vivid, convincing portrait of 1980s greed. McCann was a liar, a con artist, and a thief, who used hundreds of thousands of dollars that were not his to purchase a Mercedes-Benz, rabbit furs, rare coins, stamps, and $7,000 in tickets to sporting events. He attended football games with the likes of Donald Trump and Roy Cohn.

Even when testimony got bogged down with tax and banking jargon, the trial would be brightened by the spectators who watched from beyond the red velvet rope separating them from the accused. The courtroom was always filled with a character or two, including one old lady who took McCann's side—and a one-hundred-dollar cab ride down to the courthouse to support him. She was one of the legions of Jersey City mumblers and wackos, openly voicing her opinions in court. She reminded me of the old woman who would yell at the statues at OLC Church. One afternoon, after Chertoff danced all over McCann in his cross-examination, she yelled out, "He doesn't even look like a lawyer. He looks like a shrimp." The judge pounded his gavel and demanded order in the court, but by then everyone was laughing.

It was Hudson County theater at its best.

The afternoon the verdict was announced, McCann stood silently, his face as red as his leather chair. The jury foreman stood as well, then calmly said, "Guilty," repeating the word fourteen more times, once after each of the charges. Each time the foreman said the word, McCann's face grew a little redder, until it looked as if it might pop like a big blister, right off his shoulders. McCann was convicted of fifteen counts of fraud, including swindling the S&L out of $300,000, evading income taxes, and covering up his crimes with lies. He was acquitted of one count of mail fraud.

When it was all over, his poor mother sobbed quietly into a tissue. McCann's bodyguard—the former *Jersey Journal* police reporter, whom I had replaced—ran interference, knocking reporters out of the way as the mayor made his way from the courthouse. When he got to the front steps, McCann made no cracks about sanitation trucks, no excuses about the Bush family. His only words were a testy "Where's the car?"

The prosecutor got one last shot in, though. "All of Mr. McCann's insults and offers of jobs driving garbage trucks don't really count for much now," said Chertoff. He would go on to bigger and better things—pursuing President Clinton on his Whitewater dealings.

Clinton got off. But McCann went to jail.

Even after he got out, McCann tried to run for mayor again. And had a large group of supporters. I figured Jersey City deserved him. Luckily, a judge ruled that McCann couldn't hold office. My mother was in the courtroom that day as part of her job. She did a small, celebratory jig.

———

Since my mother worked in the prosecutor's office, I avoided covering most court cases. The only other trial I covered while at *The Jersey Journal* was a Mafia case that was tried at the federal courthouse in Newark. I looked forward to taking the PATH train there every day. Newark had a cool, 1930s-era subway system, with WPA art on the walls. There was a towering Gothic cathedral, and blooming cherry trees in its sprawling park, fresh pink and green amid the urban decay. I realized just how sad Jersey City was when Newark was a noticeable step up.

The city's razor-wire fences and graffiti were balanced by its abandoned, but still grand Art Deco buildings. It was tired and worn, but I got a sense that something great had once happened there. It even had a real skyline. Jersey City, with the slogan "Everything for Industry," had only the decaying Medical Center, abandoned factories, and contaminated playgrounds as reminders of the good old days.

Going to Newark for the Mafia trial was also a chance to get away

from disturbing personal subject matter: no chromium, Colgate development, Loew's Theatre fights, or Cold Storage memories.

My family was filled with criminals, but at least they weren't mobsters. Grandpa was once hauled in for questioning when gangster
Frank Costello was called to testify in the 1950s. He got all dressed up
for his "interview," feeling like a big shot, connected in the slightest
way to a kingpin like Costello. But Grandpa didn't know anything. He
wished he did. Every day after his interview, Grandpa sat glued to the
television, watching the Costello Senate hearings.

The case I was assigned in Newark revolved around a Hudson
County gang accused of racketeering. Their leader was charged with
ordering the murder of a New York businessman, Irwin "the Fat Man"
Schiff. He weighed over 350 pounds and had been shot gangland-
style, twice in the head, while eating his banana flambé at Bravo Ser-
gio, an Upper East Side restaurant. A mysterious blonde who had
dined with him that night and had fled the scene showed up as a prosecution witness.

Attending the trial was like watching *The Godfather.* Except better.
This was for real—and my family had nothing to do with it.

There was a petite brunette who fingered one of the mobsters in
court as we all held our collective breath. The other reporters and I
were seated in the first row, and we watched as she nervously testified
that she made eye contact with the guy the night of Schiff's murder.
He had been standing at the back door of the restaurant, keeping
watch, to make sure the murder was carried out, when the brunette
came down from her apartment to take out her garbage.

During a break in the testimony, the fingered man, Richard "Bocci"
DiSciscio of Bayonne, turned his head to get a look at the clock at the
back of the courtroom and accidentally made eye contact with me. His
eyes, dark and empty, bore right through mine to the back of my skull.
I hoped I never bumped into him in a dark alley while throwing out the
trash. I found myself rooting for the prosecution.

Bocci wasn't the only one who made me nervous. The lead defen-
dant was Bobby Manna, accused of being the head of the Hudson
County mob and the consigliere, or number-three man, in the Gen-
ovese crime family. Manna was the guy who had been placed at

Kenny's disposal years ago, the guy whose father had shot Kenny in the ass. He was also the cousin of my high school boyfriend.

When my mother heard I was covering the trial, she got worried and said, "Don't think he doesn't know who you are. Those guys keep an eye on everybody." But Manna never said a word. He never even looked my way, not like Bocci had.

Manna, Bocci, and their boys—a restaurateur named Marty "Motts" Casella, from Secaucus, and former Hoboken cop Frank "Dipsy" Daniello—were also accused of plotting to murder John Gotti and his brother Gene. Their associate, union leader Rocco "Rocky" Napoli, was charged with conspiracy and labor bribery. The Statue of Liberty was even dragged into the indictment. Manna and his cohorts were accused of instigating a territorial battle with New York unions over control of the Liberty–Ellis Island restoration project.

The least of the charges had to do with illegal gambling. An FBI agent took the stand and explained some of the phrases the jury would be hearing in the gambling portion of the trial. *Runners,* he explained, were at the bottom of the pyramid and dealt with bettors on a day-to-day basis. They would run bets into the office where the numbers were turned in. Uncle Henry had been a runner. *Hit* meant a win, and *overlook* meant that a bookie reneged on a payment. I could have explained all that to the jury.

The best part of the trial were the secretly recorded conversations, taped at the Village Coffee Shop in downtown Jersey City and at Casella's in Hoboken, mostly in the restaurant's "Chariot Room" and the ladies' rest room—used as a private meeting place for the paranoid mobsters. It seemed that very few women frequented Casella's, though I recalled eating dinner there one Christmas Day years ago with my family. My father, tired of the King's Court and Top of the Meadows, had been on a new-restaurant kick and wanted to try Casella's steak. The day we went, the dining room was empty, which we attributed to the holiday. But Casella's was often empty, I learned. Now I knew why.

I wondered if our dinner there was secretly recorded, thrown on the pile of uninteresting, non-Mob-related conversation. Did they have my mother on tape complaining that the rigatoni was overcooked? My pregnant sister worrying aloud about the possibility of varicose veins?

Or my father complaining that the wait staff was rushing us out of there?

Nothing so boring was ever played in court. The dialogue from the tapes we heard was right out of a Martin Scorsese movie. We listened each day with big headphones and followed along with a government transcript. On one tape, a government witness named Vincent "the Fish" Cafaro was overheard telling his wife that he recently had lunch with his mother—who had been dead for the past eighteen years. The defense used that tape as evidence that Cafaro was out of his mind, and therefore an unreliable witness.

Between discussions of hits, the murderous and the gambling kind, the defendants joked on tape about their sexual conquests. Rocky boasted about wanting to give his "mozzarella" to one of his female co-conspirators. Everyone in the courtroom burst out laughing. The only one who kept a straight face—barely—was the judge, Maryann Trump Barry—the sister of Donald Trump. She looked like her brother in a wig and black robe.

In another conversation Rocky complained that he wanted a hot typewriter from a guy nicknamed Trolley Car. "You tell that skinny bastard Trolley Car I want my typewriter. You got two. Richie got two. The other guy got two. And where's mine? I want one." After Rocky got his typewriter, he complained the next day, "Okay. Tell him I need a VCR. Two of 'em."

The most controversial of Rocky's conversations was with Judge Zampella, the guy who had always been such a good friend to Grandpa, the one who brushed my mother off after Grandpa tried to shoot us. The same one who had gotten Grandpa the job in the library, and had let him go that Easter week after he broke all the furniture.

On the Manna tapes, Zampella could be heard saying, "You know, I stopped the investigation and that man has never said thank-you for what I did."

"Ungrateful kid," says Rocky.

In other tapes, Rocky could be overheard discussing how he was getting Zampella's help in expunging his criminal record. "I had Judge Zampella down here the other day," said Rocky. "I know what I'm doing."

He certainly did. In December 1987, Rocky was made an honorary deputy sheriff for Hudson County.

As a result of the tapes, Zampella was forced to step down. He was never charged with any crimes, but stopping investigations for your mobster friends and expunging their criminal records are not the activities a judge is expected to engage in, in his spare time. Not even a judge in Hudson County. My family saw Zampella's fall as karma, his payback for being rude to my mother and Aunt Mary Ann and for failing to keep Grandpa behind bars. He got his. That's what people said about Zampella.

All kinds of people were popping up in the government case: Hoboken policemen, Jersey City police officials, a Hudson County sheriff's officer, an investigator from the Hudson County prosecutor's office who was tipping off the mobsters during gambling raids. Just when I started to have some real fun at the trial, an all too familiar name appeared in the government transcripts. When I read the name, I held my breath and closed my eyes. I had to be seeing things.

I let my breath out, opened my eyes, and looked again. But there it was: cousin Mike's name.

In the August 23, 1987, recording, an unidentified male looking for a lawyer is overheard asking where Mike is. Nothing more. Nothing criminal.

Though Mike wasn't indicted, wasn't on the tapes himself, and wasn't a mobster, he had been a mayoral candidate and was therefore a public figure. I started to panic, right there in the courtroom, wondering if I was supposed to call the office and tell my editor that Mike's name was mentioned in the transcripts. Where was my allegiance?

I suffered a crisis of conscience trying to decide whether to be true to my editor or true to the family. Would I embarrass a relative, one that I actually liked? The mere fact that his name was mentioned, even though it was innocent, could be embarrassing. But it was also news. I thought about those afternoons in Aunt Katie's backyard and the long conversations I had had with Mike about his Norman Rockwell prints and books like *Lord of the Flies*. But that was a long time ago. Was it my responsibility to let the city editor—and the city—know that a former mayoral candidate's name was mentioned in the

Manna tapes? Or should I call Mike and let him know that his name was mentioned?

I did neither.

Instead, I did what Kunegunda did fifty years earlier. I kept my trap shut.

But it didn't matter. Another reporter covering the trial realized who Mike was and wrote a front-page story about Mike's name popping up in the transcripts. In the story, Mike denied any wrongdoing and said he often went to Casella's for dinner, that lots of people did. He even said he planned on calling the prosecutor to offer any help he could.

The Mike story blew over as quickly as it had blown up. No one paid much attention. But I couldn't wait for the Manna trial to be over. Neither could the jury. We were all relieved when Manna and his gang were found guilty. When the foreman delivered the verdict, jurors on either side of him held his legs so he wouldn't fall over.

With the verdict in and the trial finished, I figured I was safe. But Mike's name popped up again, in an AP story I read on the wire one afternoon. This time, Mike was disbarred for misappropriating client funds. Mike's name and picture wound up on the front page of the paper. So did Paula's long, Italian last name. The $20,000 used for the closing on our Summit Avenue house ten years earlier had been part of Mike's "misappropriated funds."

My sister and her husband had no idea that their money had been "misappropriated" and had no clue Mike was being investigated. According to Mike, the problem was discovered during an automatic audit on his account. His biggest crime was simply a matter of "commingling" of funds. In 1977, a law was passed that said lawyers couldn't mix clients' money with their personal money. With the $20,000 in trust, Mike had written checks from the same account.

"Whether you intend to rob them or not, even though no one loses a penny, it's automatic disbarment," Mike explained. "No ifs, ands, or buts."

In his defense, Mike told the Supreme Court of New Jersey he had been having personal problems. His house—the one where we had visited Aunt Katie and where Beansie had been reared—burned down. The rumor was that a bookie threw a Molotov cocktail at it because either Katie or Mike owed him money. Not long after, Mike suffered a broken arm. He had two coronary operations. Chubby killed himself. Uncle Al got cancer. Aunt Katie would go to the Mayo Clinic with him and entertain all the patients on his floor. Many a patient died with a smile on his face because of Aunt Katie—Uncle Al included. Aunt Katie suffered a stroke, but she survived. As if that wasn't enough hard luck, Mike also lost both legs to diabetes.

Mike "endured more grief within several years than many endure in a lifetime," the court found, but "his suffering did not prevent him from knowing what he was doing when he misused client funds."

When I went to visit Mike afterward at his house, the house rebuilt on the ashes of the fire, we chatted about his disbarment, about politics, and about Jersey City. He didn't seem to care that much about being disbarred. He said he hadn't practiced in years anyway, that he'd just done the house closing for Paula because she was a relative. What bothered him more was his inability to run for office because of his health problems. He knew he'd never be elected mayor, and had no plans of running again. But he still had tax-reform ideas that he hoped to share with the governor and other elected officials. Whenever friends and relatives dropped by or called, he tried to explain his complicated theories.

Every time the phone rang while I was there, Mike was very eager to answer it. But each time he rolled his wheelchair over to the phone, one of his prosthetic legs would fall off. I was a nervous wreck the whole afternoon.

"Want me to get that?" I exclaimed each time the phone rang, not sure if I meant the receiver or Mike's leg lying in the middle of the floor.

"No," he joked, bending over, his sense of humor still, miraculously, intact. "It's the only exercise I get."

———

It was getting harder and harder to decide what was newsworthy and what should be kept a family secret. My family popped up yet again in a story about Hudson County voter fraud. During the Secaucus City Council election, an especially scummy politician went a step beyond using the names of the dead to vote in his favor. Patients at Meadow-view Hospital were registered to vote by absentee ballot.

Some of the people at Meadowview didn't know who the president of the United States was. Some didn't even know their own name. Michael Lari, the council candidate who uncovered the scandal and tried to get the votes thrown out, had a list of fifty mentally and emotionally disturbed voters from Meadowview who were taken advantage of. The names weren't published. But *The Jersey Journal* had the list.

Political reporter Pete Weiss noticed a Stapinski name on that list and asked me if I was related. He handed it to me. When I saw Thomas Stapinski and realized what Pete was writing about, my face got hot. I had a vision of some Hudson County political operative conning my severely retarded uncle into scribbling his name and "voting preference" on a ballot. I swallowed hard, gulping down a strong urge to cry.

I hadn't seen Uncle Tommy in a few years, but I knew his condition hadn't improved. I could just picture his squinty eyes, like my father's, and that sad, retarded smile.

After I regained my composure, the Beansie temper rose higher than ever before. I wanted to drive my Buick Skylark to Secaucus and keep driving until I ran over the council candidate responsible for this. Then I'd put it in reverse, back up, and run over him again.

When I calmed down, I decided against the hit and run. The pen was mightier than the Buick Skylark. I decided to write a column about the voter fraud, how disgusting the whole thing was. I could describe Uncle Tommy and my visits to him as a child, how he had looked the last time I saw him, at Thanksgiving dinner at our house on Summit Avenue. There was no way Uncle Tommy could voluntarily cast a vote for someone. I would write a column about it, and write it with the venom that could only come from personal involvement.

But my family asked me not to. They were embarrassed.

Uncle Tommy had been a dirty family secret for decades, and they didn't want him trotted out, no matter how just the cause. What got me, though, wasn't my family's protests. I found out that this wasn't the only time Meadowview had been raided for Hudson County votes.

This had been going on for years. Uncle Tommy had probably been taken advantage of for decades. I just hadn't been in a position to notice. I suddenly felt helpless and very small in the face of all that corruption. I was a footnote, incapable of change in such a fucked-up place.

Heartsick and disgusted, I buckled under the weight of Jersey City and my family. Instead of writing a column about Uncle Tommy, I decided to leave *The Jersey Journal*.

As I searched for a reporting job in the tri-state area, I grew more and more bitter. What I really wanted was to get away from my family, and living in Connecticut or Long Island wouldn't accomplish that. But I didn't know where to go or how to get away for good.

I moved within a five-mile radius three times in less than three years, in a desperate attempt to make myself happy. From Weehawken, I moved back to Jersey City, to a duplex apartment downtown. I loved the place, but I hated one of my roommates, a vegetarian who yelled at me for cooking chicken in her stainless-steel pots. I finally decided to move out after she went to Nicaragua on a monthlong humanitarian mission and stuck me with her three-hundred-dollar phone bill.

Next, I moved to a Heights basement apartment, in a house that my sister had bought as an investment. Every time it rained, my kitchen flooded. But what finally made me move were the upstairs tenants, noisy postal workers who played Lynyrd Skynyrd when they returned from their graveyard shift each night. The Oriental rug in the vestibule and the pictures on the hallway walls vanished. I was afraid my stereo speakers would be next or, worse, that they'd shoot Wendell when he went up and asked them for the tenth time to turn down "Free Bird."

I considered moving in with Wendell, but I figured I'd just bring him down. I was so miserable, it was contagious. Instead, I moved to Manhattan, to a mouse- and roach-infested apartment at the mouth of the Holland Tunnel, and commuted every day to Journal Square.

While I searched for a new job, my weekly column became sharper, more biting, and increasingly controversial. I lambasted the planning board for eating lavish meals at the expensive Casa Dante Restaurant, Frank Sinatra for marketing his own inedible spaghetti sauce in a jar, and a local Italian parish for not welcoming black people to its annual feast.

The pastor of Mount Carmel, the parish I took to task, delivered sermons about me on Sundays and sponsored a petition drive to try to get me fired. The paper's only black columnist, Earl Morgan, and some white clergy members came to my defense. But things got ugly. In the mail, I got a dirty maxi-pad with my column wrapped around it. I got letters telling me I should shut up and get a proper woman's job, as a nurse or a secretary.

My family was forced to defend me week after week. While out with his in-laws at an Italian dinner-dance, Stanley almost choked on his antipasto when one of the guys at the table said, "So what about that Stapinski broad?" He was the pastor of Mount Carmel and was about to launch into a tirade against me, not knowing Stanley was my brother. Dolores, my sister-in-law, had to practically sit on top of Stanley so he wouldn't jump across the table and give the priest a black eye.

We laughed about it at the next family get-together, but it wasn't really funny. Not only was my family affecting my writing, but now my writing was affecting my family.

My sister got a job as a teacher at P.S. 27, which was named, ironically, the Zampella School, after one of the judge's relatives. In my column, I tried to stay away from the subject of education altogether for fear my sister would be fired. But it seemed that whatever I wrote about, there was some family connection.

Because of the attention my column was getting, Ma was transferred at work from the record room to central judicial processing court, where the bad guys were arraigned—and where there was less confidential information floating around. Working CJP was a much harder job for my sixty-year-old mother, and the prosecutor hoped that by transferring her down there, she would quit. He didn't know her very well. She would not be manipulated. Anyway, she had seen much worse at the DMV. Many of her former customers were now the bad guys being arraigned. They'd wave to Ma as they were led away in handcuffs. "Hey, Motor Vehicle Lady," they'd say. "What are you doing here?" Ma thrived at CJP, and became indispensable.

But her demotion was just another reason for me to get the hell out of Jersey City. If I left the paper, my mother's job would get easier. I was no longer helping her by sticking around. She wouldn't die if I moved away. Besides, her job at the courthouse was a conflict on so many different levels. Every week there was swag for sale in the court-house hallways: clothes, fine china, knockoff designer watches, radios, electric razors. I wasn't sure if it was confiscated property from swag busts or if it was just plain swag that fell off the truck and directly into the courthouse hallways.

An investigator noticed my mother perusing some courthouse swag one afternoon and asked to talk to her. She was afraid that she was being caught buying swag, that the investigator was going to question her or, worse, have her arrested. Instead, he asked my mother to leave the bag of goodies under his desk for him to browse through so he could buy a few things for the wife and kids. He knew all about the swag. And so did I. So did everybody in the courthouse. Was I sup-posed to report this? My allegiance to my mother certainly outweighed any journalistic ethics.

I was struck by the irony. Just a couple of years earlier, I had yelled at a friend for voting for a candidate so his mother could get a city job. Now I was no better. Worse, really.

I told myself that journalistic ethics were for people more fortunate than I, for people without relatives in Hudson County. They were for people whose parents could afford them, whose families didn't have to rely on county jobs. I was rationalizing, but it beat ratting out my mother and her friends and the guy selling the swag.

The real reason I couldn't write about the courthouse swag was that I was wearing it. My mother had given me dozens of swag shirts, sweaters, and nightgowns from the courthouse hallways. The kids in our family played with swag toys and stuffed animals. My sister had swag china and a swag designer watch and smelled of swag perfume. There were knockoff handbags and gloves, underwear and slippers.

If I was to write about the courthouse swag, I would have to get rid of at least half my wardrobe. Then I would have to find Ma a new job, because she would be fired or, worse, ostracized from her circle of swag-buying friends.

Anyway, what was a little swag on the side? A cheap designer watch never hurt anyone, except the guy whose truck had been hijacked. I had grown up on swag. We all had.

Hadn't we?

There was only one way to solve the swag problem, only one way to help my mother get her job back in the file room, to avoid getting hit with the sadness that swirled around Mike and Uncle Tommy and to stop my brother from punching somebody in the mouth when I wrote my next column. I had to go.

At twenty-seven, I was getting gray hair from worrying so much about the conflicts of interest in my complicated little life. Vacations with Wendell weren't enough of a break. They only left me wanting more time away from Hudson County. I felt like the tired statue outside City Hall, so weary that I needed to sit things out for a while.

When Wendell left the paper and got a job at New York *Newsday,* I felt abandoned. I finally left *The Jersey Journal* and moved away. Not to Connecticut or Long Island or the Midwest or sunny California. In a moment of claustrophobic panic I moved far, far away, so far that no one—not even my mother—would visit me.

17

RESURRECTION

In a moment of insanity, I joined the Jesuit Volunteer Corps and took a job as a news director at a radio station in Nome.

Nome, Alaska, a few miles from Siberia. The station was called KNOM—*monk* spelled backward.

I had waited too long to leave. Far too long. It was as if I had been sitting on a springboard at *The Jersey Journal*. The longer I stayed and the more pressure I felt, the farther the spring was bent back. When the board finally let loose, in the summer of 1992, I was flung to the farthest reaches of the globe.

Nome seemed the opposite of Hudson County: no people, no decay, no corruption; just lots of snow and ice. Clean, cool, and empty. I went there sight unseen. I should have done a little research first.

There was crime and corruption in Nome. Since its population was only three thousand, there were fewer crimes, but per capita it probably worked out to be about the same as Hudson County. Alcoholism was rampant. Suicide was common. And worst of all, it was butt-ugly. It was the only place in Alaska that was as ugly as Jersey City.

There were rusted water tanks at the edge of town. And only three seasons: Snow, Mud, and Dust. The streets were not paved. There was a saloon on every corner. No mountain view. And there were no trees. It was so cold in Nome that there were no trees. I couldn't believe I had chosen a place that had less foliage than Jersey City. I didn't think such a place existed. But it did. And I was now a resident.

I tried to look on the bright side. When I first got there, I figured I'd be helping people through KNOM, maybe doing some kind of Christian outreach to try and make the world a better place. But the extent of our religious duty at the radio station was popping in a tape of the rosary at night, to lull the northern masses to sleep. It wasn't what I'd had in mind.

So I picked up where I had left off at *The Jersey Journal* and wrote stories about an Eskimo guy accused of stealing windows from a HUD-funded project and the state investigation into a local nursing home for native elders. There were reports of mutated walruses washing up on the shores of Eskimo villages because of the nuclear waste the Russians had dumped into the ocean. It was worse than the Jersey City chromium problem. Instead of the politics at city council meetings, I covered the politics at walrus-commission meetings.

After a few weeks of chasing stories like a madwoman, I looked around me and noticed everyone else was traveling about half my speed. Then I remembered why I was here. I had moved to Alaska to sit things out.

I put on my news blinders and decided to write only happy stories for a while, stories about sled-dog races and skating rink openings.

I tried to keep abreast of what was happening in the real world. While at KNOM, I read about the World Trade Center bombing on the AP wire. I remembered my old fear of the Twin Towers falling across the river and crushing my house. I couldn't believe it had almost happened. I was glad I wasn't there for it.

I was not surprised to learn that the bombers lived in Jersey City. I could picture them staring day after day across the river, hating those towering symbols of American capitalism, of progress, hating them enough to actually blow them up. One of the nation's biggest urban disasters was caused by a group of maniacs who felt they had something important to say but were powerless to say it—three guys from Jersey City. The place could drive you crazy if you didn't escape in time.

I was glad I did, as ugly as Nome was. I joined a bowling league, sang in a Christmas choir, and went on long walks along the town's beach, where gold prospectors still set up raggedy tents and panning equipment in summer. I wrote in a journal that cousin Gerri gave me as a going-away present and composed long letters to Wendell, who was now breaking stories about the World Trade Center bombing. At night, I put on my fur ruff and watched the aurora borealis light up the Nome sky.

Whenever I could, whenever the weather permitted, I got out of town and headed to the country. Just a short drive outside ugly Nome, you could find yourself in the middle of nowhere. Cool, clean nowhere.

After an eleven-mile drive or bike ride, it was a three-mile hike to Tom's Cabin, an old miner's cabin. A former Jesuit volunteer named Tom had discovered it and fixed it up a few years earlier. We current volunteers helped maintain it on our hikes out, chopping wood, sweeping the crooked floor, and restocking the canned food and first-aid supplies. There was a dirt road that led to Tom's, though driving was pretty rough going. Most visitors to Tom's Cabin walked it or biked it or snow-machined it, depending on the season.

Most people would stay out for the day and then hike back in and hitch a ride to town. Some spent the night. But it was sometimes tricky. Just because it was a nice day on the hike out didn't necessarily mean it would be a nice day on the hike in. If there was a blizzard, you could be trapped at Tom's for several days. And in the spring and summer there were bears. Everyone in Nome had heard about the group of volunteers who hiked out to find a bloody, broken window at Tom's— from the bear who broke in to steal the Dinty Moore stew left inside.

My bowling partners, Eric and Johnny O—short for John O'Gorman—decided to hike out to the cabin Easter weekend. And Johnny O couldn't wait to tell me.

"We're going out to the cabin on Saturday," John said, poking me in the arm on Holy Thursday. Johnny O was a big guy, so when he poked you, it hurt.

I rolled my eyes and punched him back, but negative reinforcement never worked with Johnny O. He'd poke you again the next chance he got. Besides, he was such a sweet guy, I'd always feel a little guilty after hitting him. He wasn't even aware he was hurting me.

"You should come with us," he said, his voice cracking a little in his nervous excitement. It was hard to feel enthusiastic around Johnny O. Any excitement usually paled in comparison to his. But sometimes it was contagious, like the June day he decided we should jump into the Grand Central River in our underwear.

He stripped right there on the road, and seconds later I was sitting on the metal railing in my panties and long-johns top, counting down to the plunge. The water was about thirty feet below, turquoise blue, deep, and clear right to the bottom. It was June, but there was still ice on the edges of the river. We looked at each other and laughed. "On three," he said. Together we counted, "One, two, three." And slipped off into the unknowable as everyone around us cheered.

Most people have never felt water that cold on their bodies. There's the quick ice cube down the back of the shirt now and then from the practical joker friend. But the water in the Grand Central that day was as cold as water gets without freezing. It was like a tub filled with ice cubes. That was the Grand Central in summer.

As soon as I hit the ice-cold water, the only thing on my mind was that I had to get out as soon as I possibly could. I pushed my way up to the surface and swam faster than I'd ever swum, crunched over the ice with my bare feet and ran up the embankment to my dry, warm clothes. All in five seconds flat. I thought it was a stupid thing to have done. But as the day wore on, the sun not setting that long summer's day, I was glad Johnny O had been so contagious. My body tingled for the next twelve hours. I felt more alive that day, physically, than I'd ever felt. The jolt woke me up and permanently removed the twenty-seven years of crud that had settled on my brain while in Hudson County.

Johnny O, one of my many friends and saviors in Nome, was now convincing me to take the hike out to Tom's in the snow. I wasn't very enthusiastic about snowshoes, and I didn't think I could keep up with Eric's cross-country skiing. He'd been all the way to the edge of the Bering Sea ice in storm conditions.

"I'll just slow you down," I whined.

But Eric and Johnny O insisted I come along.

On the Saturday before Easter, I took a hike out to Tom's with them. The bears were still sleeping and spring breakup, the time of year the ice on the sea cracks and floats out to sea, was just a few weeks away. There wasn't much danger of a snowstorm or a bear attack. Eric skied, Johnny O snowshoed, and, because I weighed just under a hundred pounds, my lightest since high school, I walked. Very lightly.

Traveling with two men also guaranteed a light pack. Hanging out with boys still had its benefits. Eric carried most of the water; Johnny O, most of the food. Eric, a fellow Jesuit Volunteer from Colorado, was convinced the Nome water was contaminated with nuclear waste from the Russian Far East. Johnny O, a former Volunteer, liked food even more than we did, so he carried most of it.

I tried the snowshoes for a few minutes. But they were uncomfortable and almost impossible to walk in. I had to walk with my legs far apart but keep them pointing straight or else the wooden backs would cross each other and I would trip. I traveled about fifteen feet in them, then decided I'd take my chances walking without them and tied them on the back of my pack. Though it was warm, in the forties, the snow hadn't melted in most places yet. There was a layer of ice on top of about two feet of powder. The melted snow that had frozen over in a slippery coating formed a thin but resistant shell.

One hundred pounds was just about all it could bear. Every ten minutes or so, my boot would plunge through, the white crust sucking in my entire leg. I'd struggle up out of the small hole I'd made, then push myself up with my mittened hands. That first step after a fall would plunge me right back into the snow. Once I fell in, it was as if the ice knew I was wary of falling in again. I fell in again and again, until I finally got my footing. In some spots where ice had collapsed, I'd tiptoe. Or pretend I was a deer, scurrying across the tundra. I wished myself lighter, held my breath. Where the ice looked sturdy, I'd hurry across. Where it looked like it might give, I slid slowly forward. It was not an easy way to travel three miles, but it looked a lot easier than the snowshoes Johnny O was wearing.

Most of the day, I walked in Johnny O's path. The flattened snow left by his snowshoes was packed hard and wide. Johnny O wasn't fol-

lowing any path. In the summer, there was a marked trail that hikers
could follow out to Tom's Cabin. But in winter, everything looked the
same, and I was more than a little worried we wouldn't find the cabin
and would wander off in the wrong direction. Eric, meanwhile, danced
and swerved around us, made circles in our paths, and served as an
annoying reminder that we should have brought cross-country skis. To
punish him, I placed my Walkman at the top of his backpack and set
up mini-speakers right below his shoulders. Eric was our home-away-
from-home entertainment center. While we struggled along, he played
tunes from his back. But after a while Eric yelled for me to remove the
speakers. We could hear him loud and clear, but he had no idea what
we were saying behind his back. The music was too loud.

Within the first hour of the trip, distant pops could be heard from
the Nome firing range a few miles away. Because the willows were still
covered in snow, there were no birds yet. So once we got out of earshot
of the shooting range and turned off the Walkman and stood still, there
was silence. Complete silence.

I had never known complete silence. There was always traffic, always an ambulance coming or going, someone screaming outside my
window, a clock ticking, a baby crying, the heat rising in the radiator,
muffled sounds of the next-door neighbor's home entertainment system, a family story being told. In Nome, there had been dogs howling,
drunks singing, the station humming, and snow machines roaring. Silence was something completely new to my ears. Something that took
getting used to.

I had once heard near silence on the side of a road on a trip with
Wendell. During one of our vacations from work, we pulled off the side
of the highway in Northern California to take a look at the Milky Way.
It was the middle of the night, so there were no other cars. Just some
crickets. It was so quiet that we were scared, scared of the immensity
of the heavens, of the possibility of an ax murderer lurking in the red-
woods.

Wendell and I were scared of the silence and what might fill that
void suddenly, violently. We jumped back into the rent-a-car and
turned the radio up loud. That night, with the crickets cricketing and
the road lights buzzing, we hadn't even heard total silence. But it

seemed to me that no one but the people here, the people living above the tree line, had ever heard total silence.

In the isolated spots in the Midwest, in the South, and in the rest of Alaska, there were birds singing, the wind blowing through leaves and branches. The wind rustling against something. Whistling through canyons. Past cows or moose. But out on the road to Tom's, there was nothing to rustle. Nothing to whistle past. Nothing to sing, unless we did the singing. Just smooth, aerodynamic, wind-resistant hills of ice and snow. The hard-packed white outlines cutting across the blue sky were silent for miles. White and blue, the colors of winter, didn't make a peep.

We knew we were close when we heard the sound of icicles dripping in the distance.

Eric was the first to reach the cabin, so he dug the piled-up snow from the doorway. On our fourth and last hour of hiking, I'd grown tired. But now I was charged by the sight of the one-room shack and the lengthened hours of sunlight still shining on us. Like children let out of school early on a snow day, we dropped our gear inside the wooden door, grabbed three garbage bags, and headed for the hills.

Sledding above the tree line was a special treat, since there's nothing to hit for hundreds of miles in each direction. I felt like Santa Claus riding on the electric razor in that television commercial, the one where he goes gliding up and down, up and down, into TV infinity. As we gained more confidence, we approached steeper and steeper hills, until Eric and Johnny O decided to try the kamikaze hill, the vertical drop. I just sat back on my garbage bag and watched and laughed as their bags left the surface and they entered free falls and then landed in the soft powder below.

While the boys frolicked, I climbed to the top of an adjacent hill and crawled into a narrow, ice-blue crevice, where a line of noisy icicles hung. I leaned my head out far enough to place my mouth beneath them and drink in the cold water dripping from their tips.

That night we dined on Dinty Moore stew and ramen-noodle soup cooked over the stove that warmed the cabin. Eric got the fire so dan-

gerously hot that it glowed red through the black cast iron. For dessert
we had popcorn, Gummi Bears, and an entire box of rosé wine. For
shipping purposes, most of Nome's wine came in big boxes rather than
in bottles. We smoked from Eric's pipe and danced until 2 A.M. to the
music from the tiny Walkman speakers, which were now placed on a
rickety wooden shelf. I joked that we should keep it down. The neighbors might complain.

We finally turned the music off and set up our sleeping bags. But
before I climbed in, I decided to take a look outside.

I walked out into the dark, cool night. The blue sky was now ink-
black. The only light came from the stars and moon, far above the
cabin's tin roof. I felt small and very far away from anywhere—closer to
the moon than to the rest of the world. There was a peacefulness here
that I hadn't felt on the highway with Wendell, and surely had never
felt in Hudson County. This time the vastness of the night sky and the
silence didn't send me hurrying back to the safety inside. It was the
cold, finally, that chased me back to Tom's Cabin.

We slept long and hard, rising on Easter Sunday to the silence. It
was the most solemn religious holiday I'd ever experienced. More holy
than a visit to St. Peter's. More beautiful than midnight mass at OLC.
Instead of incense, we breathed in the smoke from the chimney. The
white snow was purer than the Easter lilies I had been forced to carry
each year in Holy Thursday procession. There were no lily pots for me
this Holy Week. Just empty cans of Dinty Moore to carry back home.
To Nome.

18

VALENTINE'S DAY

I considered staying in Nome. I lived there a year and watched the ice break up and move out toward Russia. When summer came 'round again, I picked blueberries from the tundra and went soaking in the hot springs nearby.

But after twelve months in the middle of nowhere, I felt it was time to go somewhere. I considered buying a one-way ticket around the world and traveling for a year. Then I almost moved to Chicago to take a job at the *Sun-Times.* I also wondered what it would be like to live in Southern California, the colors bright and the weather warm. But the truth was, I missed Wendell. And Wendell was in New York.

I decided to go back to the East Coast, but not back home. I'd never go back there, really. I would visit from time to time, but I couldn't live there again.

There were things I missed about home, though. While I was away, I realized that not everyone knew what a brownstone looked like. I missed their smooth faces and high stoops and the solid feeling they gave you. I realized that the ingredients I needed for the food I liked to eat were not easily found in most grocery stores in Alaska, or in most of

America. I couldn't even buy a pound of rigatoni. Elbow macaroni was as good as it got at the Nome supermarket. No matter how hard I tried, I couldn't put sauce on elbow macaroni. It was a sacrilege.

The pace I was used to was not the pace of most towns, or even most cities. I talked too fast for everybody I met, and they made fun of my accent. The weather I was accustomed to, the way it changed just when I was getting sick of it, was not the same everywhere. In other words I was homesick, as much as a person could be for a place as sick as Jersey City.

On my first visit back to Jersey City after Alaska, I took my mountain bike on the PATH train, then rode up the hill to the Heights. Later, when I wasn't looking, someone stole my bike from my brother's garage.

I was lucky that the details I loved about Jersey City could be found elsewhere, namely Brooklyn, and that Wendell lived there. When I moved back to the Lower 48, I moved in with him. I announced to my inquiring Polish aunts that I was living in sin, right across New York Harbor.

The Brooklyn sidewalks were just like the ones in Jersey City, except I hadn't memorized their cracks and pockmarks. I could buy fresh mozzarella and pierogi, but while waiting in line I didn't have to see ex-classmates and politicians I had exposed in the pages of *The Jersey Journal*.

Brooklyn was like Jersey City worked over by a stretching machine: The bad neighborhoods were bigger, but so were the good neighborhoods. They spread out for miles, with their brownstones and flowering trees. Just when I tired of summer, autumn leaves fell.

Out of the many spots on the globe that I visited, Brooklyn was closest to home. The good parts of home.

Brooklyn was part of New York, and its people seemed less beaten down than people from Jersey City. It was hard to be intimidated by something you were a part of.

The buildings I had gazed at from the Hudson River's edge always looked like a crown of jewels at night, the green-copper crown of the Woolworth Building a glowing emerald, the World Trade Center two strips of diamonds, and the Empire State Building a sapphire, ruby, or amethyst, depending on the holiday. The tops of the buildings were jewels sitting silently on the head of a sleeping king, riches that Jersey City residents coveted but couldn't steal.

The skyline seemed different from the other side. The people in Brooklyn didn't act like the world owed them something. They were proud, not arrogant; civic-minded, but never small-town. Though they ate the same food, had the same accent, and walked on sidewalks made from the same blue stone as people from Jersey City, they seemed more happy. Or maybe it was just that I was happy.

My relatives were still close by, but we were separated by two rivers. They were afraid to drive over to Brooklyn for fear they'd get lost in a borough so big. I could see them whenever I wanted, not whenever they wanted. I was a freelancer, and could write about all kinds of subjects that had nothing to do with me. Or them. I could cast off those family stories.

But I should have known better. You could choose your friends, my mother said, but not your family. They chose you, ages ago, centuries before you were born. And there was really no escape.

If anything, the family stories grew closer. They entered my generation and touched my family in ways we'd never seen, pissing on the hallowed ground of Gammontown. They showed that you couldn't run away from your relatives, and that no matter how far you ran, history would catch up with you and fix you good.

––––––––

While I was still climbing mountains and mushing dog teams on the frozen tundra, one of the cousins I had left behind was establishing a career as a criminal. When I found out, it was no surprise. It's just that I had forgotten all about George, the kid with the light in his brown eyes, who had seen his father hanging in the doorway. I hadn't seen George in years.

In Jersey City, George never stood a chance. I always wondered whether if he'd grown up somewhere else, George may have turned out all right. Maybe he would have been a cop in an alternate universe. Or a famous bank robber. Or a mad scientist, his thick Barney Google glasses crooked above his crooked smile.

By the time he was eighteen, George had been convicted of aggravated assault and sentenced to seven years in prison. Four years later, let out early, George was convicted of robbery and burglary and sentenced to two and a half years. While I was away, George developed a heroin habit, like his father. He needed to support it, and in the fall of 1993, he was arrested in a chain-snatching but was let go when the victim refused to pursue the charges.

To get clean, George got a job at the Sewerage Authority, working with his mother's boyfriend, a former Colgate employee. But that didn't last. In the spring of the following year, he was arrested yet again for committing fifty-seven burglaries in a four-month-long crime spree. He complained that he'd been railroaded, that many of the crimes weren't his.

The police said that George had robbed neighbors' homes—mostly in the OLC neighborhood—on Colgate Street, Henderson Street, Morris Street, and Essex Street. One of the houses he hit was 171 Grand, right next door to where my Russian great-grandmother was killed by her husband years ago. They said he had burglarized six homes on Sussex Street, a few doors away from OLC, shattering the calm of Gammontown.

George also stole a blue Toyota van. He should have driven it to a faraway place. But he didn't. George stayed right in stinky old Jersey City. If he had to stay, he should have stayed close to home, within the safe confines of Gammontown.

In his criminal pursuits, George moved farther out of the neighborhood and into other areas of downtown, to more unknown territory. I think that the farther from home he went, the more risky his career became. Knowing your subject is essential, even in the world of crime. Knowing who owns what, who's a loudmouth, who's not, can help you stay out of jail. On Second Street, Fourth Street, Fifth Street, Eighth Street, and Pavonia Avenue, George got closer and closer to jail.

One of his most stupid crimes was count twenty-one: terroristic threats. George broke into a woman's house, and when she went to pick up the phone, he grabbed the receiver out of her hand, hung it up, and threatened to kill her if she tried anything more. It was one thing to commit crimes against property. It was another to threaten to kill the owners of that property.

But the biggest mistake George made was robbing the home of Nidia Colon, a downtown resident who also happened to be a Hudson County freeholder. George had no idea who Colon was. Which, of course, was the problem. Had he known she was a politician, George would never have burglarized her home. He just as easily could have robbed her next-door neighbor.

For George, the political became personal.

Before he was even convicted, George spent eighteen months behind bars, held on $50,000 cash only bail. Eventually, he was given a 10 percent cash option and the family raised enough money to set him free. On November 6, 1995, George made the $5,000 bail. To stay off the streets and out of trouble, he worked Bingo at OLC to earn some pocket money. Maybe he should have hopped a train to another town, or a plane to Mexico.

Valentine's Day 1996—a day short of his father's anniversary in heaven—George pleaded guilty to twenty-nine of the fifty-seven burglaries. He could wind up serving ten years. His sentencing was a little over a month away, but the prosecutor argued he should be sentenced sooner, or kept in custody. He was worried that George might get into more trouble.

But George was allowed to leave the courthouse. Outside, his mother, Mary Ann, gave him six dollars to buy a Valentine's Day rose for his girlfriend.

George went home with his girlfriend to her apartment in the Heights, just a few blocks from our Summit Avenue house and down the street from Stanley's apartment. Tired from the depressing events of the day, and probably thinking of his father, George took a nap. Around 7:50 P.M., he woke up and asked his girlfriend to go out with him. He wanted to get some air. But she wanted to stay home. They argued. And George stormed out on his own, perhaps in search of somewhere to spend that six dollars, meant for Valentine's Day flowers.

That night, George's mother was home in Gammontown. Her Morris Street apartment faced where the Colgate factory used to be before it was closed and the fresh, soapy smell was swiped forever from the air.

Mary Ann was watching the soap opera awards when she and her boyfriend, Eddie, noticed cop cars speeding past the window. Eddie ran outside to see what was happening. Mary Ann followed, not even bothering to change her flimsy three-dollar canvas shoes. It was cold out, but she wouldn't be out for long.

A friend with a police scanner told Mary Ann that the cops were chasing a kid with a gun on the roof of 207 Warren Street. That was the street where Bromirski's Funeral Home was, where Daddy had been laid out. It was the street with the unobstructed view of the Statue of Liberty. During the statue's centennial celebration, people gathered early in the morning on Warren Street to get a view of the evening fireworks.

On February 14, 1996, there were no fireworks, of course. But a large crowd congregated there again, dozens of couples pulled away from the warm glow of their TV sets, huddling in the cold, their coats thrown over housedresses and pajamas, their necks craned in the hopes of getting a glimpse of some real-live police drama. Mary Ann joined the crowd.

In the frigid night, Mary Ann's feet kept freezing, forcing her to run back to her apartment. But she couldn't stay away from the scene of the crime: 207 Warren Street, which was right across from the house where George's father had died twenty-four years earlier.

It was at 204 Warren that Mary Ann and George had found him hanging in a doorway the night after Valentine's Day.

Mary Ann stood right in front of that house at 204 Warren in her cheap slip-on shoes, gazing up at 207, across the street, where the police chase was going down, the Statue of Liberty green and glowing, its back to her and the nosy crowd.

Cop cars were zooming past. Some policemen ran through the Italian restaurant on the corner, their guns drawn. Four plainclothes cops ran up the stairs of the brownstone.

Then Mary Ann heard the gunshots. One shot, followed by three in quick succession.

Boom.

Boom, boom, boom.

It wasn't clear who had been shot, if anyone, but with so many cops around it was a good bet the robber was down.

Mary Ann's first thought wasn't for the robber himself but for the robber's mother. Mary Ann, who knew the sorrow of having a troubled kid, thought no mother deserved the pain of losing a child, no matter what that child did.

The plainclothes cops, uninjured, ran back down to the street, got into their cars, and left. Meanwhile, more than two dozen uniformed cops arrived on the scene, their blue police cars parked in zigzags in the middle of Warren Street, their lights flashing.

When she got home, Mary Ann got a funny feeling, as if something had passed through her. She got goose bumps and wondered, for the first time, if maybe the robber was George.

"Eddie," she said. "There's something wrong, Eddie."

"Don't even think that," he said, changing the TV channel. He knew what she was thinking.

"You're thinking the same thing," she told him.

Eddie didn't answer.

The only hope Mary Ann clung to was that she knew George didn't own a gun.

She kept going back to the scene, where about thirty cops and, by now, a few reporters were gathered. There were TV reporters and the new police reporter from *The Jersey Journal*.

Mary Ann ran back and forth between Warren and Morris Streets seven times that night, her feet still freezing. In her panic, she hadn't thought to put on warmer shoes. On one of her last runs outside, a neighbor told her that the robber was a Puerto Rican. Mary Ann's heart pounded in her eardrums.

George's father had been Puerto Rican, so George was half–Puerto Rican.

One of the cops, the son of Ruthie, the crossing guard/lottery winner who had died of a heart attack, was on the scene. Mary Ann stood close and listened to what he was saying to his captain, to try and prove her worst fears wrong. She overheard him say that a second robber had gotten away.

Mary Ann went home one more time and turned on the Channel 9 news, which showed paramedics taking the robber out in a body bag. She couldn't see his face. But she was scared now, and told Eddie that if anyone knocked on the door, he shouldn't let them in. She went to the bedroom, got down on her knees, and started praying. *Please, God. Let him be the one that got away.*

There was a knock on the door. It was a homicide detective, and Eddie let him in. "There was just a tragic accident," said the detective. "A terrible mistake." He showed Eddie a picture of George. "Is this him?"

Mary Ann screamed that she wanted to see her son. But the detective told her she couldn't, that George was already gone. Not just in the way that Daddy was gone, but physically gone, too. George's body was on its way to Newark for an autopsy. Mary Ann prayed that there had been a mix-up, some kind of mistake.

Before she even saw her son's body, the police delivered an envelope to her house. Inside were George's thick glasses.

———

Mary Ann never really found out what had happened that night. She didn't believe the *Jersey Journal* version, that six hours after pleading guilty in court, minutes after leaving his girlfriend's house, George committed yet another robbery, this time at a fruit-and-vegetable store in the city's Greenville section—a neighborhood he'd never hit before. When a silent alarm was tripped, police arrived on the scene. But George pointed his gun at the cops and got away.

Leading police on a wild chase through the city, George finally crashed a stolen red Hyundai downtown in our peaceful parish neighborhood, got out, ran through several backyards, then climbed a fire escape to one of the tarred roofs. Police chased him on foot, jumping from roof to roof until George eluded them by breaking through a roof hatch, then kicking in the door of the second-floor apartment.

George chose the apartment carefully, knowing full well who lived there: a distant relative named Bob, the brother-in-law of my aunt Terri, my father's sister, the one who hit 057 straight the day I was born. Bob was an elderly bachelor and lived alone on Warren Street. When George popped in, Bob was asleep. But not for long. He came out in his pajamas, holding a searchlight.

George, holding a loaded .38, told Bob to keep quiet and not to worry, that he knew him, was related almost, and that he wouldn't hurt him. He was just trying to find a way out without the police seeing him. But George had trouble opening the kitchen window. He jimmied it and punched it but couldn't get it open in time.

The police busted through the door and told George to surrender. But George had no plans of going back to jail. He pointed the gun at his own head.

That's how I see him when I picture him now: frozen in time, with that gun to his head, which was filled with that awful memory of his father swinging in the doorway right across the street. It was like George's history was weighing heavy, as if cement shoes had been dragging him down for years and years. It was easier to just drown than to fight the sinking.

Maybe the memory of his father dying was like the vague memory of a bad dream you can't really recall but that flashes for a second when you get back under the covers the next night, weary and tired, all your defenses down. Maybe for that split second, with his gun to his head, George saw his father hanging there.

"I'm not going back to jail," George told the cops. "I'd rather die." The two police officers tried to talk George out of shooting himself but said he turned the gun on them. "If I'm gonna go, you're gonna go," they said he told them. The police opened fire. George was shot four times, in the hand, rib cage, leg, and—the fatal bullet—the Adam's apple.

He still had the six dollars in his pocket that his mother had given him for the flowers. But that part didn't make it into *The Jersey Journal*. It would have made him human, and there was no room for humanity in the police report. The picture the paper ran was an ugly mug shot of George, his hair cut in a fade, his chin covered in a goatee, his glasses as big and thick as when he was a kid. No crooked smile for the camera.

As George was carried out in the body bag, the cops were treated for trauma at a local hospital. Maybe they should have taken Bob with them. George's blood was splattered all over his apartment. Bob had been injured in the war while stationed in Casino, Italy. But this was too much to handle. He could barely cut his own meat anymore because of his handicap, never mind mop up this mess. Though the police sent a crew to clean most of it up, Aunt Terri wound up getting on her hands and knees and scrubbing Bob's kitchen floor.

Mary Ann didn't believe that George even had a gun. She thought that he was simply pulling his glasses out of his pocket when the cops burst into Bob's apartment, that they mistook the glasses for a gun and blew him away.

Even if he had a gun and they thought he was going to kill himself, why didn't they back off? she thought. Why didn't they come out into the crowd and get Mary Ann—his own mother—to talk him down?

There were conflicting reports about where George was shot. Was it the second floor or third floor? Was there a female eyewitness? Were there four shots or five shots? The cops told Mary Ann no one else was involved in the robbery, despite what Ruthie's son said that night. Mary Ann didn't believe George was the one who had robbed the store earlier that evening, that it must have been the other guy, the second assailant, who fled the scene, that George was just in the wrong place at the wrong time. In with the wrong crowd. Yet again. Mary Ann wondered who the cops would blame for their unsolved robberies now that George, their scapegoat, was gone.

She tried talking to the cops, tried having someone arrange a meeting with Bob, but no one would sit down with her. She wanted to ask Bob if George had suffered. "I wanted to go up there, to the place where he got shot, just to see it," she said. "He was a human being. He was my son."

Before the shooting, Mary Ann had never noticed Bob. But afterward, at the supermarket and at the Flamingo Diner in the neighborhood, Mary Ann would always see him. He'd be standing right next to her, waiting for his groceries to be bagged or for a cup of coffee, but he had no idea that she was George's mother. She wanted to poke him. But even if she could have, she would never have gotten up the nerve to talk to him, invite herself over to his house for coffee, ask him what had really happened that night.

George was laid out for two days at the Bromirski Funeral Home on Warren Street, on the same street where he was shot. The funeral director told Mary Ann to get a shirt with a high collar, to cover the bullet wound in George's throat.

I didn't go to the wake or the funeral. After Daddy died, I found it hard to go to wakes, especially those at Bromirski's. I only went when I really had to, like when Cioci Stella or Uncle Henry died. I hadn't been close to George, so I wimped out.

As often as she could, Mary Ann visited the cemetery where George was buried. It's the same cemetery where my father is buried, Holy Cross in North Arlington, the town where Aunt Terri lived, the town with all the sinkholes. My father was buried at the back, near the road and across from a bowling alley. George was at the other end, in an older grave, near the front gates.

Though his last name was different from mine, George's grave was marked STAPINSKI, the last name of Mary Ann's grandparents, who are both buried in that same plot. There was room for one more casket in the grave. And since Mary Ann was short on money, the family told her to bury George there, where his remains would mingle with the Stapinski ashes.

Mary Ann put George's picture on a shelf in her modest living room on Morris Street, not far from the Morris Canal basin on which barges once carried coal to New York, ignoring Jersey City altogether. Next to George's picture she placed a candle, which she would light every day, then blow out before going to sleep each night. She hoped that it would help push George's soul toward the light. She prayed each night that he was headed to a better place, far from Jersey City.

19

NO FILTERS

One afternoon, I got a call from my mother that my favorite cousin, Gerri, was "in trouble." I knew right away Ma didn't mean that Gerri was pregnant. I knew it was worse than that. Before I even heard what she'd done wrong, I was ready to defend her, write letters to her in prison or in rehab or wherever she was headed, to let her know that I'd be there for her. We were a forgiving family, after all, who had seen much worse. What with Grandpa, and Great-Grandpa Peter, Uncle Frankie, and Uncle Henry, Uncle Andrew, George, and all the crooked politicians.

Gerri wasn't even the first in her immediate family to get into trouble. In 1988, one of her sisters was indicted on charges of stealing money from the Hyundai dealership where she worked, but no one really paid much attention. It was just another blot on the family name. And besides, the charges were later dismissed.

But Gerri was different. Her trouble hit us hard, like a sock in the mouth you didn't see coming.

We all loved her. My father had loved her because she loved his hot roast beef sandwiches. My mother loved her like a godmother; my sister, like a Confirmation sponsor. I loved her because she always had time to play with me and never ignored me. She had the patience to teach me to ride a two-wheeler on the dead-end streets of North Bergen. Our birthdays were the same week. She had even given me that journal to take to Alaska. I thought maybe I could send her a journal so she could record her troubled thoughts. But I thought better of it. They were probably memories she'd much rather forget.

When Ma called to tell me about Gerri, I remembered last Christmas. Gerri had had her annual holiday gathering in her bachelorette pad, but the spread she put out seemed much more elaborate than usual. There was top-shelf liquor and shrimp—not the swag off-the-back-of-the-truck kind but expensive, store-bought shrimp. Since Daddy had died, shellfish was off our family menu. It cost too much.

Between stories of Grandpa throwing the Blessed Mother salesman down the stairs and Ma and Aunt Mary Ann dropping that big chunk of ice, Gerri showed us all the new furniture she had bought. Having recently suffered through the purchase of my first couch, I knew how expensive furniture could be. And this was nice stuff. Big. Real wood. Plus, there was a new bedroom set, with a fancy Christmas bedspread. There was Christmas china kept in a kitchen cabinet that my brother-in-law accidentally leaned on and almost knocked over. Gerri had a state-of-the-art CD player with multiple carts. I remember coveting it and the many Christmas CDs revolving around inside. Gerri had diamond earrings and a tennis bracelet. She drove a Lexus.

Even with a nice car like that, Gerri picked my mother and her father up at the airport in a limousine. Ma and Uncle Jerry had gone to Florida to visit Aunt Mary Ann, and there was Gerri at Newark Airport with a limo, a wet bar and all, ready to bring them home in luxury. My mother bragged about it, and it made me feel a little envious. Why couldn't I pick my mother up in a stretch limo? What kind of daughter was I anyway? Why didn't I get a real job that paid real money?

And then it occurred to me.

Gerri was up to something. I told my mother I suspected that Gerri was dealing drugs. I guess I was being catty, jealous that she had enough money to pick Ma up in style. But Ma didn't believe Gerri was running drugs. I didn't want to believe it myself. Doing drugs was your

personal prerogative, but selling drugs was scummy. Gerri wasn't
scummy. But something did seem strange.

Time passed, and I'd actually forgotten all about the limo episode
and my drug theory until my mother called me long-distance to tell me
about Gerri's trouble. She had been arrested. Not for drugs, Ma said,
but for swindling her company out of $219,792.55. Nearly a quarter-
million dollars. It wasn't just that she stole the money, but how she
stole it that was the problem.

Gerri was the accounts-payable clerk at a laundry-supply company
in Saddlebrook, New Jersey. It was her job to pay vendors. Instead of
paying them, she placed the company checks in her own account, bit
by bit, over a two-year period. No money laundering or elaborate
schemes: Once a week or once every two weeks, she would take a
company check, no matter who it was made out to, and deposit it into
her account.

When the company discovered the missing money, they traced it to
Gerri. They blamed the bank and held it liable for accepting checks
that weren't even made out to Gerri. The big problem, what made
Gerri's crime a problem for us all, was that the bank where she made
the deposits was the same one where my brother-in-law, Basil, worked.

Basil was a bank vice-president. One terrible morning, he came
across Gerri's name in a news flash that the bank had circulated about
the crime. He almost fell off his ergonomic chair. Basil had worked all
his life to rise above his Hudson County heritage. With my sister's
help, he had bought a house, launched a respectable career, and had
two exceptional children, one of whom went on to Harvard Law
School, just like cousin Mike.

Basil and Paula had worked for years to separate themselves from
the bad reputation of Hudson County and the criminals in our family.
They even tried to get rid of their accents. They did everything to blend
in with the yuppies who bought brownstones on either side of them.
They stopped putting colored Christmas lights on the tree; only taste-
ful tiny white lights would do. And the tree itself was no longer fake,
but fresh and green. They stopped making sausage and meatballs for
Sunday dinner and instead went out for brunch, toasting each other
with mimosas.

They took Gerri's crime personally. And I couldn't blame them. The tellers in Basil's bank all knew Gerri as a familiar face, the vice-president's cousin, so they never asked any questions when she showed up at their windows with her deposit slips and her dirty laundry-company checks. Like us, they probably liked Gerri and trusted her fresh, open face and wide, white smile.

When Gerri's arrest report turned up on Basil's desk, he debated whether to keep quiet about being related to her or own up to it. If he stepped forward to face the heat voluntarily, maybe the boss would commend him for his honesty. He went to his boss and told him about the relation. Better that than let them discover it on their own and accuse him of being an accomplice.

Basil was investigated. But most of all, he was embarrassed. He had worked hard, trying to rise above his roots, his Hoboken days, and his long, difficult-to-pronounce last name. But he hadn't distanced himself from the family stories. He was now part of one. And so were we.

To prove his loyalty to the bank, and to punish her for what she did, Basil didn't defend Gerri. He showed no mercy. The bank went all the way with its prosecution.

At first Gerri pleaded not guilty, but then changed her mind and pleaded out to second-degree theft. She agreed to pay all the money back.

At her hearing, the judge asked if she had a family. Gerri said yes, meaning her parents, siblings, and us. But the judge wanted to know if Gerri had any children, because, he announced, she was going to prison. Second-degree theft carried a maximum of three years in jail.

Basil, meanwhile, got a promotion at an upscale suburban regional bank. His title was president. He'd started as a teller and was now making six figures, the hard way, the legal way, the non–Hudson County way. The white-collar way. But Gerri hadn't thought of that, I suppose. Or maybe she just didn't care. That was my sister's take on it, and the reason she couldn't forgive Gerri. It was one thing to screw people you didn't know. But it was another thing to screw your relatives.

I felt bad for Gerri and had a feeling she hadn't involved us on purpose. I secretly sent her a card once, no real message inside, just "Love,

Helene," to let her know I was thinking about her and was sorry for what was happening to her. But I felt guilty for weeks. My sister would have been pissed if she'd found out.

I figured that working so closely with all that money, day after day, the temptation to steal was just too great. That was Gerri's only excuse. But I tried to find others for her.

Aunt Millie had been sick, so maybe Gerri stole most of the money to help her pay her medical bills. Maybe she didn't realize how much money she had actually taken, since she stole it a little at a time.

Maybe growing up in North Bergen had done Gerri in: North Bergen High School, the White Castle, or running wild and being able to cook breakfast in the morning on her own. Maybe she went wrong because North Bergen was shaped like a gun, because it was filled with so many dead-end streets, or because it didn't get good television reception. Maybe it was because she didn't go to church every Sunday when she was little.

There were dozens of excuses. I could blame what happened to Gerri on local politics, on people like McCann and Mocco, who set bad examples for our generation just like Hague and Kenny had done years ago for Beansie's generation.

What I feared most was that Gerri was responding to a deep genetic pull passed on from Grandpa. She was, after all, named after him. Grandpa Jerry. And he did come and live with her longer than he had lived with us.

When it came down to it, maybe it was all just a matter of odds, like betting the number. With a grandfather like Beansie, one of us was bound to get into trouble. The criminal gene was just too strong and was sure to be passed down.

Maybe Gerri did what she did because she was there that night Grandpa tried to kill us. It was as if Grandpa had actually climbed those stairs back in 1970, past the dust bunnies and broken floor tiles, but had only one bullet in his gun. And Gerri got it. Point-blank.

She said she couldn't really remember that night, but the memory was back there, lingering like those antique bullets Frank shot into his head. Like George's forgotten memory of his father, invisible but potent, dragging him to an early death.

Stanley, Paula, and I remembered the night Grandpa tried to shoot us, and savored each unfiltered detail. Maybe it was the remembering— or not remembering—that made the difference.

Before she "went away," Gerri half-jokingly threatened to run Basil over in her car. Paula stood by her husband. And so did I. We weren't allowed to go anywhere near Gerri, especially Basil, who took extra care in looking both ways before he crossed the street.

Because of the bad blood between my sister and Gerri, we couldn't go to North Bergen and laugh about the family stories for fear that Gerri would come up in conversation or show up in the flesh, out on bail. As if she were waiting, revving her Lexus's engine.

Our other relatives didn't know about Gerri's crime or why my sister was mad. Ma was afraid of hurting her brother Jerry, so she kept quiet about the whole affair and suffered in silence. Our other cousins and aunts invited us all—including Gerri—to family engagements. We couldn't attend weddings or funerals, christenings or showers, since Gerri might be there. And we couldn't say why we weren't coming, since Uncle Jerry would have been devastated if everyone knew about Gerri. We loved Uncle Jerry too much to cause him such grief.

For seven years we stayed away and kept quiet. Our cousins thought we were just being snobby, that we didn't want to bother with them. The whole mess took its biggest toll on my mother and Uncle Jerry, who carried on their normal relationship for years, pretending not to know what the other one knew. They still traveled together to visit Aunt Mary Ann in Florida. Uncle Jerry came to my mother's house to do her taxes, and she repaid him with a big macaroni dinner. They pretended nothing was wrong. But without the family's comfort, and with that secret weighing him down, Uncle Jerry aged. And Ma grieved terribly for those lost family gatherings.

I was surprised I felt bad about missing the family functions. For years I had complained about all those baby showers where bows were taped onto paper plates and placed on the heads of my pregnant cousins as their friends oohed and ahhed. But now that the family gatherings were off-limits, I missed them. They left a strange vacuum in my life. My family was a pain in the ass, but they were my family and mine alone to complain about or avoid. I had thought they'd always be there to mock or cherish, depending on my mood.

It felt like a piece of furniture was missing from my living room. It was mostly crummy, secondhand furniture, but it was mine and had its particular place in the room. I couldn't get used to the brand-new hole it left when it was gone. And it seemed that every time I went out, there was something else missing when I got back.

During the family blackout, Aunt Katie died. My Brooklyn apartment was only a few miles from Jersey City and from the funeral parlor but two rivers, two tunnels, and one family fight removed. I was close enough to Jersey City that from my living room window I could tell the time on the red, glowing Colgate clock. I could see the stepped buildings of the Medical Center and the railroad terminal that Irene and Vita had passed through over a century ago.

From that same window I could see the Statue of Liberty—not the back view like the one on Warren Street or the tired version outside City Hall Park, but the real thing, her face, green and glowing, staring straight at me, daring me to cross New York Harbor for Aunt Katie's wake.

Feeling sad and homesick, I got up the courage and went.

The first thing I noticed was that Aunt Katie had on a pink dress that matched the drapes behind her. I imagined her getting up and joking about it, making a reference to Scarlett O'Hara sewing her outfit from the curtains.

Aunt Katie had always looked all wrong in a dress, too formal and ladylike. Now she looked especially wrong. I wondered if she had her strange-looking partial dentures in, too, for this special occasion. The last of Aunt Katie's special occasions. I tried to get close enough to see, but stopped short of sticking a finger into her mouth. It wouldn't have gone over well, even in my family.

As I knelt before the casket I pretended to pray, but instead, I just gazed at Aunt Katie. Her body looked especially small in its coffin, shrunken almost, and so awkward in that dress.

Great-Aunt Katie. She had seemed so much taller in life. She was so wise, with her advice on how to stop a mad dog and how to get your husband to stop drinking. But she was never full of herself. Aunt Katie was flawed, and was always the first to admit it.

I remembered her reciting a poem when I was a kid. She said she wrote it, but knowing Aunt Katie, it was probably plagiarized. It was about getting a chance to live your life over again. And it all came back to me now in the funeral home. In metered verse, Aunt Katie said she would be more careful the next time around, tell her sons that she loved them, take more long walks. I remember her stopping and choking back tears before she was done. We likely didn't get our lives to live over, she said, "but knowing me, I'd make the same damn mistakes again."

They weren't such bad mistakes, especially in the context of our family. There were worse things you could do.

Hardly anyone came to Aunt Katie's funeral. When I looked around and saw all those empty seats, I winced. Had the family been on speaking terms, there would have been more people there. But I wondered where all those men and women were that Aunt Katie had helped during four decades as a committeewoman. It was time for all those favors to be repaid. All those potholes she got filled, the broken traffic lights she got repaired, all the people she helped move in to the neighborhood, all those she helped get jobs and food baskets, the couples she counseled through family fights, the pastors whose raffles she sold. Where were they now, the ungrateful bastards?

But then I realized where they were. All those people were dead, of course, their souls joining the long parade of barely missed Jersey Citizens, marching on with the sad subjects of all those feature obituaries toward permanent oblivion.

At eighty-six, Aunt Katie had outlived them. I smiled my half smile, blessed myself, and got up from the kneeler, no longer so upset about the empty seats behind me. I sat in one of them and stared at Aunt Katie some more.

She had talked for years about how one shot of Canadian Club a day would keep her going. And she was right. Maybe Aunt Katie was even right about those Lucky Strikes.

It was the filters that killed you.

20

BORN AGAIN

Gerri was sentenced a month after her thirty-sixth birthday, and served seven hard months in a women's penitentiary, let out early for good behavior. While behind bars, she found God and was born again. She sent Paula a long, penitent letter, apologizing to her. In the letter, Gerri told Paula she hadn't meant to hurt her.

Because of the letter and because Gerri did her penance, my sister finally forgave her for her sins. Seven years was long enough. At a family party, complete with a cheesy karaoke machine, she and Paula got up together and sang the Sister Sledge anthem "We Are Family." It was a corny but poignant moment. Gerri practically cried, the prodigal daughter so happy to be back in the fold.

Paula and Gerri made up at my cousin Jamie's wedding, at a big restaurant on the Jersey shore. It was the first time the whole family had been together in seven years. We all excitedly posed for a group photo on the restaurant's giant, echoing porch, the unfamiliar sea air sticky and damp as we linked arms and held hands. If you looked closely at the picture, you could see that my cousin Susan and I—the babies in our families—were both pregnant with babies of our own. It was a new beginning, in a way. The beginning of an era. Or the end of a bad one. Life had come full circle in the blunt, poetic way it usually does.

Susan had a son with a sense of humor so sharp he made his grandfather—Uncle Jerry—sound like a mortician. Amid the family turmoil, the comedy gene not only survived but thrived. I was glad the fighting was over, that I was able to get to know little Alan and see what a pisser he was.

Optimist that I was, I naturally started worrying about negative traits that might get passed down from the family, like cancerous cells incubating year after year, waiting to cluster into a tumor and wreak havoc. A good sense of humor was a wonderful family trait. But what about a desire to kill? A penchant to steal? To run numbers? I was afraid to research the topic of criminal genetics, scared of what I might find. And, besides, what was the point?

There was little I could do, other than choose a good husband. It was no accident that Wendell's grandfather was a judge—the upstanding, righteous kind, not the nickel-pork-chop variety that usually got assigned in Jersey City.

"We have a lot in common," I told Wendell on one of our first dates at Boulevard Drinks. "Your grandfather's a judge and mine was a criminal." I figured the judge genes might outweigh the criminal genes if we ever decided to get married and have kids.

Maybe there were other measures I could take to guard my offspring from the evil genes. Though I'm not a believer in Original Sin, I planned to have my baby baptized. I figured that in my family, with all those sins floating around, it didn't hurt to get spritzed with a little holy water. Just in case there was such a thing as a soul, heaven, hell, and limbo, my baby would be protected.

Most days, I was still too sophisticated to believe there were such things. But once I became pregnant, I started to wonder. At night, when all was quiet and my mind let down its defenses, I thought about the drawings Sister Isabelle had made us sketch in third grade in anticipation of the coming end of the world, our own versions of heaven and hell—angels on downy wings and devils with pitchforks. Then my mind wandered to places like the Sistine Chapel and the museums hung with Bosch paintings, the Cold Storage, the piles of dead rats, and the emergency room into which Daddy disappeared, and I worried that maybe there was a heaven and hell after all. That there were souls that needed to be saved and prayed for, and souls that floated into the heavens on their own lightness.

With the baby fluttering inside me, I felt a sudden panic and a helplessness. Now that I was contributing to the family line, I was connected to something huge, to eternity or a continuum that would make my life a mere star in a Milky Way of lives that came before me and would stretch on after me. Long after me. I was part of it but so, so small. The thought made me feel lost and scared, like I had that night I got out of the car with Wendell on the California highway.

If there was such thing as a soul, were there billions of them circling the heavens or were they recycled? My family members were firm believers in reincarnation. It was really just another version of genetics, with a religious spin to give it all a sense of mystery. The rule was that the newborn baby inherited the soul of the dead person who had just exited the planet or was on his deathbed. The death and birth, or rebirth, usually occurred within months, weeks, or days of each other, although the difference could stretch as long as a few years.

Uncle John was convinced my mother was Great-Grandma Irene reincarnated, with her face, her wit, her straight black hair, and her love of dancing.

When my brother was born, Dziadzia was on his deathbed, which explained why my brother's name was Stanley. Dziadzia's real name had been Stanislaw. My father begged my mother to name my brother after him. Then, in an extra cosmic twist, Stanley was coincidentally born on St. Stanislaw's feast day. Ma had no choice. Stanley it was, even though Stanley never really looked like a Stanley.

Right after Babci died, I was born, and came out looking just like her, squinty eyes, big nose, thick, dark hair.

When Stanley had a son, just a couple of years after Daddy died, Alex came out looking exactly like Daddy. He even acted like him, quiet but observant, coming out with a great one-liner every now and then. I had wondered where Daddy had gone off to in that emergency room. And now I knew. Alex was Daddy all over again. It was as if someone had boiled Daddy down to his essence and then poured him into a much smaller mold. I could just picture this kid years from now, broiling a few lobster tails just like his grandfather.

I was all for reincarnation: Take a soul to give a soul. It seemed like a resourceful, environmentally correct way to run a universe. As long as my kid was recycled from someone I liked, someone good.

But in my family it was slim pickin's.

I wondered whose soul—if anyone's—my baby would inherit. I wondered if cross-gender reincarnation was possible. My mother was a good soul, but I didn't want her dying anytime soon. So her soul was off-limits. Maybe Aunt Katie would come back in my kid. Short, squat, smoking Lucky Strikes, throwing back shots of Canadian Club.

I had a boy and we named him Dean, after no one in the family. We simply liked the name. Fresh and new. It was an added bonus that Dean Street was not far from my Brooklyn apartment, the street where Grandma came to live with her brother right before she met Grandpa. Dean Street was where Grandma had nearly escaped.

When I took Dean home from the hospital, I stared hard at his face and searched for clues in his features. With each twist, his face would completely change, like a kaleidoscope, leaving little trace of the last pattern I viewed. Daddy was in there. But so was Ma, with Wendell's lips curled into my smirk. And he hadn't even been to Jersey City yet. Aunt Katie was nowhere to be found.

Mornings he looked like Stanley, and evenings, like Paula. He had my sister-in-law's toes, my father-in-law's piercing stare, and my mother-in-law's round head. But he seemed to have my attitude, thoroughly unimpressed with everyone around him.

Sometimes he was like one of those Stapinski smorgasbords, with all my Polish relatives bringing something different to the table. When he frowned, my baby was Daddy. When he was sad, Uncle Tommy. When he cried, Uncle Eddie. When he scowled, he was Cioci Stella. And when he lifted a toy too close to his face and his eyes crossed, Uncle Henry.

But when he smiled, my baby was Grandpa. The first time I noticed, it scared the shit out of me.

I asked my mother if I was seeing things, and she shook her head.

It's Beansie, all right. He only appeared in charismatic flashes. But there he was, Grandpa, smiling up at me, more often than I liked to admit. Grandpa the charmer. Grandpa the handsome guy who Grandma fell in love with seventy years ago.

I hadn't seen Grandpa smile much in my lifetime, but I recognized the grin from family photos he hadn't gotten around to destroying. It wasn't so much the smile itself. That was more like Wendell's and my own. It was more in the cheeks and around the eyes that Beansie came out to play.

My cousin Jamie—on a roll from the family reunion that occurred at her wedding—dug up some old family movies and had them transferred to videotape. I saw Grandpa in motion for the first time since childhood. Eyes blinking, lips moving, bald head nodding. The movies were from my mother's wedding: Grandpa in a white tuxedo jacket, looking slightly demented, walking my skinny mother up the St. Mary's Church steps. I watched the film several times, and each time I rewound and watched Grandpa ascend those stone steps, the less I hated him. The ice-truck dent on the left side of his head was clear as could be. I had always thought that was just an excuse. But there it was.

There was also a sad, vacant stare in his eyes that most snapshots couldn't capture, and a timid smile, a remnant of the charming one I knew from those pictures and from my baby's face.

Grandpa was pathetic, not scary. Now, when I looked at his picture, I felt an unfamiliar ache, one I associated with seeing Uncle Tommy at Meadowview. It was sorrow. Maybe it was because of motherhood, but for the first time in my life, I actually felt sorry for Grandpa. I preferred anger over sorrow. It hurt much less.

For years, my mother had said she believed that Grandpa had been in purgatory and that she should pray for him, to try and move him along. I had always assumed Grandpa had gone straight to hell.

When I asked my mother why she prayed for her father, she said she felt he had done his penance on earth and that he didn't deserve the fires of hell.

After we kicked him out back in 1970, Grandpa went to live with Gerri and her family. But he drove Aunt Millie and Uncle Jerry crazy, yelling all the time that the television was too loud. Once, when they went out, they left Grandpa to baby-sit. He screamed at my cousins all night, scaring the memory deep into them. My cousin Susan remembers him accidentally stepping on her Barbie Dream House and crushing it. He promised to buy her a new one for Christmas.

Because he was impossible to live with, Grandpa wound up alone again, wandering the streets by himself until he had a heart attack and wound up in the Medical Center.

My mother took mercy on him one more time and visited him there with Uncle Jerry. When they got there, Grandpa cursed and yelled and scared them away for the last time. The exasperated doctors sent him to the Trenton State Hospital psychiatric ward for over a year. While there, he wrote a letter to one of his sisters—his handwriting still impeccable and sane—begging her to take him out, to save him. He told her in the letter that he didn't belong there.

I imagined what that was like and how much worse it was than being like Uncle Tommy, retarded and unaware of what was happening around you. I imagined being trapped in a psychiatric ward, knowing that you're simply mean, not crazy.

Six months later, Grandpa wound up in John F. Kennedy Hospital in Edison, New Jersey. That's where he died, alone, Christmas morning.

The hospital was a half mile from my uncle Robby's new house, and when he heard that Grandpa had died there, he thought that Grandpa had been stalking him and his family. But it was just another one of life's little coincidences. Grandpa didn't even know that Uncle Robby had recently moved there. His son lived less than a mile away and Grandpa didn't even know it.

Now that I had a son of my own, I understood why my mother prayed for Grandpa. He had suffered in the worst way, alone. Though he deserved to be left all alone, it was still sad. And besides, family was family. If they didn't pray for your soul, who would?

No matter whose soul my son inherited, he would turn out just fine if I raised him right. But how did you raise a child right? Would I send him to Catholic school, to try and instill a sense of morality? Would I let him run wild, or watch his every move? Make him eat organic vegetables, or let him eat hot dogs from Boulevard Drinks? Should we stay in the city, or move to the country?

I decided I would hold him close but not too tight. I would sing to him and brush his hair and find trees for him to climb. I would protect him from oncoming traffic and head injuries, and would avoid putting him in a crib for as long as possible, so he wouldn't have to stare at the world through a set of bars those first few months of life. When he got a little older, I would teach him right from wrong. I wasn't sure how to go about it, exactly, but I figured it would come to me. I would take him to church on Sundays to give him some grounding and something to rebel against in life besides me and Wendell. He would know who was good and who was bad and how to tell the difference, and that sometimes there really was no difference. That most people were angel and devil, Beansie and Grandma rolled up in a complicated mess.

He would know about Vita's card game, about Peter beating Irene, about Grandma and Aunt Helen and their brothers, Uncle Sam and Uncle John and their brownstone on Grand Street and the books on their shelves. He would know about Dziadzia's bootlegging and Babci's accident, epileptic Uncle Tommy and Meadowview, Kunegunda and Uncle Andrew and the Polish revolution that never was, Uncle Henry the bookie, and Uncle Eddie and the bull, about Hague and Kenny and my mother dancing with the mayor-to-be at Victory Hall. My son would get to know my mother, and know her well, learn about how she was so much like Aunt Katie in her old age. He would know about Aunt Katie's job as a committeewoman and as a riveter, about the night of cousin Mike's campaign party, the night I wore my first pair of glasses, about everyone hitting the number the day I was born, about the igloos Paula and Stanley built on Sussex Street, about how Grandma died on Ash Wednesday, about Daddy and the lobster tails and the trips to Bubbling Springs and the Loew's Theatre. I'd eventually tell him about Frank, Kelsey, and the backyard; the OLC nuns and priests; Aunt Julie and cousin Stephen and the day John was shot in Arizona; about the stolen Blessed Mother and the salesman that Grandpa threw down the stairs. He would hear stories of Grandpa from Uncle Jerry and Uncle Robby, the bad stories and the funny stories, like the one about the day Aunt Mary Ann and Ma carried that block of ice and then let it go, only to carry it up again in the next retelling, forever and ever. He'd know about the day Uncle Sonny died, and, once he was old enough to understand, why Grandma married Grandpa. About Carvel and the stolen ice cream, Venice and the Stanley Theatre, *The Jersey Journal* and the night Stanley almost punched the priest in the mouth, the Manna transcripts, Mayor McCann and cousin Mike running one more time, Uncle Tommy voting, and my running away from home finally. He would know about cousin George seeing his father dead and then dying right across the street, about Gerri teaching me to ride a bike and stealing all that money. I would point to Jersey City from the apartment window, to the railroad terminal and the new shiny buildings, and sometimes I would even take him to visit.

On an overcast day, Jersey City could still bring me down, with its aluminum siding, junkies, and crumbling highways. But on a good day, a sunny, clear day, Jersey City didn't look quite as bad as I remembered it. And it wasn't just the distance that softened me.

The New York skyline was even more spectacular with the Colgate factory buildings demolished, no longer obstructing the view. A new Colgate development was filling the hole left by the old factory, the pile drivers so loud that they broke the windows of George's mother's house on Morris Street. Development spread farther inland, to other neighborhoods besides the waterfront areas, and was rising at a furious pace.

Activist Colin Egan founded a farmer's market right in the shadow of the horrendously ugly PATH building, where sallow Jersey City residents, deprived for years of good, fresh produce, could finally buy a nice tomato. The farmer's market was a footnote in Colin's list of good deeds. He, Joe Duffy, and Ted Conrad, before he died, eventually convinced the planning board that the Loew's Theatre was worth saving. It was being rehabbed and was fully supported by the new mayor, Bret Schundler.

The first Republican in nearly a century, Schundler was elected the year I went to Alaska. He was an investment banker with money to burn, so corruption was no longer an issue. He didn't need to steal money. He had enough. Finally, a mayor of Jersey City who had enough.

Schundler was all right in my book, Republican or not. Some people disliked him because he wasn't Hudson County born and raised. The worst accusation they could dredge up was that he owned a house in Jersey City but lived most of the time out of town in a second home in the suburbs. They said the first chance he got, he'd leave Jersey City flat and follow his ambitions for higher office. But I didn't think that was so bad. It was better than taking kickbacks and stealing taxpayer money earmarked for new schools and nontoxic playgrounds. In an imperfect world, I would take a politically ambitious, conservative commuter over a born-and-raised corrupt swindler.

Schundler was one of the legions of yuppies who had moved to downtown Jersey City in the mid-1980s. When he pulled up in front of his apartment in a cab in those first few months in town, the driver noticed the address and gestured to the front door. "My brother was shot to death right on your stoop," he told him.

Less than a year later, the day before he closed on his brownstone, Schundler was walking in the neighborhood and watched as police cars zoomed past him and his wife. When they got to the house they were about to buy, they saw that the cop cars were parked out front. They had just arrested two kids who tried to rob the house. Schundler's house.

Schundler thought twice about closing. But he went ahead and made Jersey City his home. Vice and all.

He knew, firsthand, that the city could be a tough place. At the turn of the new century, crime was down 40 percent from the time he took office. But it still had a long way to go.

There were still chopped-up bodies and floaters pulled from the Hudson River each spring. But times were changing. There was the lesbian-rough-sex murder case in Bayonne, and the Internet case, in which a Jersey City guy was accused of luring a California girl online and then murdering her. In the autumn of 1999, a Hudson County real estate baron who had bought Mayor Hague's fourteen-room luxury

Kennedy Boulevard apartment was allegedly gunned down by his dis-gruntled doorman, a three-hundred-pound former Board of Ed worker known as Big Daddy. The only witness to the murder was an eight-year-old boy. Bad news didn't get much more colorful than that.

The crime story that fascinated me the most, though, happened the summer before. A time capsule placed under the Christopher Colum-bus statue on Journal Square was missing when the statue was moved for construction. The time capsule, including photos, newspapers, and other mementos, had been sealed at the base of the statue in October 1950 by Judge Zampella and Hudson's other well-connected Italians.

The oblong copper box was supposed to be opened in the year 2000 and resealed until 2050. But when workers moved the bronze explorer from his perch on a hot August afternoon in 1998, to make way for a $7.5-million Journal Square face-lift, the box was nowhere to be found. The construction crew searched the base and dug through the construction rubble, but it was gone. Who could be low enough to steal a time capsule? It was almost as bad as stealing the Blessed Mother.

Jersey City was so corrupt it couldn't even hold on to its history.

But then again, neither could I.

As a freelance reporter, I stole other people's hard-luck stories and wrote about them. It was my job to sneak into their lives and take notes. Five-finger discount. Secondhand. I wrote about crime victims and celebrities battling cancer, infertile couples and union workers phased out from jobs they'd held for fifty years, people losing their businesses and kids dying of drug overdoses. They weren't my stories. But I took them and put my byline on them. I made them my own.

My family's stories were different. For years, I felt a sense of enti-tlement to them, the way rich kids must feel about the family fortune. True tales about stolen encyclopedias, lobster tails, a statue of the Blessed Mother, a hospital bed, rare coins, a quarter of a million dol-lars. They were my only inheritance—save for a few stolen objects that I got to keep along the way.

But I had been away too long, had missed too many family gather-ings. Maybe it was that seven-year hiatus. Even the old stories were told less and less frequently, an eerie foreshadowing to what was happening to people like George and Gerri. The crime stories, funny at first, grew closer and closer to home, eating their way to the heart of the family, until they almost devoured us altogether. Gerri's crime had nearly wrecked us. And no one wanted to talk about it. It wasn't a funny story, and it wasn't mine to tell, really.

I wondered if any of the stories were mine to take with me wherever I went, like the books from Aunt Mary Ann and the stolen dictionary that went with me whenever I moved. Now that I was gone, I felt like I had to steal the family stories back, bit by bit, phone call by phone call, like a thief in the night, my relatives rightfully suspicious of my motives.

I wanted my son to know those stories, to show him where his mother grew up, to see it, taste it, smell it. But the smells I smelled at his age, both good and bad, were all gone. No more coffee or chocolate, soap or blubber. The factories had moved out long ago. The restaurants Daddy took us to were gone, too. Lobster tails, I discovered, were very expensive and difficult to cook. Daddy, like a champion figure skater, had only made it look easy.

I wanted Dean to meet the good people of Jersey City, the few I encountered throughout my lifetime. Though many Jersey Citizens were not worth meeting, there were some who'd surprise you with their no-bullshit attitude and willingness to do you a favor.

I wanted him to know that Jersey City had prepared me for the world—a harsh place, filled with jerks and criminals, no matter how far you traveled. In Manhattan, I once tripped and fell and watched people step over me at the curb. In Brooklyn, my apartment was broken into three times. In San Francisco, a big fat guy stole my wallet on a bus, then treated all his friends to the movies on my credit card. In Hong Kong, people pushed me out of the way to get a seat on the ferry. And in Cairo, a guy tried to grab my butt as I walked past him. I punched him hard in the chest and told him to go paw his wife like that. He had no idea what I was saying. But he heard the tone in my voice, and looked apologetic.

Because Jersey City had been so tough, I was always prepared for what might come my way.

I wanted my son to know that Jersey City was the world in high relief, stark black and white, with no punches pulled. The bad was especially bad, so the good stood out. When you met a good person—a truly good person—in a place as ugly and as awful as that, it could choke you up and make you want to cry.

I wanted my kid to know that, to know the characters I knew, to show him where his mother played, the wall on which I slammed a handball at age five, the pole I climbed, the door to my building, where the junkies came to hide, the door to the Majestic Tavern that I had pushed open with hands as tiny as his. But the Majestic was replaced by a Pakistani restaurant. And those doors opened the way for stories that were barely mine anymore, told in an accent that was slowly, surely fading.

ACKNOWLEDGMENTS

Thanks to Jennifer Rudolph Walsh and Ann Godoff; Tony Petrosino for his Web searches and for the poster of Journal Square; Jamie Vena Gottschall for her family research; Bob and Joseph Vena, Robert Vena, Jill Worthington, Susan Yenni, Edward and Elaine Stapinski, Michael Bell, Julie and Stephen Nowatkowski, Terri Gradowski, Mary Ann Koch, Mary Ann DelGreco, Eddie Meehan, Paula Muia, Colin Egan, Bret Schundler, Frank Culloo, Marcos Navas, Gene Scanlon, Anthony Cucci, Jaime Vasquez, Angie Wendolowski, Marybeth McGovern, Guy Catrillo, Bill Miller, William Rashbaum, Bob Leach, and Fred Friesendorf for their memories and expertise; to Pete Weiss, John Petrick, Olga Torres, Margaret Schmidt, Judy Locoriere, and the staff of *The Jersey Journal*; to Bessie Jamieson, Tom Boyle, Maria Schembari, Doug Roy, Brenda Tyson, Peg Latham, and the Millay Colony for the Arts, for giving me the space, both physical and mental; Sara Eckel, Laura Kriska, Jerome Gentes, Russell West, Kurt Jaskowiak, Andrew King, Luc Sante, Le Anne Schreiber, Kim Rich, Jodi Honeycutt, Jim DeRogatis, Deirdre Fretz, and Lauren and Paul Spagnoletti, for their encouragement; Ken French, Bruce Brandt, Charlie Markey, and John Norton in the New Jersey Room, Paula Spagnoletti, Stanley Stapinski, and Kathy and Walter Jamieson, for the answers to my many questions; my mother, Irene Stapinski, for her astounding memory and her nurturing skills; Dean Jamieson, for the luck and love he brought; and most of all, to my husband, Wendell Jamieson, for his countless edits, his boundless faith, and his incredible patience.

BIBLIOGRAPHY

Several books provided background and historical information. The most comprehensive was Thomas F. X. Smith's *Powerticians* (Lyle Stuart, 1982). Dayton David McKean's *The Boss: The Hague Machine in Action* (Houghton Mifflin, 1940); Richard J. Connors's *A Cycle of Power* (The Scarecrow Press, 1971); George C. Rapport's *The Statesman and the Boss* (Vantage Press, 1961); J. Owen Grundy's *The History of Jersey City* (Jersey City Chamber of Commerce, 1976); and John M. Kelly, Rita M. Murphy, and William J. Roehrenbeck's *Jersey City Tercentenary 1660–1960* (1960) were also essential. Other important sources included Bob Leach's *Saloon Stories*, his piece on Frank Hague, "To Touch His Garment," his story on Newsboy Moriarty, as well as his *Hague Picture Book* (Jersey City Historical Project, 1998); Joan Doherty Lovero's *Hudson County: The Left Bank* (American Historical Press, 1999); Kenneth T. Jackson's *Encyclopedia of New York City* (Yale University Press, 1995), Carlo Levi's *Christ Stopped at Eboli* (Farrar, Straus and Company, 1947), Helen E. Sheehan and Richard P. Wedeen's *Toxic Circles* (Rutgers University Press, 1993). Also helpful were Randall Gabrielan's *Jersey City in Vintage Postcards* (Arcadia Publishing, 1999); Robert R. Goller's *The Morris Canal, Across New Jersey by Water and Rail* (1999), and Patrick B. Shalhoub's *Jersey City* (1995), both from the Images of America series (Arcadia Publishing).

Several magazine and news articles were used as sources, including Thomas J. Fleming's "I Am the Law," from *American Heritage,* June 1969; William F. Longgood's "Jersey City Is Hard to Be Believed," from *The Saturday Evening Post,* April 3, 1954; an article on Hague from *Life* magazine, February 7, 1938; Brent Cunningham's "The Newhouse Way," from *Columbia Journalism Review,* January/February 2000; Frank Gallagher and Debra Kindervatter's story on the Central Railroad terminal, *N.J. Outdoors,* September/October 1989; Joan Cook's February 26, 1979, *New York Times* obituary on Newsboy Moriarty; Ronald Sullivan's December 2, 1970, story in the *Times* on the Mosquito Commission trial; and Frederika Randall's September 3, 2000, *Times* story on Matera; the *Hudson Dispatch*'s June/July 1934 coverage of Uncle Andrew's death; and Kevin M. Meyer's December 31, 1989, corruption roundup in the *Jersey City Reporter.*

A legion of anonymous *Jersey Journal* reporters and editors provided me with a rough draft of Hudson County's history: articles on the murder of Frank Kenny, from April 1916; the Black Tom explosion, from July and August 1916; Great-Grandma Irene's death, from November 3, 1922; the Majestic heist, from October 1923; Uncle Andrew's death, from June/July 1934; Grandpa's crimes from April 1, June 14, and September 6, 1935, October 18, 1943, July 25, 1948, September 19, 1951, and August 5, 1970; the death of Uncle Sonny on August 10, 1944 (once I tracked it down); Kenny's rally from May 6, 1949, his election, and Kenny's own article, "Cork Row, a Bit of Heaven in Downtown"; the closing of the Stanley Theatre, from October 1953; and Frank's DMV shooting, from September 1972 and July 1976.

A long list of bylined *Jersey Journal* reporters deserve credit as well. For information, I mined Peter Weiss's incredible body of work, including, but not limited to, his February 12, 1999, story on the Medical Center; his and Patricia Ford's coverage of the City Hall fire, from September 14, 1979; William Worrell's "race riot" story from August 3, 1964; Patricia Scott's jail coverage; Dan Rosenfeld's September 9, 1991, story on contamination at Liberty State Park, among dozens of other articles on toxic waste; Bernie Rosenberg's column on the Newark Bay Bridge accident; Joseph Albright's October 5, 1991, article and Nat Berg's March 29, 1965, story on cousin Mike; John Petrick's, Earl Morgan's, Emily Smith's, Bill Campbell's, and Peter Weiss's coverage of the Manna trial; John Petrick's October 19, 1991, story on his Medical Center tour; Deborah Yaffe's November 18, 1991, story on Aunt Katie; Michael Finnegan's, John Oswald's, John Petrick's, Peter Weiss's, and Bill Campbell's 1991 coverage of Mayor McCann's indictment, trial, and conviction; Elaine Pofeldt's, Kristen Danis's, and John Petrick's coverage of the Union Terminal odor stories; Agustin Torres's, James Efstathiou's, and Peter Weiss's stories on the Secaucus Council election; Agustin Torres's December 4, 1998, coverage of the Columbus monument; Stan Eason and Gilbert Martinez's February 1996 stories on cousin George; Greg Wilson's Secaucus election coverage; and Christina Joseph's and Melody Tanti's September 1999 stories on Barry Segall.

Helene Stapinski began her career at her hometown newspaper, *The Jersey Journal,* and since then has written for *The New York Times, New York* magazine, and *People,* among other publications. She received her B.A. in journalism from New York University in 1987 and her MFA from Columbia in 1995. She lives in Brooklyn with her husband and son.

A NOTE ON THE TYPE

This book was set in Fairfield, the first typeface from the hand of the distinguished American artist and engraver Rudolph Ruzicka (1883–1978). In its structure Fairfield displays the sober and sane qualities of the master craftsman whose talent has long been dedicated to clarity. It is this trait that accounts for the trim grace and vigor, the spirited design and sensitive balance, of this original typeface.